When the Eagle Screams

When the Eagle Screams

*America's Vulnerability
to Terrorism*

Stephen Bowman

A Birch Lane Press Book
Published by Carol Publishing Group

A Birch Lane Press Book
Published by Carol Publishing Group
Birch Lane Press is a registered trademark of Carol Communications, Inc.
Editorial Offices: 600 Madison Avenue, New York, N.Y. 10022
Sales and Distribution Offices: 120 Enterprise Avenue, Secaucus, N.J.
  07094
In Canada: Canadian Manda Group, P.O. Box 920, Station U, Toronto,
  Ontario M8Z 5P9
Queries regarding rights and permissions should be addressed to
  Carol Publishing Group, 600 Madison Avenue, New York, N.Y. 10022

Carol Publishing Group books are available at special discounts for
bulk purchases, for sales promotion, fund-raising, or educational
purposes. Special editions can be created to specifications.
For details, contact: Special Sales Department, Carol Publishing Group,
120 Enterprise Avenue, Secaucus, N.J. 07094

Manufactured in the United States of America
10 9 8 7 6 5 4 3 2 1

Library of Congress Cataloging-in-Publication Data

Bowman, Stephen.
   When the eagle screams : America's vulnerability to terrorism /
by Stephen Bowman
        p.   cm.
   "A Birch Lane Press book."
   ISBN 1-55972-228-2
   1. Terrorism—United States.   2. Subversive activities—United States.
I. Title.
HV6432.B68   1994
363.2'2'0973—dc20   93-47233
                                                         CIP

To Kate and Zach

Contents

Introduction:
An Interview With
William Colby

One month after the terrorist bomb exploded at the World Trade Center in New York City on February 26, 1993, I met with William Colby, the former director of the Central Intelligence Agency, to discuss his views on the terrorist threat to the United States. I had been researching terrorism for about four years, so I was prepared to produce a timely book on the subject.

There was a very real sense of urgency at the time of our meeting. My initial outline for this book had predicted that the World Trade Center would be the first target of a new wave of foreign terrorist actions and that the next targets would be New York's busy traffic tunnels. Watching the book come to life before I could get the words on the page was disturbing, and when the plot to attack the United Nations and the New York City traffic tunnels came to light, the message of this book suddenly took on a new importance. I was eager to get Bill Colby's opinions on the subject. Not only was he the former director of the CIA (1973-1976), but he had spent most of his life in covert operations, dating back to the beginning of his career as a soldier working behind enemy lines during World War II. He had also witnessed or participated in some of the most trying times of our intelligence agencies when both the FBI and CIA had been accused of going out of control in their zest for gathering information on private citizens as well as accusations, never confirmed, that the CIA had trained assassins and targeted nonmilitary personnel. Who better than Colby to reflect on the threat of terrorism?

Since this was our third meeting, he invited me to his home in Georgetown, where we conducted the interview in his living room. I was surprised by his candor.

Bowman: As I mentioned, I am writing a book on terrorism—the threat of terrorism inside the United States. The World Trade Center bombing obviously spurred me to action to complete the book, but I view that as rather cosmetic, really, as compared to what might be coming and what we can do about it.

Colby: Well, I think two things.

Greater public awareness will make the public accept the various rules necessary to fight this kind of environment. For example, we all accept the minute or two delay it takes us to get on an airplane because of the screening—because it's such an obvious point of vulnerability and the screening has been a great success in stopping hijacking. Not that you've eliminated every [threat], but you have certainly reduced the number enormously by that type of procedure.

Now you're seeing—with companies and big buildings—that a similar identification access procedure is generally accepted.

There is some doubt as to how efficient some of those are. One has the impression one could sign the name Adolph Hitler and walk in and nobody would pay any attention in a certain number of cases, but some of them are a little more serious than others. And it's this sort of thing [the World Trade Center bombing] that makes things a little more serious and puts the heat on the guard services to be more serious. It's all an educational effort.

The second thing is stimulating the public to take a role. You remember the terrible case in New York years ago—Kitty Genovese, a young woman who was murdered while thirty-seven people saw it happen outside their windows and did nothing? That was a shock, just a terrible lack of public interest and a terrible crime. On the other hand, the Son of Sam case in New York also had the city terrorized by murdering young women in various parts of the city. But sooner or later he was picked up because some neighbor noticed something funny about his car and tipped the police to it.

So there's the difference: public engagement.

If the public is aware that there is a terrorist problem—instead of just ignoring that package sitting on the bus all by itself, alerting some authority—[they can help] avoid disasters. If terrorists see that the public will report their activities, that puts a certain deterrence into the problem.

So public involvement and interest are important elements of fighting terrorists.

B: What about more sophisticated terrorist attacks?

C: I think terrorism—if it gets serious—will be suppressed. It will either be suppressed by use of the lawful means of aroused government, or by aroused people taking the steps necessary to conquer it.

The Italians did a brilliant job on the Red Brigades, which was bombing and killing people throughout the country and even kidnapped and murdered the prime minister. It was a major threat. And the Italians rallied to put their police force and security services to work. They used the courts. They used the law. They did not develop death squads or anything like that to fight it. And the Red Brigades are practically nonexistent now. Why? Because they [the Italians] put their minds to it and worked at it. Because it was serious. If it is a marginal thing, you probably can't get people interested in it. That's the problem. But if it's serious, they will.

Now, some governments have gone over the edge and gone to illegal ways of fighting terrorists. A prime example is Argentina, which did launch death squads, and a lot of people disappeared. They did suppress terrorism, but they did it at a terrible cost, and they are still suffering the results of it because of the way they went about it. So, in that sense, I think (a) terrorism can be defeated and (b) you have to use legal means to do it.

B: What about international terrorism?

C: International terrorism has a complication where you've got nations such as Libya, Iran, and others that are now stimulating various fundamentalist terrorists—through Sudan against Egypt, Sudan against Tunisia—these are real problems. But they can be defeated. It takes a lot of guts and a lot of strength to go at it.

B: Marenches, the ex-head of the French intelligence, refers to the battle against terrorism as the Fourth World War.

C: Well, I'm not sure it's quite to that extent. Terrorism is a problem, but let's face it: the most serious terrorist threat most Americans face is walking through a center city at night. That is the home of terrorism. It has nothing to do with Middle Easterners coming and planting bombs, but it is a form of terrorism. We've had terrorists in this country. We've had the Ku Klux Klan, which was a terrorist organization, no doubt about it. So this is a phenomenon that does exist.

Being terrorized is a very broad concept. That's the Fourth World War—it's a normal problem of keeping order in a society against extremists. And there are extremists around. Some of them consider America a Great Satan, and therefore a blow against the symbol of America, such as the Trade Towers, something like that is supposed to be a rewarding kind of a thing to do. Well, we have to make sure it is not rewarding.

I don't think it's a Third World War or a Fourth World War. Believe me, you cannot equate the problems of terrorism with the fact that we and the Russians faced each other, each of us, with twenty-five thousand warheads. We weren't talking about death and destruction. We were talking about elimination of life on earth. We are very fortunate to have gotten through that period. We still have a clean-up job to do, and one of the things we have to worry about is nuclear terrorism, of course. But, believe me, there's nothing that matches the potential destruction of that situation.

B: Do you find it frightening that Iran and North Korea are jointly developing nuclear capabilities?

C: Sure. But again, proliferation is a threat and one we have to worry about. But let's face it—it's a threat of one bomb, not twenty-five thousand. We have to keep the pressure on these countries not to develop that kind of nuclear power. But we have to show the example. We have to show the leadership. For too many years the United States has refused to consider a variety of potential steps that would, I think, help us in that process. No first-use pledge. And we have continued to test until Congress stopped it, a few months ago, until next July.

But the other nations say, "What do you mean? We're not supposed to have any, and you go ahead and make more and more? That doesn't make any sense." And it doesn't make any sense. Indira Gandhi once said in a somewhat sharp way, "Don't you superpowers give us lessons about nuclear warheads until you get your own act under control." Well, now I think we are beginning to do exactly that. The United States and Russia have agreed on major reductions in nuclear arms, but it's still an absurd number. We can continue to go down much further than that. The nuclear potential in some of these irresponsible hands does and should worry us. We should use all possible diplomacy, certainly, and go to sanctions if necessary to dissuade them from developing nuclear weapons.

B: What about the general fundamentalist threat?

C: We tend to think of terrorism as some great, centralized net coming out of some major war center somewhere. To a degree, that exists—there were those kinds of networks and conscious support of known groups and other countries. But there is another phenomenon, and it may be that the World Trade Center [bombing] represents this.

This has to do with the inflammatory spreading of terrorism which is not enacted by specific recruitment and dispatch of agents. It's designed to encourage extremists to think up on their own what they might be able to do. Now that's a tougher problem because even if you get an agent or a source in one of these networks, you may get a pretty good idea of what's going on, but you cannot tell who is picking up the point and what he is doing with it. We may see that this World Trade Center thing was like that—people get inspired by an extreme mission and go ahead and figure out on their own what they might do to make a blow for their beliefs. It doesn't take a large network. It just takes a few people. And your chances of having an agent in that small group are not very much.

Again, if the neighbors are conscious of the problem, it makes it more difficult. You can hardly set up a bomb shop without, in most areas, somehow showing that you're trying to hide something.

B: What if terrorism reaches truly sophisticated levels where the actual infrastructure of the country is the target?

C: A country picks itself up because of its huge redundancy. If you have a revolutionary situation where you have lots of this going on, then it can have a real impact. But if it's an external thing, you're not apt to get that much loss. You can drive yourself crazy with the nuclear bombs in the crates in New York Harbor, and so forth. And we have to worry about things like that, but I don't think we have to go crazy over it tomorrow morning.

What we should do is try to think of ways to plan for the future. If we have an enemy nation and we know they have a nuclear bomb but no missile to send it, which would be the silliest way to send it anyway, how might they send it? What should we do to protect ourselves against that kind of problem ten years from now? Do the war planning. We have to prepare for the unexpected without doing it through paranoia.

B: What do you think the dangers are of government-sponsored terrorism becoming more organized?

C: I believe in being serious and reasonable, developing the proper kinds of measures, there's no question about it. But you can't scare me to death. Nobody's prepared for terrorism. One of the lessons that the Middle Eastern and other countries are gradually learning is that any attempt to separate themselves from the rest of the world leads to their going backwards.

Look at Iran, who declared war on the world, and they've gone backwards in terms of development. Look at Cuba. They're still stuck in the Fifties because it's all by itself. So there they are, stuck in the time warp of the Fifties, and if you offered the people a chance to get out and go to Miami, a good half of them would go tomorrow morning. So, any of these countries that think they can be independent of the rest of the world, they're not going anywhere.

It's only by opening up and joining the rest of the world that you begin to get the flow of ideas and experience and trade and services and all the rest of it that create progress and advancement. Look at Russia after seventy years of isolation. They've got a great army but lousy shoes. In Iran there's a second line there, not exactly what I'd call moderate, but one which says "let's start the process of going back to the world." The second line is clearly starting to have an impact in Iranian politics. And part of that is not engaging in terrorism against other states.

B: In relation to some of the theories that countries will start to use terrorism as an actual military tactic, could we have rendered Iraq just as helpless with ten thousand dollars' worth of terrorism as we did with the billions of dollars spent on Desert Storm?

C: Well, again, we should have nothing to do with terrorism on innocent people. On the enemy, sure, sneak in and shoot the leadership on the other side. The young men on one side are killing the young men on the other side. As far as I'm concerned, the leaders are fair targets, and that's not terrorism.

B: Don't we have a law against that, or is it . . .

C: We have a Presidential directive which says we will not engage in assassination. But I think it's understood that assassination does not include shooting an enemy soldier or his commander. If you're in a time of war, you're entitled to anything. I would have cheerfully carried a bomb into Hitler's bunker and tried to get rid of the commander of the enemy forces.

The most absurd story I've ever heard was that in the Battle of Waterloo, in the middle of all this carnage, the Duke of Wellington saw that Napoleon had fallen within range of the British guns and he told the guns not to fire because generals don't shoot generals. Well, the hell with that. If you're shootin' privates, you sure as hell can shoot generals, as far as I'm concerned.

B: How confusing does that get in these days when we very seldom declare war?

C: Well, that's all right, too. I'll still apply it to when young men are killing each other.

The one thing you have to remember—and Americans are very poor on this—is that the primary job of defending against terrorism is nonmilitary. It's police security and the intelligence role. We don't understand police— the role of the police—because we have a military tradition. That guy over there is the enemy. Whereas the policeman thinks that guy over there is a citizen who needs to be controlled. Take Kent State, where some poor National Guardsman confronted a mob of screaming students and all he could think to do was shoot at them. That tore the country apart. Dumb. Whereas a policeman never would have shot at them. He would have gotten in the middle of them and pushed them away, and that's about it. It's more prevention than punishment.

I thanked Bill Colby for his time and proceeded to conduct interviews with antiterrorist experts in the Washington area. There were a number of frightening contradictions revealed in these interviews. One of these was to hear each source emphasize the need to make the public aware of the terrorist threat, but then to see their concerns mitigated by official statements made by their superiors to the newspapers later that same day. It was also disturbing to hear the military mentality of "acceptable civilian losses" being applied to this domestic threat. I saw this attitude as representative of a major problem our officials face in learning to abandon their cold war methods in order to deal with a new kind of terrorist war that would take place inside our cities.

This recurring cold war mentality resulted in a major theme of this book: In today's age of advanced weaponry, when even an unsophisticated lunatic can wipe out a city, we cannot afford to allow history to repeat itself by repeating mistakes of the past.

Preface

We are witnessing one of the most historic periods in human existence—a collision of cultures, political ideologies, religious doctrines, economic struggles, and national-security measures. The forces with which these evolutionary powers clash are strong enough to obliterate national boundaries, cause a superpower to self-destruct, release the pent-up angers of suppressed racial hatreds, and introduce to another generation the horror of ethnic cleansing.

Amid these collisions, both on a global scale and within the borders of each nation, terrorism erupts and does its work. Terrorism reminds us not only that we are witnessing an historic moment, but also that we are fully participating in the creation of a new world for the next century.

Our political and social reactions to terrorism may well present some of the greatest challenges to definitions of freedom and democracy. Surrounded by issues of immigration, economic strife, religious fundamentalism, energy and environmental needs, and antiquated political structures, the growing conservative movements in every nation and every religion are leading to the creation of reinforced borders, strict laws, and unforgiving moral codes, all of which will be conceived as unbending. The stage will be set for a new form of cold war, albeit not so cold as before.

This war will be fought not on one front, but on numerous cultural fronts which simultaneously transcend national borders and help assure that terrorist acts become the war strategy of the future.

Governments today attempt to meet these new challenges with old, cold-war political and military methods, which are the only methods they know. As massive armies march fruitlessly and superweapons prove themselves useless (except for encouraging other nations to build similar arsenals of mass destruction), the terrorist trend builds, bringing the world's conflicts to the doorstep of every citizen.

Nations that were prepared for the feared explosion of the cold war are not prepared for the terrorist war. Western nations, and the United States in particular, are most vulnerable to attacks designed to cripple or destroy their fragile infrastructures, which are wholly dependent on oil deliveries, fragile technological support, and computer controls—any or all of which can be destroyed in a single night while armies and their arsenals sit in darkness.

All of these threats are transitional problems related to the profound changes taking place. The violence connected with this transition can either be prolonged by the wrong response, or shortened considerably by common-sense solutions. In light of shocking events of today—both positive and negative, but shocking nonetheless—the answers to these problems appear to be confusing and obscure. But, as always, asking the right questions is a key to finding the answers.

This book is written with four primary premises: (1) terrorism is a symptom of political, social, and religious issues basically ignored by federal agencies in charge of national security; (2) terrorism can no longer be treated as an obscure criminal risk now that terrorists have access to weapons of mass destruction; (3) national infrastructures lie naked to terrorist attack; and (4) terrorism is ineffective against a stable society.

It is my hope that these four observations will considerably broaden the scope of terrorist study, an exercise which no official agencies have been willing to undertake. This book paints these issues with a broad brush in order to boldly illustrate theories which, if followed, might well point the way to meaningful solutions.

Acknowledgments

I have accumulated many debts of gratitude as a writer, and with this book in particular. First and foremost is my thanks to Jan Finken and Kitty Cappellano, who together took over the responsibilities of my "other life" and enabled me to concentrate on research and writing. They have shared my vision that through creative communication we can have an impact on building a better world.

Paula Albert, who has dedicated her time over the past few years to provide astute research assistance on this and other projects, has added her own rare brand of bright intelligence to the work.

Among the many sources of expert personalities, none stand out more than William Colby, former Director of the Central Intelligence Agency. Mr. Colby not only was a gracious host but was kind enough to provide most critical objections to the first draft of the book.

I am also grateful to the many people I interviewed connected to the State Department, the Department of Defense, and the Intelligence agencies who shared frank conversations and personal insight with me even though they knew I would often be critical of the bureaucracies to which they owed their allegiance.

Lastly, I want to thank my editor, Bruce Shostak, and my copy editor, George Rowland. Together they helped weave the complex issues of this subject into a productive work. And my literary agent, Mitchell Rose, who recognized the important message hidden in my original notes and scribbles.

Part I

THE AWAKENING

CHAPTER 1

When Terrorism Hits Home

What happens if sophisticated terrorism finally erupts in the United States to the point where the nation faces the kind of devastating and prolonged battle it has long known (and been warned) about but has steadfastly remained unprepared to handle? Since the United States no longer is invulnerable to terrorism (and in fact is sure to become its primary target), this question, like its future answer, takes on tremendous importance.

The American Experience in the twentieth century, tough though it has been, has left no comparison which allows us to imagine the consequences of terrorism run rampant on U.S. soil. For many Americans, World War II and the cold war "conflicts" of Korea and Vietnam are but far-off memories, and for most they are mere footnotes to history romanticized in films and novels. But those who lived through the wars remember them as series of battles fought on distant shores, their grim details and effects reported primarily by radio, movie-theater newsreel films, and (at least after World War II), TV—and their costs further made evident in such varied ways and means as shortages, propaganda films, and the dreaded telegrams to service-personnel homes. Even the GI's who fought those wars recall the battle sites as places to which they went to fight so they could return to a nation that had traditionally (with but two or three brief exceptions, historians point out) been spared harmful invasion by a foreign power. The bombs, the crushed cities, the desecrated national shrines and demolished homes, the death camps, the millions of dead civilians and homeless orphans, the diseases and countless other hardships—all of those were the kind of horrible events that in the future could happen to only foreign people in foreign lands. Not to Americans in the good old U.S.A.—or anywhere else.

Because Americans have been so generally safe from foreign invasion, there has existed for nearly all of America's history since 1776 a peculiar inequality with almost all other nations—a lack of common experience which cannot help but prohibit Americans, including our political scholars, from fully understanding the psyche of other countries.

Terrorism promises to be the great equalizer.

Even our contemporary experience with terrorism has been viewed as a foreign problem, something that might happen to innocent Americans only while traveling abroad. Strikes against the United States have been mostly limited to bombs on airplanes, an explosives-filled car crashing through an embassy gate, or the kidnapping of an American diplomat or businessman. Our only protection against these events has been the security forces of foreign hosts, which we assume are far better than ours due to their familiarity with terrorist actions. But we have yet to see bodies littering the streets of our cities—a certainty we do not wish to consider as such, and thus one for which we have yet to prepare.

For most Americans, the word *terrorist* conjures up images of psychologically dysfunctional creeps sneaking clumsily around with unsophisticated bombs. We envision them as grubby little bands of disgruntled illiterates driven by religious or political fanaticism and with little purpose other than spreading general, sporadic terror. We see them as foreigners looking for a public spot at which to cause havoc.

Unfortunately, the February 26, 1993, bomb explosion at the World Trade Center in New York City supports those images. A van full of nitroglycerin, urea nitrate and sulfuric acid exploded in a basement parking lot, killing five and injuring hundreds. A couple of days later, the FBI picked up a rather sorrowful Arab who had returned to the rental agency to redeem his $400 deposit on the van, which he had rented under his own name. All around the country the next day, people were asking: "Did you hear the one about the stupid Arab . . . ?"

But these are false images which do little more than give us a false sense of comfort and keep us from taking the proper steps toward protecting ourselves from the world's newest form of war.

Count Alexandre de Marenches, the former head of French Intelligence, referred to the present and future battle against terrorism as "The Fourth World War" in his 1992 book of the same name coauthored by David Andelman. In his epilogue he said of terrorism: "The threat is truly awesome in its reach and scope. It requires a whole new strategic system to address and cope with it. . . . All of our institutions must keep pace with those changes or we are lost."

Most Americans would say that Marenches is an alarmist, but then most Americans have little idea how vulnerable their country is to terrorist attack or how wrong their stereotype of a terrorist may be when compared to the trends. Before we can relate to their awesome potential for destruction in this country, as indeed in every other Western nation (as will be described in this book), we must understand the following trends:

1. Terrorism is becoming the war strategy of the future.
2. Terrorists will reach new heights of sophistication.
3. The motivations for terrorist attacks will have greater purpose. Targets of the future will be countries and economic systems, not buildings and airplanes.
4. Our military experts and strategists of World War II and the cold war are at a loss for a solution. They cling to methods that have no place in the future.
5. Our military weapons arsenal, along with the sophisticated weaponry on the drawing boards, combine to be obsolete for a war on terrorism.
6. The U.S. infrastructure has been built without regard to terrorist threats. Our entire system can be brought down with striking ease.
7. Terrorism is a greater threat to democracy than communism or socialism ever were.
8. The United States is the target of the future.

As with any of the few turning points in history, like the industrial revolution or the discovery of atomic power, there are some who will throw up their hands with Doomsday gloom and consign the entire population to living as if in an armed camp featuring great amounts of prison bars and barbed wire. There are others who will insist that the future won't be different from the present for at least the remainder of *their* lifetime, even as they fail to recognize the changes going on all around them.

We can afford neither of these views. Changes are taking place now and will be firmly in place within most of our lifetimes. We can look to the future with optimism, but only if we recognize it for what it is becoming, and grow to be part of it.

This book reveals for the first time to the general public America's true vulnerability to terrorism. These chapters take the sophisticated terrorist scenario and play it out to its conclusion through documented facts and examples. These pages reveal how a small group, or sometimes even just one person, can: bring our nation's oil supply to a halt; incinerate an entire city; upset the world's money supply; destroy our electrical grids; cause a

major city to self-destruct—a series of likely events which will challenge
our society, our democratic and economic principles, our civil-rights
beliefs, our entire way of life.

When research for this book began in 1988, one of my initial concerns
was that it might prove a realistic blueprint for terrorism. This concern
was quickly alleviated, partly because basic research found the information readily available. Careful documentation regarding America's vulnerability to terrorism was found in open-to-the-public congressional
reports. Detailed instructions on how to cripple the United States were
found on library shelves. The resource list of readily available books,
reports, pamphlets, and articles numbers in the thousands.

More frightening were exclusive interviews with terrorists themselves.
In the darkened basement of a small home somewhere in middle America,
terrorists parroted their attack plans, converting them from paper-plot to
actual war-tactic status. Further exclusive interviews with their rival counterterrorist experts added still more credibility to what might have originally been considered an incredible possibility. In fact, it was concluded
that terrorists and most governments know about this plot, and its awesome potential, but the American public and the publics of the rest of the
Western world have been kept in the dark. In the interest of national security, however, some locations and specific details of this plot have been
altered in (or deleted from) these pages.

Just how lost are we in our present situation?

Because the World Trade Center bombing reawakened our awareness
of the terrorist threat in this country, let's take a look at some of the related
activities during the period of February/March 1993. The following examples give insight as to where we are, the dangers we face, the trends developing, and where we must go to combat the physical and psychological
terrorist threat.

Happening concurrently during that sixty-day period were: the bomb
explosion at the World Trade Center; the siege of a cult compound outside
Waco, Texas; the federal trial of four policemen in Los Angeles, for the
Rodney King beating which had kicked off the LA riots two years earlier;
and the release of a final report from the State Department on the actual
effectiveness of our bombing and missile raids in the Persian Gulf War
against Iraq. The commonality of these four events is not in their inception but in their results and our responses to them. Each of these events
brought into question both the nation's authority and its ability to deal
with domestic violence.

The bombing at the World Trade Center brought home the basic elements of terrorism. It demonstrated that almost anyone can make a bomb and that (as Paul Ragonese, a former member of the New York City bomb squad, told *USA Today*), "If you have the mentality to hurt people, it's pretty easy" to use a bomb. That particular unsophisticated bomb went off in a garage which the Port Authority had been warned was susceptible to attack, causing over $300 million damage to the city's twin tallest buildings. The economic loss amounted to over $1 billion when business losses by building occupants were taken into account.

The bombing also gave America a taste of the terror that rudimentary terrorism often employs—the terror of random acts by unknown perpetrators for unclear reasons.

While the nation applauded the FBI's efficiency in tracking down the suspects, weeks later it was still not clear whether the attacks could be tied to any foreign group, and FBI director William Sessions warned a House hearing committee that weeks or months would pass before they would know for sure.

The House hearings had not yet begun, however, before another crisis developed in a small enclave on the outskirts of Waco, Texas. David Koresh, a self-proclaimed Christ figure who had changed his name from Vernon Howell, was the leader of a religious commune calling themselves Branch Davidians—a Christian Fundamentalist division. Koresh and his followers of thirty men, forty women, and eight children declared their own little war on federal agencies. On day one of the initial invasion of the compound by agents of the Bureau of Alcohol, Tobacco and Firearms, four ATF agents were killed and fifteen were wounded. Three weeks later, over four hundred federal officers and an array of armored military equipment were still in a siege mode against the heavily armed compound. The estimated cost of the siege was over $2 million a day, according to the FBI's published statement, while the agencies waited for Koresh to call the next move.

When asked why the attack had gone so poorly, one agent said they were simply "outgunned" by the civilians inside. Although a recent newspaper report had printed accounts of the cult's plans, and given details of their arsenal, the state and federal officials had entered the compound carrying only handguns. The agency offered no reason for this apparently foolish move, but since at least some of the occupants inside the compound were considered hostages or innocent bystanders, it is easy to imagine a decision not to barge in with automatic weapons blazing. Also, in all prior situations of this kind, one hundred trained agents with handguns would have been sufficient to do the job. As things went, for the first few days Koresh held the federal agencies virtually hostage while they met his demands for television and radio air time designed to spread his propaganda to the public.

While four hundred federal agents waited on the plains of Texas and an even larger combined force of federal, state, and city personnel responded to the World Trade Center explosion, a trial was going on in California which officials worried would set off an uncontrollable race riot.

Twelve jurors listened to testimony while trying to determine whether four police officers had violated Rodney King's civil rights. They pondered both the testimony and their decision, knowing full well that an acquittal of the officers might set off another riot even more destructive than the initial one of 1991. They were aware of the threats by black groups that this time the riots would spread out from the inner city and into the white suburbs. They remembered that the National Guard had been helpless to stop the murders and destruction the last time.

While most viewers of the videotape of the Rodney King beating were shocked by the actions of the officers, they also had a sense that the riots, and the threat of further riots, were holding the twelve jurors hostage, along with the entire federal judicial system. Confirming this feeling of our legal system's being under siege was the order by the presiding judge that helicopters be ready to whisk jurors away from the roof of the courthouse after they delivered their verdict.

Back in Washington, D.C., on the same day that Rodney King took the stand to testify, Americans were still pondering the meaning of the World Trade Center incident. The kind of attack that we had avoided for over two hundred years had finally happened—and all of the fantastic weaponry at which we had marveled during the Persian Gulf War with Iraq had proved useless against a small group of terrorists. Suddenly the very hype from the war about our fantastic technical superiority emphasized that bringing the problems to our home turf quickly neutralized the weapons.

The State Department had even more bad news when it reported updated statistics from the Persian Gulf War. Two years earlier, military experts had stated that the incessant bombing of Iraq, which American audiences had watched live via satellite, had killed over one hundred thousand Iraqi soldiers. It had been easy enough to believe those figures. We had watched as the Air Force, Army, Marines, Navy, National Guard, and multinational troops pounded the country with billions of dollars' worth of bombs and missiles. We had listened and nodded while the technocrats rushed to the cameras to laud mechanized war and to marvel at the first opportunity to demonstrate the miraculous weapons in our arsenal. The televised carpet bombings themselves seemed to guarantee complete annihilation.

Two years later, after intensive research, the State Department produced a final report on the actual damage to Iraqi positions. Instead of one hundred thousand soldiers killed, fewer than fifteen hundred were actually killed by the massive raid. And, adding insult to (non)injury, even though American and allied losses were small, the report also revealed that 30 percent of American and allied deaths were caused by "friendly fire" from American guns. In other words, our modern weaponry was impressive, but did little actual damage. More important, to the mind-frame of the third world, the updated outcome confirmed that Saddam Hussein was victorious!

An official military response to this criticism would likely be that the real value of the raids was to wipe out important Iraqi installations, disrupt Hussein's ability to rule, and prohibit Iraq from operating as a country by knocking out its technical and industrial infrastructure. This is probably true; our goals had nothing to do with claiming territory or killing people. Keep this in mind as the terrorist plot unfolds.

Compared to the possible disruption posed by terrorism in this country, these four incidents, including the forty-day Persian Gulf War, were rather minor occurrences. And yet our response to these events provides a hint to our present answers to these important questions regarding terrorism:

- Are our federal, state, and local agencies prepared to handle large-scale terrorist attacks? How would they respond without the luxury of weeks and months of postattack investigation time?
- How many days can the nation go without oil, gas, or electricity before it grinds to a halt and heads into a forty-five- or fifty-year depression?
- What happens to the world economy if United States financial institutions are suddenly stopped from operating?
- With our health-care system in turmoil, and property-casualty insurers reeling from the (predicted) effects of recent earthquakes and hurricanes, will terrorism bankrupt the nation's property-casualty insurance industry?
- What are the possibilities of the FBI's greatest fear becoming a reality— foreign and domestic terrorist groups working together to coordinate their activities?
- Will racism, anti-Semitism, and cultism reach new heights if terrorism drives the nation's misery index to unbearable levels?
- What constitutional rights will be challenged if the federal government takes steps to thwart terrorism?
- For the average citizen, what effects will these actions have on our daily lives?
- Do our present limitations on the presidency, Congress, and our federal agencies prohibit them from taking the proper steps to defend us?

•Do present laws make it illegal for us to join the war of terrorism—fighting terrorism with terrorism? Are we willing to do so? Is our military willing to abandon outdated methods for the new war strategies experts like Count de Marenches say are necessary?

•What are the likely targets? Why have we left them all unprotected?

In the House committee hearings on terrorism held shortly after the World Trade Center explosion, FBI director William Sessions was asked what citizens should do to protect themselves. His answer: "Be careful." There was not much more he could say.

The committee would do well to go back through their own records and review the hundreds of pages of congressional reports at their disposal that predict the consequences of terrorism. These reports detail our country's vulnerability, not just to attacks which cause public hysteria, but to attacks which could actually challenge the existence of the United States, and the continuation of democratic principles everywhere. The reports also detail what most citizens currently sense: As future national and international terrorists walk past our arsenals and in the shadows of our billions of dollars' worth of weapons rendered obsolete because they cannot be used against domestic targets, the United States waits almost helplessly for a sophisticated terrorist plot to unfold.

And the plot is in the making, as revealed in the following chapters.

Is there some type of CIA or FBI conspiracy to keep this information about our vulnerability from the public? Are they conducting a campaign of misinformation? No. It seems that these agencies would *like* the general information to be made public—perhaps with the goal of enlisting public and media support for legislative and procedural changes meant to provide the agencies weapons with which to protect the nation. FBI and government requests in March 1994 to give the FBI greater freedom to conduct wiretaps and to allow secret monitoring of computer transmissions are recent examples of this goal—emphasizing that a climate of fear of terrorism may conflict with civil rights.

On the political side, the reaction to the warnings of our vulnerability to terrorists has been typical: the tendency to ignore a problem until it becomes a pressing issue. And in the case of terrorism, the issue is escalated to new levels of confusion because our traditional experts, the military strategists and cold war warriors, are unable to apply old methods to these new problems.

Now is the beginning of a new age of war. And it promises to be the most challenging period in the American Experience.

CHAPTER 2

The Players

Since 1968 over 8,500 terrorist acts worldwide have been claimed by over seven hundred different terrorist groups. More than half of these acts have been aimed at the United States or U.S. citizens.

If terrorism did not work, there would be no terrorists. But in fact it works very well—particularly if one of its primary goals is to get a message to the media for global distribution. Through terrorism the most obscure individual can suddenly position himself as a world personality. Such power and visibility might last only a few hours or days, as in the case of airline skyjackers, or it could last a lifetime and be the foundation for real world strength, as with Yasser Arafat and his rise to the top of the PLO, or as in the case of Nelson Mandela, whose lengthy imprisonment made him a living symbol of black rights and whose popularity legitimized the African National Congress (which had been considered a terrorist organization since its formation in 1912).

Modern advances of mass communication, international travel, and the development of weapons of mass destruction have helped terrorists move their causes from a local status to a global one.

Most leading experts have agreed that there are two types of terrorists: national terrorists, who work within one nation; and international terrorists, who recognize no boundaries. A common denominator required for a group or act to fit the definition of terrorism is that it be politically motivated. For example, John Hinckley's attempt to assassinate President Ronald Reagan is not considered terrorism because his only motivation was to impress an actress.

Terrorist groups are further segmented by their means of support: either self-funded or state-sponsored. State-sponsored international terrorists are the major concern for U.S. officials. These are terrorist groups who are financed—and often physically protected and directed—by governments such as those of Libya, Iran, and Iraq. Middle East countries are best known for state-sponsored terrorism, usually justifying their participation as another front for their religious war against Jews and Christians.

Again, the success of these groups promises the creation and proliferation of still more state-sponsored terrorism, as we are already seeing with the creation of Croation and Serbian terrorist cells abroad, including their active movements in the streets of New York.

It is at this level, the state-sponsored level, where terrorism promises to escalate not only to the military tactics of the future, but to new heights of technological sophistication and aspiration alike whereby hundreds of coordinated terrorist cells—with a combined total of thousands of individual members spread across the globe, financed by unlimited resources—will actually be in a position to topple whole economic systems and governments.

It is important to keep in mind that while some of these groups are small and disorganized, others are small but extremely effective, and still others are large and well-established, having been in existence longer than many recognized political parties, and even longer than some countries.

The majority of established terrorist groups today were formed between 1965 and 1975. Most of these groups have been under continuous leadership since inception, while the United States and other target countries have undergone multiple changes in administration, as well as constant bureaucratic personnel changes in national and international security forces.

The Defense Department's annual report, "Terrorist Group Profiles," and other sources provide the basis for the following listing of only the most well-known and active international and national terrorist groups. The reader is invited to skim over this listing and refer back to it as a glossary as the groups are mentioned in future pages.

Middle East

Abu Nidal Organization
Formed: 1974
Headquarters: Libya (previously Syria and Iraq)
Leader: Abu Nidal
Operations: worldwide

Abu Nidal's goal is to undermine the Israeli-Palestinian peace negotiations and affirm the Arab commitment to the destruction of Israel. Has carried out over ninety terrorist attacks since 1974 in twenty countries, killing or injuring almost nine hundred people. Targets the United States, the United Kingdom, France, Israel, moderate Palestinians, the PLO, and various Arab countries, depending on which state is sponsoring it at the time.

Major attacks include Rome and Vienna airports in December 1985, the Neve Shalom synagogue in Istanbul, the Pan Am Flight 73 hijacking in Karachi in September 1986, and *The City of Poros* day-excursion ship attack in July 1988 in Greece. Suspected of carrying out assassination on January 14, 1991, in Tunis of PLO deputy chief Abu Lyad and PLO security chief Abu Hul. ANO members also attacked and seriously wounded a senior ANO dissident in Algeria in March 1990.

Arab Organization of May 15
Formed: 1979
HQ: unknown
Leader: Abu Ibrahim
Operations: Western Europe

Committed to destroy Israel and to intimidate moderate Palestinians and other Arabs, this group was more or less absorbed into Colonel Hawari's Special Operations Group of the Fatah. Best remembered for bombing the Pan Am flight from Tokyo to Honolulu in 1982, which killed a Japanese teenager.

Democratic Front for the Liberation of Palestine
Formed: 1969
HQ: unknown, previously Syria
Leader: Nayif Hawatmeh
Operations: Lebanon and Israel

DFLP is a Marxist group that split from the PFLP in 1969. Believes in revolution of the masses as the only way to accomplish Palestinian goals. Split into two factions in 1991, one supporting Arafat, and a more hardline faction headed by Nayif Hawatmeh. Receives financial and military aid from Syria and Libya. Attacks have taken place entirely inside Israel and occupied territories.

Fatah

Formed: 1957
HQ: Tunis, Tunisia
Leader: Yasser Arafat
Operations: worldwide

Seeks to establish an independent, secular Palestinian state and recognizes the PLO as the sole legitimate representative of the Palestinian people. The Fatah, headed by Yasser Arafat, joined the PLO in 1968 and won the leadership role in 1969. Its commanders were expelled from Jordan following violent confrontations with Jordan forces in 1970–71, beginning with Black September in 1970. The invasion of Lebanon by Israel in 1982 led to the group's dispersal to several Mideast countries, including Tunisia, Yemen, Algeria, and Iraq.

Maintains several military and intelligence wings, including Force 17 (formed in early 1970s as Arafat's personal security force, then expanded into terrorist attacks) and Hawari Special Operations Group. Colonel Hawari died in an automobile crash in 1991. Support, which has come from almost every Arab state at one time or another, was interrupted during the 1990–91 Gulf War. Is known to receive weapons from China and North Korea, and extensive training and assistance from former Soviet Union and Eastern bloc countries.

Al-Gama's al-Islamiyya (The Islamic Group)

Formed: late 1970s
HQ: unknown
Leader: unknown. Preeminent spiritual leader is Sheikh Omar Abdurrahman.

Egyptian Islamic extremist group whose goal is to overthrow the government of President Hosni Mubarak and replace it with an Islamic state. Several thousand hardcore members and several thousand sympathizers.

Targets Egyptian security and officials, Coptic Christians, Western tourists, and Egyptian opponents to Islamic extremism. Assassinated the speaker of the Egyptian assembly in 1990, and launched a series of attacks on tourists in Egypt in 1992. Appears to also have support from unemployed graduates and students.

HAMAS *(Islamic Resistance Movement)*
Formed: 1987
HQ: unknown
Leader: unknown
Operations: Israel and Jordan

HAMAS was an outgrowth of the Palestinian branch of the Muslim Brotherhood and has become Fatah's principal political rival in the occupied territories. HAMAS has thousands of hardcore members, and tens of thousands of sympathizers and supporters. Through both political and terrorism methods, it advocates an Islamic Palestinian state in place of Israel.

Terrorists of the Izz al-Din al-Qassam Forces are particularly active. In 1992 and 1993, the HAMAS were responsible for many Israeli border raids and ambushes of military units on the West Bank. They receive funding from Palestinian expatriates, Iran, and private benefactors in Saudi Arabia and other Arab states, and some funding from sympathizers in Western Europe and North America.

Hizballah *(Islamic Jihad—Islamic Holy War)*
Formed: 1983
HQ: Beirut, Lebanon
Leader: Consultive Council
Operations: Middle East and Europe

Also operates under the names of Revolutionary Justice Organization, Organization of the Oppressed on Earth, and Islamic Jihad for the Liberation of Palestine.

Radical Shia group formed in Lebanon and dedicated to the creation of an Iran-style Islamic republic in Lebanon and removal of all non-Islamic influence from the area. Its several thousand members are often directed by Iran.

The Hizballah also has cells in Europe, Africa, South America, and elsewhere. Bombed the Israeli embassy in Buenos Aires in March 1992. Is remembered for bombing the Beirut Marine barracks in 1983 and the U.S. Embassy annex in 1984.

Lebanese Armed Revolutionary Faction
Formed: 1979
HQ: Lebanon
Leader: George Ibrahim Abdallah
Operations: Lebanon

LARF is another splinter group of the Popular Front for the Liberation of Palestine. Attacks Israeli and U.S. interests, mainly in France. Wants the U.S., Israel, and France to withdraw interests in Lebanon. Few members are of Palestinian origin. Most are Lebanese Christians from the villages of Qubayyat and Andaqat in northern Lebanon.

LARF has an extensive network of safe houses, bank accounts, and arms caches throughout Europe. Tactics include assassinations and bombings, including letter bombs and car bombs. It is expected that attacks will continue against Israel, France, Italy, and the U.S. because those countries are either holding members prisoner or are pressing charges against them.

Organization of the Armed Arab Struggle
Formed: 1978
HQ: Libya and Syria
Leader: "Carlos" Apparat (Illych Ramirez Sanchez)
Operations: Western Europe and Middle East

The reputation of "Carlos" has grown to mythical proportions among terrorist groups and security forces alike. Carlos was born in Venezuela, the son of a prominent Marxist lawyer. He became involved in revolutionary tactics while a student at the Patrice Lumumba University in the Soviet Union, from which he was expelled for not being serious about his studies. Carlos was extensively involved with the Palestine Liberation Front–Special Operations Group in Lebanon. He was one of the original trainers of many of the resultant splinter groups.

Carlos became one of the established leaders and orchestrated the 1975 OPEC oil ministers hostage incident in Vienna, after which he went into retirement and became a consultant to terrorist groups worldwide.

Carlos was training Syrian intelligence troops in 1984, and was reported to be in Libya and Syria recently. There also are reports that he is dead—although no one is counting him out.

Palestine Islamic Jihad
Formed: 1970s
Leader: unknown

Committed to the creation of an Islamic Palestinian state and the destruction of Israel through holy war. Targets the U.S. as a supporter of Israel. Opposes moderate Arab states it believes have been tainted by Western secularism.

Operates primarily in Israel, the occupied territories, Jordan, and Lebanon. Receives support from Iran and Syria.

Palestine Liberation Front
Formed: 1977
HQ: Syria, Iraq, and Libya
Leaders: Muhammed Abu al Abbas, Abd al Fatah Ghanem, and Tal'at Yaqub
Operations: Lebanon, Israel, and Europe

Terrorist group that broke away from the Popular Front for the Liberation of Palestine–General Command. Later split again into pro-PLO, pro-Syrian, and pro-Libyan factions. Pro-PLO is led by Abbas, who left the PLO executive committee in 1991.

Abbas's activities include the aborted seaborne attack from Libya against Israel in 1990, and the 1985 attack on the cruise ship *Achille Lauro* during which U.S. citizen Leon Klinghoffer was murdered. Receives support from the PLO, Libya, and Iraq.

Palestine Liberation Organization (PLO)
Formed: 1964
HQ: Tunis
Leader: Yasser Arafat

The umbrella organization of Palestinian nationalists dedicated to the establishment of a Palestinian state. Control devolved to the leadership of various fedayeen militia groups after the 1967 Arab–Israeli war, with Yasser Arafat's Al-Fatah being the dominant group. Arafat became chairman in 1969. The PLO fragmented into several groups in the 1980s, each holding various views on terrorism, but the PLO remains the lead organization. Arafat publicly denounced terrorism in 1988, but the U.S. holds the PLO responsible for terrorist acts of the many factions, and broke off official dialogue after terrorist attacks in 1990.

Arafat's Fatah and Force 17 members are active terrorists who hold high positions in the PLO in embassies throughout the world.

The PLO was finally recognized by Israel as part of the 1993 Mideast Peace agreement toward Palestinian self-rule.

Popular Front for the Liberation of Palestine
Formed: 1967
HQ: unknown, previously Syria
Leader: Dr. George Habash
Operations: Middle East and Europe

The PFLP is a member organization of the PLO. After the Fatah, it is the most important military and political organization in the Palestinian movement. Advocates a Pan-Arab revolution, with Habash openly differing with Arafat on many issues. Conducts terrorist attacks primarily in Syria, Lebanon, and Israel.

Popular Front for the Liberation of Palestine–General Command (PFLP–GC)
Formed: 1968
HQ: Syria
Leader: Ahmad Jibril
Operations: Middle East

Split from the PFLP in 1968 to concentrate on fighting rather than politics. Opposed to Arafat and all Arab moderation. Probably directed by Syria. Receives support and safe haven from Syria, Libya, and Iran.

Popular Front for the Liberation of Palestine–Special Command (PFLP–SC)
Formed: 1979
Leader: Abu Salim

Broke away from the PFLP. Has claimed responsibility for numerous notorious attacks in Western Europe, including the 1985 bombing of a restaurant frequented by U.S. servicemen in Torrijon, Spain, killing eighteen civilians. Operates out of Lebanon and in various areas of the Middle East and Western Europe.

Popular Struggle Front
Formed: 1967
HQ: Syria and Libya
Leader: Dr. Samir Ghawshah
Operations: Lebanon and occupied areas

A splinter group from the PLO. Receives support from Syria, and in 1991 rejoined the PLO. Carries out attacks throughout the Middle East against Israeli and U.S. interests.

Sa'iqa
Formed: 1968
HQ: Syria
Leaders: Issam al-Qadi and Sami al-Attari
Operations: Middle East and Europe

Also known as The Thunderbolt and Eagles of the Palestinian Revolution, the Sa'iqa want to destroy Israel and replace it with a pro-Syrian Palestinian state. It has established a pro-Syrian Palestinian army. The Sa'iqa was established by the ruling Baath Party not only to conduct terrorist activities against foreign countries but to help the Syrian rulers control citizens.

Western Europe

Armenian Secret Army for the Liberation of Armenia
Formed: 1975
HQ: unknown
Leader: Monte Melkonian
Operations: worldwide

ASLA was formed in 1975 with the stated intention of compelling the Turkish government to publicly acknowledge its responsibility for the deaths of over 1.5 million Armenians in 1915, to pay retribution therefor, and to cede territory for an Armenian homeland. Led by Hagop Hagopian until his assassination in Athens in 1988. Also known as the Orly Group and the 3rd October Organization.

Through the 1970s and 1980s targeted Turkish, French, Swiss, and U.S. airline offices. Suffering from internal strife, the organization has been relatively inactive since 1990, although it claims responsibility for the

1993 attack on the Turkish ambassador to Hungary. Receives aid and safe haven from Syria, along with some support from Libya.

Basque Fatherland and Liberty (ETA)
Formed: 1959
HQ: Basque provinces of Spain and France
Leader: Jose Ternera
Operations: Spain and France

Aims to create an independent homeland in the Basque region of Spain. Has muted commitment to Marxism. In 1974 split into two factions: ETA-Political-Military, and ETA-Military. The former has been inactive since limited home rule was granted in 1982. ETA-Military continues to conduct lethal attacks despite several arrests of leaders in 1992 and 1993. Over forty people were killed and two hundred injured by ETA attacks in 1991. Has received training in Libya, Lebanon, and Nicaragua. Has close ties to PIRA in Ireland. Operates primarily in Spain and France, but has hit Spanish political and cultural targets in Italy and Germany.

Combatant Communist Cells
Formed: 1984
HQ: Brussels
Leader: Pierre Carrette
Operations: Belgium

Belgium was once a refuge for international terrorists, until the CCC began operations to foster a revolution inside the country. Pierre Carrette and three other militants were arrested by police in 1985. It is believed that the group is rebuilding and will resume operations.

Devrimici Sol (Dev Sol)
Formed: 1978
HQ: unknown
Leader: unknown
Operations: Turkey

Originally a splinter faction of the Turkish People's Liberation Party/Front, espouses a Marxist ideology and is intensely xenophobic and virulently anti-U.S. and anti-NATO. Seeks a national revolution.

Responsible for the murders of four retired military officers and thirty police in 1991. Resumed operations against foreign interests in 1991, killing two American contractors and one British businessman. Attempted the murder of a U.S. Air Force officer, and conducted over thirty bombings against Western diplomatic, commercial, and cultural facilities.

Direct Action

Formed: 1979
HQ: Paris, Lyons
Leader: unknown
Operations: France and Belgium

Their goal is to further close confrontation between the masses and western imperialization. Police successes in 1987 severely crippled the Direct Action group. Remaining hardcore members maintain ties with the Italian Red Brigades, the Irish National Liberation Army, and the Lebanese Armed Revolutionary Faction.

First of October Anti-Fascist Resistance Group

Formed: 1975
HQ: unknown
Leader: Camarada Arenas
Operations: Spain

Fewer than a dozen operatives loosely associated with the Spanish Communist Party–Reconstituted. Seeks to remove U.S. military forces from Spain and establish a revolutionary regime. Has ties to the French (Direct Action) and the Italian Red Brigades. The German RAF has sought ties to the group as well. During 1991, bombed railroad lines and segments of the NATO oil pipeline in Spain.

Iraultza

Formed: 1982
HQ: unknown
Leader: unknown
Operations: Basque provinces of Spain

Iraultza is earmarked by intelligence agencies as having the potential for becoming a future threat. It wants to establish an independent Marxist Basque nation and protests U.S. foreign policy, particularly in Latin America.

Irish National Liberation Army
Formed: 1975
HQ: Dublin
Leader: Harry Flynn
Operations: Belfast and Londonderry

The INLA wants to form a united thirty-two-county Socialist Republic in Ireland. Active in urban areas such as Belfast and Londonderry. Most of the original leaders were either killed or arrested (Flynn). It received widespread notoriety after the assassination of leading British Conservative Party member Airey Neave in Great Britain. The explosive device used in the assassination indicated a new level of sophistication among Irish terrorist groups. The INLA remains a brutal and unpredictable organization.

Justice Commandos of the Armenian Genocide
Formed: 1975
HQ: unknown
Leader: unknown
Operations: worldwide

Believed to have become the Armenian Revolutionary Army, it wants to establish the independent Armenia as it existed in Turkey after World War I.

Kurdistan Workers Party (PKK)
Formed: mid-1970s
HQ: probably Lebanon
Leader: unknown
Operations: Targets Turkey and Western Europe while maintaining locations in Iran, Syria, and Iraq

Also known as the Kurdistan Labor Party, it is composed of Turkish Kurds who want to set up a Marxist state in southeastern Turkey. Is becoming increasingly active against Turkish and rival Kurdish groups, as well as NATO targets. In 1993, orchestrated massive raids against Turkish business, government, and cultural interests throughout Europe.

Popular Forces 25 April
Formed: 1980
HQ: Lisbon, Oporto, and Barcelos
Leader: Lt. Col. Otelo Saraiva de Carvalho
Operations: Portugal

Anti-U.S. and NATO, wants to violently overthrow Portuguese government to establish a Marxist state. A small group operating in Portugal which attacks Portuguese, U.S., and NATO targets. Sometimes calls itself the Armed Revolutionary Organization.

Provisional Irish Republican Army
Formed: 1970
HQ: Ireland
Leaders: Gerry Adams and Martin McGuiness
Operations: Ireland, England, and Europe

A radical terrorist group formed as the clandestine armed wing of Sinn Fein, a legal political movement dedicated to the removal of British forces and the unification of Ireland. Organized into small, tightly knit cells under the leadership of the Army Council.

Several hundred hardcore members, and several thousand sympathizers, conduct assassinations, bombings, kidnappings, extortion, and robberies against British targets in Ireland, Britain, and Western Europe. Stepped up operations on the mainland in 1992.

Receives support from Libya and the PLO, maintains links with the Basques, and receives considerable economic support from U.S. sympathizers.

Red Army Faction (Baader-Meinhof Gang)
Formed: 1968
HQ: Germany
Leaders: Barbara Mayer, Inge Viett, Sigrid Sternbeck, Tomas Simon, Wolfgang Grams, Horst Meyer, Birgit Hogefeld, Silke Maier-Witt, and Susanne Albrecht
Operations: Germany

Supported by the intelligentsia, wants to destroy western capitalism to precipitate a worldwide Marxist revolution. A small and disciplined group which is the successor to the Baader-Meinhof Gang, it originated in the student protests of the 1960s. Organized into hardcore cadres that carry out terrorist attacks, and a network of supporters who provide logistic and propaganda support. Has survived despite numerous arrests of top leaders over the years.

Some ties still exist with Middle Eastern terrorist groups, and it appears to be developing closer relations with the First of October Antifascist Resistance Group in Spain.

Red Brigades
Formed: 1970
HQ: Rome, Naples, Genoa, Milan, and the Tuscany region of Italy
Leader: unknown
Operations: Italy

Wants to destroy the Italian government through revolution, and opposes the presence of NATO and U.S. or other Western multinational companies. Maintains ties with Palestinian terror groups. Recent arrests indicate a presence in Spain.

Revolutionary Cells
Formed: 1973
HQ: Berlin and Frankfurt
Leaders: Rudolph Raabe, Sonja Suder, Christian Gauger, Rudolf Schindler, and Savine Eckle
Operations: Germany

Opposes the U.S. military presence in West Germany as "colonialization." With significant caches of weapons hidden in forest areas, the Revolutionary Cells are competent, what with advanced weaponry and the making of sophisticated time-delay bombs.

Revolutionary Organization 17 November
Formed: 1975
HQ: Athens
Leader: unknown
Operations: Greece

A radical leftist group named for the November 1973 student uprising protesting the military regime. Anti-U.S., anti-Turkey, and anti-NATO. Committed to removal of Turkish/U.S. interests in Cyprus, and severing

Greece's ties to NATO and the European Community. Affiliated with other Greek terrorists.

Very active during the Gulf War against Turkish targets and with rocket attacks in Athens. Added rocket attacks in a stepped-up campaign which continues against U.S. and European Community interests.

Revolutionary Popular Struggle
Formed: 1973
HQ: Athens
Leader: unknown
Operations: Greece

Anti-NATO and U.S. presence in Greece. Promotes revolution against imperialism. Organization is unclear, but probably consists of a loose coalition of several small and violent groups and affiliates, including the 17 November.

Has targeted U.S. military and business facilities since 1986.

Terra Lliure (Free Land)
Formed: 1970s
HQ: unknown
Leader: unknown
Operations: Catalonia

Left-wing Catalonian separatist terrorist group with the goal of establishing an independent Marxist state in the Spanish Provinces of Catalonia and Valencia. Leadership announced in 1991 a cessation of terrorist activities, but hardcore members remain active. Attacks foreign banks and travel agencies.

Latin America

Alfaro Lives, Damn It! (Alfaro Vive, Carajo!)
Formed: 1983
HQ: unknown
Leader: unknown
Operations: Ecuador

Most senior leaders were arrested or killed in 1986. Wants to force withdrawal of U.S. interests in Ecuador. Collaborates with forces in Colombia, Peru, and Bolivia.

Bandera Roja (Red Flag)
Formed: 1969
HQ: unknown
Leader: unknown
Operations: Venezuela

A small group whose membership declined in the late 1980s, but is expected to find new support among the economically depressed with the hardship of the oil market in Venezuela.

Cinchoneros Popular Liberation Movement
Formed: 1980
HQ: Tegucigalpa, Honduras
Leader: unknown
Operations: Honduras

With Cuban and Nicaraguan support, as well as some assistance from the Salvadoran Farabundo Martí National Liberation Front, this group seeks to overthrow the Honduran government and oust U.S. interests. The movement appears to be rebuilding for a future explosion of activity.

Clara Elizabeth Ramirez Front
Formed: 1983
HQ: San Salvador
Leader: unknown
Operations: San Salvador

Conducts high-visibility acts of violence to erode public support for the government. Targets U.S. citizens and Salvadoran government. Recently has stepped up recruiting efforts on college campuses and among labor union members.

Farabundo Martí National Liberation Front
Formed: 1980
HQ: El Salvador and Nicaragua
Leaders: Joaquin Villalobos, George Handal, Leonel Gonzalez, Eduardo Castaneda, and Francisco Jovel
Operations: El Salvador and Honduras

Pro-Cuban, wants to create a sustained war of attrition against the elected government of El Salvador. Receives direct support from Cuba and the Sandinistas in Nicaragua, along with significant financial support from sympathetic groups in the United States and Europe.

Composed of five leftist groups: Central American Workers' Revolutionary Party; People's Revolutionary Army; Farabundo Martí Popular Liberation Forces; Armed Forces of National Resistance; and the Communist Party of El Salvador's Armed Forces of Liberation. A peace agreement with the government of El Salvador was reached on December 31, 1991. Carried out bombings, assassinations, economic sabotage, arson, and other urban and rural operations.

Guatemalan National Revolutionary Unity
Formed: 1982
HQ: Mexico, Cuba, and Nicaragua
Leaders: Rodrigo Amado, Jorge Garcia, and Ricardo de Leon
Operations: Guatemala

Through a united guerrilla front, works to defeat the power of national and foreign wealth and to install a democratic people's government. An umbrella organization of many small guerrilla groups in Guatemala: the Revolutionary Organization of the People in Arms, the Guerrilla Army of the Poor, and the Rebel Armed Forces. It is the militant wing of the Guatemalan Committee for Patriotic Unity.

Has a history of attacking oil pipelines and oil wells, along with U.S. military and business targets.

Lautaro Youth Movement (MJL)
Formed: late 1980s
HQ: Santiago
Leader: unknown
Operations: Chile

Sometimes known as the Lautaro faction of the United Popular Action Movement, or the Lautaro Popular Rebel Forces, it is a violent, anti-U.S. extremist group led by leftist elements but recruiting heavily among criminals and alienated youths from poorer areas of the cities. Has been linked to several assassinations, bank robberies, bombings, and burnings of Mormon chapels. May receive support from Cuba.

Lorenzo Zelaya Popular Revolutionary Forces
Formed: 1978
HQ: Tegucigalpa and San Pedro Sula
Leader: unknown
Operations: Tegucigalpa, San Pedro Sula, and Honduras

Has the goal of carrying out the war on U.S. imperialism, targeting U.S. companies, military facilities, Peace Corp members, and embassies. Wants to revive the Honduran revolutionary movement, which the government crushed in 1983.

19th of April Movement
Formed: 1970
HQ: Cali, Colombia
Leaders: Carlos Leon-Gomez, Antonio Navarro, and Otty Patino
Operations: Columbia

The group takes its name from the date of the 1970 election defeat of former President General Gustavo Rojas Pinilla. Membership has come from students and intellectuals, with recent expansion of recruits into the peasant areas. Revenues from drug trafficking are a major part of the group's support base.

Macheteros (Machete Wielders)
Formed: 1978
HQ: unknown
Leader: unknown
Operations: Puerto Rico

Wants to wage war against U.S. imperialism. They are an extremely tightknit and violent terrorist group, with a reputation for their good security and detailed attacks.

Manuel Rodriguez Patriotic Front (FPMR)
Formed: 1983
HQ: Santiago
Leader: unknown
Operations: Chile

Named for a hero in Chile's war of independence against Spain, the FPMR is the armed wing of the Chilean Communist Party. The group splintered in 1987 into two factions, with the main movement laying down arms in 1991 to become a political movement, and the smaller, dissident group, FPMR-D, becoming one of Chile's most active terrorist groups.

Responsible for many attacks against U.S. businesses and Mormon churches from 1986 through 1993. Attacked U.S. military and embassy targets in 1991. Probably cross-trains with Peru's MRTA.

Morazanist Patriotic Front (FPM)
Formed: late 1980s
HQ: unknown
Leader: unknown
Operations: Honduras

A radical leftist terrorist group that attacks in protest of U.S. intervention in Honduran economic and political affairs.

Mainly attacks U.S. military targets. Bombed a bus in 1990, wounding seven U.S. servicemen. Bombed a Peace Corps office in 1988. Wounded three U.S. servicemen in 1989. Attacked a U.S. convoy in 1989 and conducted a grenade attack that wounded seven servicemen in Ceiba.

Movement of the Revolutionary Left
Formed: 1965
HQ: Havana and Santiago
Leaders: Andres Allende, Herman Donoso, Manuel Donoso, and
Nelson Gutierrez
Operations: Chile

Wants to establish a Marxist state in Chile, and conducts terrorist acts in an effort to force the Chilean government to take oppressive measures against the public. Attacks U.S. military and business interests, to force withdrawal from Chile.

National Liberation Army–Bolivia

Formed: claims to be the revived organization that was formed by
Che Guevara in the 1960s
HQ: Colombia
Leaders: Manuel Martinez and Nicolas Bautista

Seeks the "conquest of power for the popular classes" to build a
Marxist-Leninist state. Operates as an umbrella group over numerous
small Bolivian subversive movements that include the CNPZ (Nestor Paz
Zamora Commission). Attacks against U.S. interests continued through
1992 and 1993.

National Liberation Army–Colombia

Formed: 1963
HQ: Colombia
Leaders: Manuel Martinez and Nicolas Bautista
Operations: Colombia

Rural-based, anti-U.S., Maoist-Marxist-Leninist group which engaged
in unsuccessful peace talks with the Colombian government in 1991.
Attacks and kidnaps foreign employees for large ransoms. Conducts
extortion and bombing attacks against U.S. businesses. Has inflicted
major damage on oil pipelines since 1986. Has received aid and training
from Cuba and Nicaragua.

Nestor Paz Zamora Commission (CNPZ)

Formed: 1990
HQ: unknown
Leader: under ELN umbrella group
Operations: Bolivia

Extremely violent and anti-U.S. radical leftist group named after the
deceased brother of President Paz Zamora. Attacked the U.S. Embassy
Marine guardhouse in 1990. Probably has only 100 members who operate
under the National Liberation Army–Bolivia umbrella.

Popular Liberation Army

Formed: 1967
HQ: Colombia
Leaders: Francisco Caraballo and Javier Robles
Operations: Colombia

This small group continues to be supported by Colombian intellectuals who follow a Maoist philosophy. Moved its operations to a rural uprising campaign in 1987, but maintains cells in cities throughout the country.

Revolutionary Armed Forces of Colombia (FARC)
Formed: 1966
HQ: Colombia
Leader: Manuel Marulanda
Operations: Colombia

Established as the military wing of the Colombian Communist Party, its goal is to overthrow both the government and the ruling class. The largest guerrilla group in Colombia, it is anti-U.S. and attacks U.S. interests and Colombian government targets. Traffics in drugs and has well-documented ties to drug traffickers.

Ricardo Franco Front
Formed: 1984
HQ: Colombia
Leader: José Alvarez
Operations: Colombia

Its stated goal is to overthrow the established order to form a "people's government." Strong U.S. opposition. After a bloody, internal purge in 1985, wherein over 100 members were found murdered and buried in a mass grave, the group has become more of a bandit group without the organization of a guerrilla cell.

Shining Path (Sendero Luminoso)
Formed: 1969
HQ: Peru
Leaders: Manuel Guzman, Julio Mezzich, and Carlota Cutti
Operations: Peru

Peru's largest subversive organization is among the world's most dangerous and ruthless terrorist groups. Goal is to destroy existing Peruvian institutions and replace them with a peasant regime as well as to rid Peru of foreign interests.

Has extensive ties to narcoproducers and narcotraffickers working in and out of Peru. Works with Colombian traffickers as well. Receives support from sympathizers in Latin America, North America, and Europe.

Tupac Amaru Revolutionary Movement
Formed: 1983
HQ: unknown
Leaders: Nestor Serpa and Victor Polay
Operations: Peru

Traditional Marxist-Leninist movement to rid Peru and the region of "imperialist" influence and establish a Marxist regime.

Responsible for more anti-U.S. attacks than any other group in Latin America. In 1990–91, attacked the U.S. Ambassador's residence, bombed the U.S. consulate and U.S.-Peruvian Binational Center, and attacked U.S. businesses and Mormon churches. Attacked Peru's presidential palace and presidential airplane in 1991. Victor Polay was arrested in 1992.

Asia

Chukaku-Ha (Nucleus or Middle-Core Faction)
Formed: 1963
HQ: Japan
Leaders: Takuji Mukai and Higeo Yamamori
Operations: Japan

An ultraleftist radical group which originated in the fragmentation of the Japanese Communist Party in 1957. Largest domestic group with political arm and small, covert action wing called the Kansai Revolutionary Army.

Participates in mass protests and snake-dancing in the streets. Supports farmers' protest of construction of the Narita airport, among other causes. Wants to abolish both the current constitutional democracy and the monarchy. Presses for termination of the U.S.–Japan Security Treaty and the removal of U.S. forces from Japan. Sabotaged Japanese railroad in 1985 and 1986. Sporadic rocket attacks, including anti-U.S. attacks against military and diplomatic targets.

Japanese Red Army
Formed: 1971
HQ: Lebanon
Leader: Fusako Shigenobu (Miss Yuki)
Operations: Western Europe, Middle East, and Asia

An international terrorist group formed after breaking away from the Japanese Communist League Red Army Faction. Stated goals are the overthrow of the Japanese government and helping to foment world revolution. May have ties to the Anti-Imperialist International Brigade, and links to the Antiwar Democratic Front, an overt leftist group inside Japan.

Recent movements indicate the formation of cells in Asian cities, including Singapore and Manila, while it keeps close relationships with Mideast terrorist groups.

The JRA bombed the USO Club in Naples in 1988. One of its members, Yu Kikumura, was arrested then on the New Jersey Turnpike in possession of explosives—apparently planning an attack to coincide with the USO bombing. Receives support from Syria and Libya, and sympathizers inside Japan.

Liberation Tigers of Tamil Eelam
Formed: 1972
HQ: Sri Lanka
Leader: Vellupillai Prabhakaran
Operations: Sri Lanka

Wants to create a separate Tamil state in the northern and eastern provinces of Sri Lanka and force Indian troops to leave that area. The group is known for its vicious attacks, including the hacking to death of innocent villagers.

New People's Army
Formed: 1969
HQ: Philippines
Leaders: Rolando Kintanar and Benito Tiamzon
Operations: Philippines

The guerrilla arm of the Communist Party of the Philippines, an avowed Maoist group formed with the aim of overthrowing the government. Rural-based, but with active urban cells to carry out terrorist attacks. Uses city-based assassination squads called "sparrow units." Receives economic support from locals, and extorts protection taxes from businesses. Also receives support from sympathetic private citizens in Europe and North America. Has links to Libya.

The New People's Army has killed ten American civilians and military personnel since 1987, besides attacking U.S. businesses which have refused to pay the revolutionary taxes.

Sikh Terrorism

Sikh terrorism is sponsored by a number of Indian and expatriate Sikh groups who want to carve out an independent Sikh state, called Khalistan (Land of the Pure), from Indian territory.

Sikh violence outside India surged after the Indian Army's attack on the Golden Temple, Sikhism's holiest shrine, and remains high. Groups that have carried out attacks include: the Dashmesh, or 10th Regiment (active in India, Germany, and Canada); Dal Khalsa; Babbar Khalsa (India, Western Europe, and Canada); and the All-India Sikh Students Federation, a militant wing of the Akali Dal, a main Sikh party now splintered.

Dal Khalsa
Formed: 1978
HQ: Punjab
Leader: Gurbachan Singh Manochahal
Operations: India

Dashmesh Regiment
Formed: 1982
HQ: Punjab
Leader: unknown
Operations: worldwide activities from India headquarters

Africa

Mozambican National Resistance
Formed: 1976
HQ: Mozambique
Leader: unknown
Operations: Mozambique

With a 20,000-member strength, operates in Mozambique and border countries of Zimbabwe, Malawi, and Zambia. Originally formed as a secret service to protect the government, it now operates as an insurgency against the government and civilian targets alike. Receives aid from South Africa and from sympathizers in South Africa, Europe, and elsewhere.

Each of the above sixty-five groups lists the United States, U.S. citizens, or expulsion of U.S. interests in their respective countries among their primary targets—as do most of the other (approximately six hundred and fifty) smaller groups around the globe. To most Americans the above names are but a mishmash of unrecognizable foreign symbols. We remember various acts of destruction, but we mentally lump them all together under the heading of "terrorism" and pay little attention to who were the perpetrators of the crimes. We have had that luxury in the past.

We remember the terrible day in 1972 when most of the members of an Israeli athletic team were seized at the Olympic Village in Munich and shortly thereafter killed by their abductors during a failed rescue attempt—but we forget that the terrorists were from the Fatah, led by Yasser Arafat and supported by the PLO, China, Iraq, Iran, and other Arab nations.

We watched with great sympathy as hostages were released in 1992 during the Bush administration, but we have little recollection that the Hizballah, a single organization of over five thousand active members working as an arm of the religious leadership of Iran, was the primary force behind the kidnappings. And we have only a vague idea of just how large was the number of Americans they held hostage for extended periods of time. They kidnapped Lt. Col. Richard Higgins; U.S. journalist Charles Glass; university at Beirut professors Jesse Turner, Alan Steen, and Robert Polhill; Edward Tracy Austin; Joseph Cicippio; Frank Reed; Thomas Sutherland; David Jacobsen; Associated Press journalist Terry Anderson; Fr. Lawrence Martin Jenco; Rev. Benjamin Weir; William Buckley; Jeremy Levin; and Frank Regier—along with a score of other non–United States citizens.

The Hizballah is also the organization which became known for its "kamikaze" car-bomb attacks, including its April 1983 attack on the U.S. Embassy in Beirut, which killed 49 and wounded 120. This was followed by a similar attack, in October of the same year, on the combined U.S. and French military barracks, which killed 241 Americans and 56 French. Here again we remember the car bombs, but not the Hizballah.

The Hizballah, sometimes called the "Islamic Jihad," is perhaps the largest example of the new fear in terrorism—a separate organization carrying out its own missions, but under the general philosophical direction of a religious order whose vague instructions from Iran to thousands of members and millions of believers worldwide can be delivered through the media. When the World Trade Center bomb exploded, it was the Islamic Jihad that was first on the FBI's list of suspects.

Under a worldwide religious order of this kind, a religious leader can go on international television or radio and make as vague a statement as, "All believers must fight the Great Satan," and within a few hours hundreds of small cells of terrorists start making or implementing plans to wreak havoc in their local areas, *wherever* they may be.

Patterns of Proliferation

Beyond the description of any particular terrorist group, it is the *pattern of proliferation* these groups supply us that is important. The spawning of terrorist groups, their expansion, their division and multiplication, and their coordination of activities are the patterns that are troublesome, because there is every reason to assume that these patterns not only will continue, but will accelerate, in our post–cold war atmosphere.

One of these patterns is the splintering of groups.

The Popular Front for the Liberation of Palestine (PFLP) is best remembered for its 1976 hijacking of an Air France airliner to Entebbe, Uganda, in which four passengers were killed during the now-famous rescue operation by Israeli paratroopers. One of its members, Ahmad Jibril, left the PFLP to form the Popular Front for the Liberation of Palestine–General Command (PFLP–GC), introducing the application of conventional military tactics to terrorist acts. Later, two more groups splintered from the PFLP to form the Arab Organization of May 15 (May 15), headquartered in Western Europe, and the Lebanese Armed Revolutionary Faction (LARF), headquartered in Lebanon but operating throughout Western Europe.

As these splinter groups appear, terrorism proliferates. And each group takes on its own modus operandi or "signature," from expertise in kidnapping to car bombing, from assassination to military-weapons attacks on public utilities.

Another trend of the past that will haunt security officials in the future is the extent of cooperation among terrorist groups—even the cooperation between groups which share no apparent belief or ideology. For example, the PFLP–GC trains terrorists from all over the world in its base and camps in Lebanon. Abu Nidal, the most feared terrorist in the world, contracts his network out to other groups and other state sponsors. Carlos, a terrorist who has reached mythical proportions in both the underworld and among international security forces, has become a consultant to groups worldwide. And the Red Army Faction (Baader-Meinhof Gang) of Germany has cooperated with the Japanese Red Army, which receives training in Lebanon, in the bombing of airports.

All of these actions of splintering and intratraining demonstrate not only the proliferation of terrorism, but the complex and sophisticated network of members which is now in place in almost every country. Yet none of this compares to what is coming.

Nothing reveals the potential of the new terrorism more than a look at Abu Nidal, the world's most infamous terrorist and number one on the "Most Wanted" list of every secret service agency in the Western world. A composite taken from the U.S. Defense Department's 1992 "Patterns of Global Terrorism," and two extensive books about the corruption scandal of the Bank of Credit and Commerce International (BCCI), *False Profits* by Peter Truell and Larry Gurwin, and *A Full Service Bank* by James Ring Adams and Douglas Frantz, along with information gleaned from *Jane's Defense & Aerospace News* provides a look inside the movements and power-links of today's terrorist organization, digested in the following example.

It is July, 1980. The manager of BCCI's most prestigious branch on London's Sloane Street, in the heart of the Knightsbridge shopping district, informs the senior assistant that an important customer is coming to the bank, to open a large account. He is told that the customer is a representative of the Iraqi government.

An hour later, the man arrives at the branch and is escorted immediately to the office of the manager, who then instructs Senior Assistant Ghassan Qassem to handle the new client's affairs with the utmost efficiency and discretion. This is not an unusual request, since the Sloane Street branch is the BCCI bank of choice by the royal families of the Middle East while they are in London.

Qassem's first task is to transfer $50 million from Midlands Bank to the new account at BCCI, which he will handle personally. The account, which the client agreed would receive no interest payments, provides a no-cost source of funds for BCCI, and is soon used to transfer $32 million in the first two transactions.

About this same time, across the channel in Brussels, the Abu Nidal organization kills the Israeli Commercial Attaché.

Qassem notices that his mysterious new client often travels to Europe and the Middle East. And that, when in London, he uses the branch as a personal office, spending entire days placing calls around the world and sending telexes. While this is not an unusual service for the bank to extend to prominent clients, there *is* one thing that sets these telexes apart: They are coded. Qassem has never seen a customer so concerned with security as is Samir Najmadeen, who Qassem concludes is obviously an arms dealer.

BCCI prided itself for its support of Iraq and other Middle East concerns, as well as its attitude that the doors are open to anyone—no questions asked.

BCCI's client list included all Middle East countries and royal families, along with Manuel Noriega, the CIA, the Israeli Mossad, and just about anyone who dealt internationally in arms, drugs, dirty money, or dirty causes of any kind. BCCI had sprung up during the 1973 oil embargo, representing itself to its Mideast partners as the opportunity to take economic control of the third world away from Western influences even as it put on a show for the West as the financial big brother of worthy third world causes.

Through huge donations to favorite charities and special attention to United States politicians and influence peddlers, (including publicized assistance to ex-president Jimmy Carter's charitable activities), BCCI was to be the Mideast's link to power in Washington and other capitals around the globe. BCCI was the perfect bank for anything from drug financing to terrorist payoffs, and for anyone who needed to move money around the world quickly. It had offices in fifty-nine locations throughout Europe, ninety-three in the Middle East, fifty-eight in Africa, thirty-four in Asia, and fifteen in North America and the Caribbean.

It is for these reasons that the senior assistant is not surprised that a representative for the Iraqi government is using BCCI to transfer funds for lucrative arms deals. Nor is he surprised in 1981 when Najmadeen asks him to pick up "an extremely important contact" at Gatwick Airport outside London.

The contact is approximately forty years old and carries an Iraqi passport which identifies him as Shakar Farhan. He tells Qassem that he lives in Kuwait and deals in electronics and photocopy equipment, but he speaks so little that Qassem is not even sure of how well he might actually speak English. Qassem, who was born in Syria in the mid-fifties, grew up in Jordan and went to school in London, before joining BCCI in 1973. He is only about ten years younger than his wealthy client.

Qassem drives Farham to the hotel and, in a pattern to be repeated many times throughout the coming years, escorts him on a shopping spree around London. Farhan purchases suits at a tailor's on Oxford Street, and cigars on Jermyn Street, and stocks up on a number of items at Selfridges, a department store.

During that first year, the bank account always stays in the range of $50 million, with payments going out for arms transactions, and commissions coming in from a variety of sources.

While Qassem goes about his business in May 1981, the Abu Nidal organization murders Viennese city councilman Heinz Nittel and threatens to kill Austrian chancellor Bruno Kreisky. In August, they machine-gun a Vienna synagogue, killing two and wounding seven.

By 1982, Farhan is utilizing the BCCI services extensively, while the activities of Abu Nidal pick up across Europe. In June 1982, Nidal's organization, the ANO, attempts to assassinate Israeli ambassador Shlomo Argov in London, and kills a PLO official in Rome with a car bomb. In August they machine-gun and grenade a Paris restaurant frequented by French Jews, killing six and wounding twenty-two, and attempt to murder the United Arab Emirates consul in Bombay. They wound a UAE diplomat in Kuwait. A few days later, in September, the ANO kills a Kuwait diplomat in Madrid, and in October another grenade and machine-gun attack on a Rome synagogue kills one child and injures ten other people.

In 1985, BCCI provides the financing for the shipment of riot guns and ammunition intended for Syria, but the British authorities refuse to approve the export—so the bank arranges for an African diplomat to act as a front for the shipment. The guns and ammo are then diverted to East Germany and divided between East German state police and the Abu Nidal Palestinian organization. At about the same time Abu Nidal, no longer welcome in Baghdad, moves his headquarters to Syria.

It is not until 1987 that Qassem realizes that his most important client, Shakar Farhan, is none other than Abu Nidal himself: A friend at the bank shows him a copy of the French newsmagazine *L'Express*, and there is a picture of Farhan. Except that he is captioned as Abu Nidal, the most wanted terrorist in the world.

By this time Nidal, with almost three hundred deaths to his credit, was known to almost everyone. One of his more infamous escapades had been the hijacking of an Egyptian airliner to Malta, where three Abu Nidal terrorists started killing American and Jewish passengers before being overpowered by a rescue team. In fact, the hijackers killed sixty passengers before they were stopped. (In July 1993, Omar Mohammed Ali Rezaq, who had killed many of the passengers, was released from his Maltese prison "for good behavior.")

Three months later, the ANO bombed and machine-gunned the Rome and Vienna airports, killing sixteen people—including a child—and wounding sixty.

Qassem, having seen the *L'Express* revelation, went to MI5, an English secret-service branch, and agreed to cooperate with them by revealing as much as he could about the activities of the secret Abu Nidal account. MI5, along with European and U.S. agencies, uncovered a complex web of activities which enveloped the globe, including lucrative weapons businesses owned by Abu Nidal in Poland and other East-bloc countries.

Bank deposits also linked Syria to terrorist plots, revealing that all of the moderate Arab states were paying what amounted to Mafia-style protection fees to ward off any Nidal attacks. Sheik Zayed himself, who had more-or-less financed the making of BCCI, paid Abu Nidal $17 million in protection fees in 1984 alone.

Until the closing of BCCI on July 5, 1991, the British and American secret-service agencies attempted to use the BCCI accounts to track Nidal's activities. Of course, it can be assumed that this worked the other way around, too—and it is ironic to think that one of the first persons to know about the CIA's involvement with the Iran-Contra scandal, or the CIA payoffs to Manuel Noriega, was Abu Nidal.

Nidal probably was not harmed by the BCCI closing to any great extent, but he *was* damaged by the period of détente with the East-bloc countries and the eventual ending of the cold war. To add to his woes, Poland shut down his arms operation at the suggestion of U.S. intelligence services, and he lost many of his safe havens.

It was at about this time that Abu Nidal began looking directly to the United States as his next target—or perhaps even as his next safe haven.

By 1990, even before the BCCI closing, it was widely believed that Abu Nidal was in ill health, although as yet no one writes him off as a potent threat. He reportedly has terminal cancer and remains in his heavily armed camp at the outskirts of Tripoli, where Libya has said they have him under "house arrest" to appease extradition requests from Egypt.

The ANO has lost many of its members to the PLO, due to an internal struggle for power and a rejection of Nidal's attempt to take over total control of the Fatah. At the same time, PLO sources say the fifty-six-year-old Nidal is bedridden with a heart condition brought on by his habit of chain-smoking.

"Abu Nidal, whose real name is Sabri Khalil al-Banna, has been written off before but re-emerged to carry out new atrocities," *Jane's Defense* warns.

He was reported to have flown from Baghdad to London in an Iraqi jet for open-heart surgery in 1979.

He reportedly died of a heart attack in Bulgaria in 1983, but surfaced a year later, after undergoing bypass surgery.

In 1984, reports said, he died in Baghdad, where he was headquartered, of a heart attack. At the same time, others had him undergoing surgery, somewhere in Eastern Europe, for a brain tumor.

Facts about Nidal are sometimes sketchy, but there is no doubt about his paranoia. He has executed scores of his men suspected of working with Western, Israeli, or Arab intelligence agencies, *or* the PLO. He also ordered the assassination of his nephew in Jordan, and once even suspected his wife of being a CIA agent.

One report said that he had undergone facial surgery to change his appearance, but the French article which published a picture of Nidal that was recognized by the BCCI manager would seem to discount this.

He has camouflaged his organization under a number of different names, including Black June, Black September, Revolutionary Cells, Revolutionary Organization of Socialist Moslems, and the Arab Revolutionary Brigades.

Recent defectors have said that Nidal has an aversion to the telephone, fearing it would be tapped or intercepted by electronic surveillance monitors. He also fears telephones could be booby-trapped with remote-controlled bombs similar to devices favored by Israel's Mossad secret-service agency to assassinate Palestinian operatives in Europe throughout the 1970s.

In 1989, Nidal dissolved the politburo of the Fatah in a move to take total control of the organization, a move which deepened the internal strife. Three of the leaders were among twenty-two senior members Nidal had killed in Tripoli. The nearly two dozen bodies are said to have been buried under tons of concrete by his bodyguards in what is now a parking lot behind his residence.

Even with his troubles, it is believed that Nidal holds on to his hardcore members, perhaps with even deeper resolve than before, and that they are available for hire by any government or organization that needs them.

The Nidal history demonstrates how easily even the world's best-known terrorist can travel without disguise while manipulating millions of dollars through global financial networks to finance terrorism. Though Nidal is likely to be hampered by ill health and deep psychological problems, officials worry that these same ailments may drive him to a devastating "swan dance." The fact that these announcements happen to coincide with the immigration of Nidal terrorist members to the United States is also most disturbing, to say the least.

CHAPTER 3

Profile of a Terrorist

All the old rules and definitions change when the foreign problem of terrorism is suddenly redefined as a domestic crisis. Profiles no longer are reliable. Motivations are different. Networks of underground circulation and protection change. Counterterrorist experts no longer are expert. Politicians and academic strategists in Washington and in the universities who viewed past terrorist actions as small tacks on a wall map now are suddenly held accountable for their convenient theories, and these same tacks suddenly represent a potential for devastation far greater than ever imagined.

One of the greatest misconceptions promoted by terrorist experts is that the United States does not have a population base that would support terrorism. Shortly after the World Trade Center explosion, Robert Hunter, National Security Council expert on the Middle East, told *USA Today* that the United States lacks "a terrorist culture. We don't hide terrorists. There's no sea for the fish to swim in." Other experts have made similar comments.

The most frightening aspect of these statements is that our experts may actually believe them. Just a brief look at the facts reveals how ridiculous their positions are, and it is worrisome indeed that the people who are advising our national-security planners practice such head-in-the-sand thinking.

Part of our information base comes from what we already know about terrorists—from foreign terrorist profiles that have been developed over the years. These profiles can easily be applied to the United States.

The first profile is that of the front-line soldier, without whom the leaders of the groups could not operate.

Writer D. Keith Mano reported in *National Review* in 1987 the results of an interview with Yaron Svoray of the Israeli police. Svoray gave an example of the recruitment of a young Palestinian: how one day a Mercedes-Benz pulls into a country village; a man in uniform steps from the automobile amid the gathered crowd and selects a seventeen-year-old; the boy rises to heroic stature as he accepts membership into a renowned rebel group and leaves for his induction into not only the cult-like life of terrorism, but also a world he has never known, as he suddenly grows from boy to man. He learns simple weapons, and for the first time meets unveiled women. He is sent on a mission to submachine-gun an airport, and told that when he is done he should just walk away. Not to worry, because nothing will happen to him.

And the boy believes what he is told. Why? Partly because he has been indoctrinated to become a zealot. And partly just because he is a teenager.

As Dr. Louis J. West, who heads the psychiatry department at the University of California in Los Angeles, told *Scholastic Update* magazine May 16, 1986: "Teenagers make very good zealots. They make excellent soldiers. They have strong feelings of comradery, you can excite their courage toward risk-taking behavior. They aren't as likely to believe in the possibility of their own death or serious injury as are older people, who have lived longer and seen more." Also, the boy came from a village where he had no prospects for a future, and not much to lose in death.

Sound familiar? It should, if you have read any of the reports about the reasons behind our epidemic rise of youth gangs in the United States, or the explanations for the millions of Americans who belong to Koresh-type religious cults, or the rising numbers of neo-Nazi groups in Germany, England, France, Canada, and the United States.

In just the past ten years, the youth gangs of Los Angeles known as the Crips and the Bloods have spread to every city in the nation. They are mostly black, but not always. And they have been matched by rival gangs from every minority community including Hispanics, Chicanos, Puerto Ricans, Chinese, and Vietnamese, along with Caucasian youth gangs from white slums, in addition to white-supremacist offshoots bringing young recruits into neo-Nazi and skinhead factions.

Every large to midsized city in the country has elements of gang problems which, for the most part, the cities have found insurmountable. As urban and suburban areas continue to fractionate into minority groups, youth gangs with common race or religion will continue to appear for as long as social conditions encourage that.

Almost every police officer and official in the country will admit that law enforcement has lost control over its youth gangs. The gangs are so large and powerful that they are encouraged to have citywide and nationwide conferences to settle their differences. Millions of Americans, locked and barb-wired into their own homes and apartments, live in fear of youth gangs and youth crime. When they step out of their fortresses, they do so in even greater fear. Imagine the consequences if an individual or foreign power suddenly gave one or more of these gangs a political agenda.

The profile for recruitment of members in Middle East villages is remarkably similar to the profile of gang members in the United States, as summarized here from a report distributed in 1993 to police in all U.S. cities:

GANG STRUCTURE:

Some gangs will mark an area or neighborhood with graffiti to claim the territory for drug distribution. Often drugs are distributed from a network of well-fortified houses and apartments. In addition to narcotics, some gangs are involved in terrorism, illegal arms and munitions dealings, robberies and burglaries.

Gang members often use intimidation to discourage citizens from reporting illegal activity. The citizens fear retaliation.

Some gangs align with one another to become larger and more powerful, forcing other neighborhood gangs to join or fight. Youths will gain higher status in a gang by committing violent acts.

"Original Gang" members now in their thirties and forties are held in high esteem by younger gang members—and are the source of supplying cocaine. The OG's care less about gang activity at their age and only have interest in profits from their drug trade.

Hard-Core "gang-bangers" are usually within the ages of 16–24. They wear the colors, the tattoos, engage in the drive-by shootings and deal the bulk of cocaine. "Baby Gangsters" are usually age 12–16. They aspire to be gang-bangers, act as mules running to and from the crack houses, and engage in a small quantity of crack sales. An initiation into the Hard-Core level could involve surviving a beating by an older gang member (referred to as being "jumped in") or by performing a criminal act.

"Tiny Gangsters," usually age 9–12, serve as runners and lookouts. They sometimes make as much as $200 a day.

"Associates" hang out with gang members and many deal the bulk of the drugs without engaging in gang activity. "Peripherals" are often girlfriends, hangers-on or wanna-be's who aspire to join the gang. They are often at the elementary grade level.

MENTALITY:

A need for instant gratification. "I'm gonna die anyway, so I'll take mine now."
"I'm ready to die for my homeboys." The highest honor you can give your set is death.
"My homeboys are the only ones who care for me. They love me. They accept me. They pay attention to me. To them, I'm okay."
"If I want what you have, and can take it, I will."
"If anyone messes with you, kill them."
No remorse for their actions. No sense of right or wrong. No interest in others. No compassion for others.

Gang members may come from dysfunctional, neglectful or abusive families. They have low self-esteem. They may have grown up poor without seeing any real chance for success in life and no way to make it for themselves. While their behavior may not be socially normal, they feel normal with one another.

Given a purpose, a political agenda of any kind, it is amazing to ponder what this existing force of misguided youth and willing violence could accomplish. And there are examples that this power is already recognized by foreign enemies.

In the 1960s, many of the youth on our college campuses who poured into the streets and resorted to violence had no idea they were, in some cases, being manipulated by organizations financed by the USSR. Perhaps fewer than 1 percent of the demonstrators believed they were fighting to create a socialist government, but the few who adhered to their cause fervently, most notably the members of the Students for a Democratic Society, were extremely effective in motivating a wave of millions who thought they were merely protesting the Vietnam War.

More recently, and more directly related to the youth gangs, a national wave of violence was narrowly avoided when a post-office worker in Oregon discovered a box of explosives, along with disturbingly specific instructions, sent from a gang on the west coast to one on the east coast. Similar packages had in fact gone out to every major city. From these packages the FBI discovered that a coordinated plot to enact a simultaneous attack on police nationwide was about to take place on a specific date in 1991.

In Chicago, shortly before the U.S. Air Force raid on Libya, it was discovered that members of the Black September group had proposed a $3 million contract with Libya to conduct terrorist attacks in this country on Libya's behalf. And for the past thirty years there have been periodic reports of young people traveling abroad—to Cuba, Syria, Palestine, or Lebanon—for instruction in terrorist activity.

It takes only a small stretch of the imagination to realize not only that millions of our youth are primed for recruitment into terrorist activity, but also that the organizational structures are already in place to allow them to be recruited thousands at a time.

Like the poor, illiterate Palestinian goatherd, these millions of youth-gang members are representative of what could be the national network of "grunts" for terrorist organizations. They would not likely be the leaders behind the overall plots. Instead, they would be the ones to carry the bombs, pull the triggers on their submachine guns, drive the car bombs into nuclear plants or public utilities, act as lookouts and runners, or simply provide millions of safe houses for terrorists to hide in. The biggest difference between their behavior now and in the future—and it is a big, *big* difference—could be that their targets would be both preassigned and coordinated to accomplish a common purpose.

If the idea that a specific individual or organization would mastermind this organizational network is too great a stretch of the imagination, it is even more sobering to realize that these connections are likely to evolve naturally, due to another new trend in terrorism: a growing involvement in trafficking drugs and illegal weapons.

These common connections of illegal drug and arms trafficking, and the economic interests they imply, will not only introduce the various factions but will give them reason to cement relationships.

In South America, connections between drug kings and terrorist chapters have become common. They share economic interests and the government as a common enemy. This combination of underground connections, access to arms and undercover networks, cooperative political dealings, and access to unlimited funds raises the terrorist group to new heights of unrestricted power not reliant even on any particular state sponsor.

With unlimited wealth and unrestricted power, the new terrorist represents a greater threat yet.

The fall of the Berlin Wall and the disintegration of the Soviet Union marked the end of the cold war—but almost immediately we discovered that the cold war had *some* benefits, including the comfort that small, independent communist countries would not take any overt action without permission from Soviet leaders. This Soviet control over a large portion of Europe and Asia reduced the chances of indiscriminate terrorist attacks. If anything did happen, regardless of how terrible, it usually had some sense of organization and strategic thought in relation to Soviet goals— and it was this order that allowed the West to protect itself with a similar degree of orderly counterattack planning. At the very least, Western diplomats had a good idea of whom to talk to on the other side in order to deal with the problems.

In the post–cold war climate we have *each* of the former East-bloc countries to worry about—with no central control to handle such items as arms proliferation, terrorism, nuclear weapons buildup, ethnic cleansing, border conflicts, environmental issues, and trade matters. The new, independent forces pose a similar problem of unbridled terrorist actions.

Again, the Abu Nidal Organization (ANO) provides us with a good example. Since 1986, the Vice President's Task Force on Combatting Terrorism has called the ANO "the most dangerous terrorist organization in existence, and its area of operation one of the most extensive." A major reason for this claim is the ANO's success in becoming independent from state sponsors, thus freeing it from all sense of political propriety.

In the late 1960s and early 1970s, Abu Nidal was a part of the Fatah, along with Yasser Arafat. The Fatah was one of the largest and most vicious terrorist organizations of the time. After the Israeli victory in the October 1973 Arab-Israeli War, Arafat decided to restrict terrorist actions of the Fatah to Israel and any Israeli targets in the occupied territories. Against Abu Nidal's wishes, this marked the beginning of Arafat's move to take over the Palestine Liberation Organization (PLO) and his long-term campaign to become recognized as a respectable world leader in the Middle East. Nidal left Arafat's organization, and the two became bitter rivals, with each man issuing a death warrant against the other.

Nidal's ANO is against any moderation in the Arab-Israeli conflict. While the PLO attempts to convince the Western world that it is moderate, Nidal attacks Israeli and U.S. targets worldwide, along with any Arab pro-Arafat targets—or any country that demonstrates sympathy for Israel.

This goal of moderation has been a continuing source of inner strife for Arafat's PLO. In August 1993, his peace negotiators left the peace talks with Israel and resigned their commissions because they did not agree with Arafat's latest round of accommodations to the Jews. The eventual peace accord signed a month later forced even more severe splits among anti-West groups and within the PLO itself.

While the PLO has struggled for recognition over the past twenty years, Nidal's ANO has grown to total independence from state sponsors. It has been sponsored variously by Syria, Iraq, Libya, and other nations who have wanted to make use of the Nidal network, but only one-third of its resources are derived from state sponsorship. Another third comes from blackmail and extortion, and fully another from a worldwide network of businesses and front organizations.

According to the CIA, Nidal's ANO is so well established that it would go on operating "without a blink" even if Abu Nidal were to die or finally be captured.

This tremendous financial independence allows the ANO to take action not bounded by political correctness or economic (or even military) considerations that might otherwise cause a state sponsor to behave more moderately. Nidal and the ANO have provided some of the best examples of terror unleashed over the years via a long list of car bombings, assassinations, skyjackings, restaurant bombings, and machine-gun and grenade attacks in airports and synagogues. When the World Trade Center's explosion occurred, it was Nidal whom the authorities first feared was personally behind the act—in conjunction with Jihad.

It is this kind of unrestricted movement that the new, economically independent terrorist groups will both employ and enjoy with money raised through drug and arms trafficking as well as state-sponsorship fees.

Abu Nidal Has Already Arrived in the U.S.

Even though President George Bush stated in his terrorist report that "Americans must be informed about terrorism," the government has downplayed the existence of foreign terrorist group members already residing within the United States.

A 1993 indictment in St. Louis, Missouri, demonstrates not only the extensiveness of the Abu Nidal terrorist group, but again undermines the experts who say our country does not have a population base to support terrorism. The following headline appeared January 17, 1990, in the *St. Louis Post–Dispatch*:

MURDER SUSPECTS BUGGED.
SECRET U.S. INQUIRY
NETTED "CHILLING" TAPE OF KILLING

On November 6, 1989, Zein Isa and his wife, Maria Isa, waited for their teenage daughter to come home. Once again, sixteen-year-old Palestina "Tina" Isa had broken curfew, and her parents were waiting to kill her. Literally!

Defense attorneys would argue, a slow three years later, that the murder was a product of culture clashes. Zein, a Palestinian grocery-store owner in St. Louis, was a naturalized United States citizen who spoke little English, and Maria was a Brazilian who spoke only Portuguese. Both mother and father clung to old-world Islamic traditions. Palestina was the youngest of four daughters. A straight-A student at Roosevelt High School, only Palestina among them had become Westernized.

Three years of periodic and plodding court testimony revealed a pattern of dissent within Palestina—from her sneaking out to attend the school prom (where her family showed up to escort her home) to not showing proper respect at home, to getting a late-night job at a fast-food restaurant, and even to dating a black boy against her parents' wishes.

For months prior to the killing, her father told relatives and friends that his daughter was beyond redemption and deserved to die for disgracing the family honor. "You know, for me this one has become a burned woman, a black whore, and there is no way to cleanse her except through the red color that cleanses her," Zein told a friend over the telephone.

Zein told another daughter that he would claim self-defense if he killed Palestina. "Let me put in my teeth and tell you a harsh word," he said to Palestina's older sister, Fatima. "If God makes my wish, I'll put her in the grave." Fatima responded with her own curse for her little sister, "May God pain her, may God make her sleep and not get up. She is a whore. She will never enter my house."

Zein told another friend, "There is no way to teach her manners. Teaching her must take place in the hotel under ground."

Another sister, Soraia, called the next day to offer support by suggesting that Palestina be chained in the basement and that her passport be sent back to the homeland. Zein Isa said that he would have to send her home "in a box." Soraia assured her father that if he killed Palestina, the family would defend him—after all, he had acted in accordance with his homeland and Islamic law.

It all came to a head on November 6. That had been Palestina's first night on the job at the fast-food restaurant. Her black boyfriend met her after work, to walk her home. Palestina anticipated another row with her folks, so she asked her boyfriend to wait outside—and that if he heard a lot of yelling and screaming, she would come back out to leave with him. The boyfriend waited on the sidewalk, and Palestina stepped into her home.

The prosecution told the jury that Palestina's mother, who weighed two hundred pounds, grabbed Palestina by her hair from behind, and held her daughter steady while the father stabbed Palestina seven or eight times in the chest. While she fell to the floor, gasping for breath and life, Zein said to his daughter repeatedly, "Die quickly, my daughter. Die quickly."

When Zein was arrested he claimed self-defense, revealing a small cut on his arm as proof. But a few days later, both Zein and Maria were charged with murder, and denied bail—and a confoundingly tardy three years later were finally convicted of murder, and sentenced to death.

As complex as the murder investigation was, it was even more complex due to information presented by the FBI. The key evidence in the trial was an FBI tape-recording of the murder itself!

Unknown to Isa, the FBI had obtained permission from the Foreign Intelligence Surveillance Court to wiretap Isa's telephone with an unmonitored automatic taping device. By pure chance, when the Isas' telephone was accidentally knocked off the hook, the automatic recorder picked up the entire murder sequence, along with all of the conversations recorded previously between Zein and his friends and relatives.

Throughout the trial, the FBI refused to reveal why the Isas had been under surveillance—but the court ruled that it was indeed a legal wiretap, and therefore admissible in court. It was implied that the Isas were suspected of being PLO sympathizers.

It was not until April 1993 that the FBI revealed the reason behind their surveillance, when Zein Isa and Maria Isa, along with three other Palestinians, were indicted for suspicion of plotting terrorism on behalf of Abu Nidal—and actually charged with racketeering. The three coconspirators included Saif Nijmeh, thirty-two, who was arrested at his St. Louis home; Luie Nijmeh, twenty-nine, in Miamisburg, Ohio, and Tawfiq Musa, forty-three, of Milwaukee, who was arrested in Racine, Wisconsin.

The FBI further reported that Zein made periodic trips to Palestine, and Maria made similar trips to South America. Even though the family had little money, she was in the process of purchasing a business in South America—probably with funds provided by Abu Nidal and the ANO.

Even though much of the terrorist-related information became available after the murder trial was over, Jim Nelson, special agent in charge of the

FBI office in St. Louis, told the *Post–Dispatch* that he thought these terrorist links were the real reason why Palestina had to be killed. He said the men were concerned that Palestina would inform authorities about their activities and her father's ties to Nidal.

FBI tapes also faithfully repeated discussions between Zein and his coconspirators about killing individuals of Jewish extraction in the United States, and "about blowing up the Israeli Embassy in Washington, D.C."

It may also tie to the drug-related terrorist financing trends that one of those indicted for racketeering, Luie Nijmeh, was out of jail on bond at the time of his arrest from a previous charge of possession of cocaine.

This one small story about a teenage girl's murder offers a unique, composite view of terrorist profiles: immigrant Middle Easterners with strong bonds to their homeland, surrounded by neighbors and friends who support their non-Western views in a close-knit community; active participants in the world's most feared terrorist group residing in the heartland of America, with economic distribution routes to both the Middle East and South America—and at least one of the terrorists involved in drug trafficking; and a Palestinian who makes little attempt to hide his strong racist views against blacks or any other non-Islamic group.

Clash of Cultures

While America has long taken great pride in being the melting pot of the world, the new wave of legal and illegal immigration presents new problems. The massive immigration in the latter part of the 1800s and the early 1900s was primarily of Anglo-Saxon and European origin, people with value systems similar to those of the majority of Americans. Most of the immigrants were eager not only to come to America, but also to become Americans.

Much in keeping even with our romanticized version of early European and Asian immigration, these early immigrants tried in earnest to learn to speak English, to memorize the Constitution of the United States, and to earn the right to vote. There were no welfare programs waiting for them as they accepted the lowest positions in the capitalist economic system. They adopted the system and worked their way up through it. Catholics, Protestants, and Jews did not reject their religions, but rather Americanized them to fit the new society. For the most part, the Old World became a sweet memory as they fully incorporated the New World into their daily lives. There were generational problems, of course (like those depicted in *West Side Story* and *Flower*

Drum Song), but these were small when compared to those of the new immigrants.

The *new* wave of non–Anglo-Saxon immigrants, and especially Middle Eastern and Asian immigrants, arrive (either legally *or* illegally) with strong ties to their homeland, their race, and their religious leaders—ties to beliefs, customs, and value systems most Americans and Westerners are hard-pressed to understand fully. We have to go back to the American Revolution to find a conflict representative of this dilemma, when the population of the thirteen colonies was almost evenly divided over allegiance to England versus a desire for independence.

Today, the growing number of Middle Eastern immigrants who are neither Christian nor Jew may serve to cause growing cases of misunderstanding and disassociation among communities. In just the past five years, the United States has taken in over 7 million *legal* immigrants, and over 21 million annually who arrive on temporary visas, according to the U.S. Immigration and Naturalization Service.

In the 1980s, over 2.5 million legal immigrants arrived from Asia, 5.8 million from Europe, 2 million from Mexico, the Caribbean, and Central America, 370,000 from South America, and 156,000 from Africa. The Asian figures included 341,000 from China, 231,000 from India, 129,000 from Iran, 17,000 from Iraq, 36,000 from Lebanon, and 17,000 from Syria. These figures do not include the 4 million illegal immigrants who enter the United States annually, nor the large number of illegal immigrants who overstay their visas indefinitely—as was the case with three of the suspects in the World Trade Center bombing.

In many cases, these tightknit nationalities are making America look much less of a melting pot, and much more of a jumble of third world countries often reluctant to be assimilated.

When investigating the World Trade Center explosion, authorities were quick to take steps to protect the Arab community—to assure the public that this was the work of individuals, not of a people. But these authorities told Bruce Frankel of *USA Today* that they *did* encounter what amounts to a code of silence in Middle East neighborhoods in New York and New Jersey.

CIA counterterrorism chief David Whipple has observed: "This radical Muslim international is almost automatically coherent, because people owe clan loyalties and religious loyalties that transcend any duties to a country. This is a notion that's foreign to people in the U.S."

When the culture clash involves the extremities of conflicting religions, the problems and possibilities become *even more* severe.

The Fundamentalist Factor

To many people the word "fundamentalism" has come to be associated with extreme violence, Armageddon survivalists, cult torture, brainwashing, mass suicide, child molestation, and terrorism. Christian Fundamentalists, Muslim Fundamentalists, Islamic Fundamentalists, Jewish Fundamentalists—all are held suspect by the American mainstream of being borderline "weird." (To a lesser extent, the word "orthodox" sends a similar message.)

Christian Fundamentalism is an idea followed, expounded, propagated, and bastardized by a variety of cults across the United States, many led by one or another individual whose primary interest is to use religious themes and ritual practices to brainwash members into a state of absolute physical, spiritual, and psychological submission.

Different reports on the David Koresh experience outside Waco, Texas, varied in their estimates of how many Americans were under the "spell" or control of a similar leader. They ranged from estimates as low as three million to as high as ten million no longer having control over their own lives—people whose minds (and presumably souls) have been taken over by someone else.

The Waco cult was typical of a Christian Fundamentalist group wherein the tie that binds is a belief in the soon upcoming Armageddon, or a similar belief in some calamity that would destroy either the world or (at least) the group and its beloved leader.

One problem with these extreme beliefs is that members begin to lose faith when the calamity *doesn't* come—causing the leaders to take action, either through attacks on the government or other allegedly oppressive groups, or by actually creating a private Armageddon, as in the case of the mass suicides (and associated murders) in Jonestown, Guyana. *Without* an enemy, these extremist groups have no reason for being—so they *create* an enemy. And often the government is the most convenient scapegoat—because the government as a target of their ire ties closely to the groups' very recruiting efforts.

These groups seek lonely people who are in turn seeking some center (or meaning) to their lives. Often the prospects for recruitment are honest people whose lives have taken a bad turn—a failed business, a failed marriage. (Throughout the 1980s, membership in various such groups rose sharply in the Midwest as thousands of farmers went out of business.) In these groups a leader is found who tells his more-or-less hapless followers that the fault—the cause of their woes—isn't theirs, but rather (more than not) the government's, or the blacks', or the Jews'—perhaps a combination of the three. And they in turn find other candidates who have had similar problems, and welcome them into the clan, for the most part without question.

Economic strife almost always kicks off a rise of insecurity which causes people to seek the comfort of others and this phenomenon accompanies periods in United States history when cult membership rises. In fact, the same holds true for almost *every* kind of membership—active church-participation figures go up, enrollment in the National Rifle Association skyrockets (as it has since 1991), even memberships in professional organizations boom. But it is the truly downtrodden and desperate who are the targets of the cults.

Ironically, the recruiting propaganda of the cults and extremist groups is not all that different from the techniques of established religions. Except that the cult leaders take the methods to a new level of psychological submission.

"Do you believe in God?" the leader asks.

"Yes."

"Do you believe I am a messenger of God?"

"Yes."

"Do you love God? And do you believe this love will save you from burning in hell for all eternity?"

"Yes."

"Do you love me?"

"Yes."

"Is there anything you wouldn't do for God?"

"No."

"Would you die for God?"

"Yes."

"Would you die for me?"

"Yes."

"Would you kill for God?"

This ritual of psychological programming can take place over a period of weeks, months, or years. It is usually augmented by tests, in which the leader slowly breaks down all of the things the members once knew as right versus wrong. What was once right is now punished, and what was once wrong is rewarded. In the case of David Koresh, husbands willingly encouraged their wives to submit to him sexually. Then they gave their daughters, as young as ten. And since the girls and women were now "married to The Lamb," it would then be a sin for the husbands to make love to their wives ever again.

After a while, a Catch-22 situation is firmly in place when the leader asks for yet another "sacrifice." "Wait a minute," the member says to himself, "If I don't want to blow up that nuclear plant or kill that cop, then maybe I was wrong about letting my wife and daughter have sex with him, too." Rather it becomes easier to go ahead as instructed than to struggle with the possibility that some other sin has previously been committed.

When surviving members of the Koresh group were interviewed on television, they seemed like intelligent, rational individuals—which observation served to emphasize just how persuasive a cult leader can be, and how gullible a lonely person can become. If they can give their body, then they can give their soul—*and* their life, and *other* lives. It all falls under the guise of sacrifice. The next step of the cult is to believe that anyone who does not agree simply must not understand, and therefore must be innocently sacrificed against their will for the greater cause in order to be "saved."

Christian Fundamentalist beliefs become easily and dangerously entwined with militaristic white supremacist and anti-Jewish policies. For example, everyone remembers the surprising following that David Duke managed to draw when he ran for president. The "ex" Ku Klux Klan member was also a master of public relations, looking more like actor Robert Redford than Redford himself did in his 1972 movie *The Candidate*. Duke brought out feelings that still run deep in the Deep South.

Though not as clever as the Duke candidacy, there are other white supremacist plots just as bold—and even more deadly. Most people are only vaguely familiar with the Aryan Nations, a group which operates nationwide but is headquartered primarily in Idaho and Michigan. Their stated aim is the creation of a new United States, its capital relocated to Idaho. On the surface the prospects of this may sound ridiculous, but the degree of success the group has realized is disturbing.

Idaho was picked for three reasons: a small population base, a noticeable absence of blacks and Jews, and a history of sympathy for racist policies. Setting up camp near Lake Hayden, the Aryan Nations began a national campaign to convince members to move to the small communities of Idaho. Their initial aim was to slowly win over the state not with arms, but with votes and intimidation. In some towns, Aryan Nations activists legally voted themselves into chief of police and mayoral positions, and proceeded to fill all city and county posts with fellow followers.

By their own report, these radicals teach their children (in private schools) the four R's: Reading, 'Riting, 'Rithmetic, and Racism. They also hammer across the message that America has been taken over by blacks and Jews, and that therefore the only way to save the country is to destroy it. They have been particularly successful lately in recruiting failed farmers and ranchers, in addition to southerners.

Many people choose to view the Aryan Nations groupies as a crazy bunch of rednecks with gun racks in their pickup trucks. But they deserve a closer inspection. As detailed in Chapter 6, they have assassinated news personalities who gave them unfavorable attention. They have murdered blacks and Jews, and families of various descriptions who got in the way of the creation of the new country. *And* they have entertained foreign terrorists, right on their private lands near Hayden Lake.

In 1984, while the FBI stood by helplessly, terrorists from all around the world convened in Hayden Lake for their first three-day World Conference of Terrorists. The Baader-Meinhoff Gang was in attendance. The Japanese Red Army was there. The PLO (by some accounts) was there. All meeting in the only country in the world where it was actually safe for them to do so. It must have been frustrating indeed for the FBI agents to sit there with cameras clicking while the most wanted terrorists in the world entered the gates to the private property.

The FBI stated that there was no doubt the aim of this conference was to discuss coordinating terrorist attacks globally, along with arms-shipment and drug-smuggling agreements.

An offshoot of the established white supremacist groups ties back to the youth gangs. The skinheads and other youth groups who have adopted a white supremacist philosophy are becoming the front troops of the older sects. These groups have caused trouble in the northwestern states (for example, being responsible for killings and beatings in Oregon and Washington), yet so far they have been leniently viewed as sort of a youth fashion statement in most other areas.

But that view is rapidly changing—and especially could it change with the rise of neo-Nazism in Germany and neo-Fascism throughout Europe, where governments have been most lenient with racist hate crimes. The U.S. headquarters for the Nazis is in Lincoln, Nebraska. From this location, a small staff sends hundreds of thousands of dollars to related European factions, along with millions of printed and electronic neo-Nazi propaganda for distribution in Germany, where all neo-Nazi propaganda is officially illegal.

A July 1993 report issued by the Anti-Defamation League of the B'nai B'rith takes a serious view of the increasingly violent acts of the skinheads: "The skinheads are today the most violent of all white supremacy groups. Not even the Ku Klux Klan, so notorious for their use of the rope and the gun, come close to the skinheads in the number and severity of crimes committed."

Irwin Suall, fact-finding director of the League, told the *New York Times* that the July 15, 1993, arrests of a skinhead group which had planned to attack a black church in Los Angeles, just three days after the League's report was released, indicated that the skinheads were prepared to move to more large-scale attacks on blacks, Jews, homosexuals, immigrants, and members of other minority groups. Suall credited the skinheads with twenty-two deaths since 1990. "I think we are in a period of transition in the white supremacist movement," Suall said. "Clearly there are trends within it to move toward more serious violence. Whether the arrests in Los Angeles will serve for a time at least to deter further action of that type, we'll have to wait and see."

The Anti-Defamation League estimates that skinheads number between 3,300 and 3,500 nationwide in forty states and are split into as many as 160 groups. Danny Welch, director of the Klan-Watch project of the Southern Poverty Law Center in Alabama, also told the *New York Times*, "What makes skinheads noteworthy right now is their random violence. They have been responsible for the majority of the violence committed by organized racists. They get out and just beat the heck out of anybody that's a minority or anybody that doesn't agree with them."

One of the dangers of the skinheads is similar to that of the rise in the Islamic extremist religious movement—the seemingly disorganized actions by many small groups which, although they might complement an overall goal, seem to have no direction and leave no trail to the inception of a plot. "In some ways, the disorganized nature of skinhead groups, many of which regularly break up and re-form, has kept the groups from becoming more of a force. At the same time, their fluid nature has made the groups harder to monitor and combat," Welch concluded.

What is clear is that the skinheads tend to serve the more established white supremacist organizations; and the idea that they will be foot soldiers in a reenactment of the white supremacist push of 1984, which could have resulted in as many as 400,000 deaths (covered in chapter six), can be expected.

Much to the chagrin of German authorities, one of the leading supporters of the neo-Nazi movement is the Lincoln, Nebraska, office which calls itself the "AO," the Overseas Organization of the National Socialist German Workers Party, or (transliterated) NSDAP—the formal initials for the Nazi party. The AO was founded, and is led, by

Gerhard Lauck, a third-generation American whose grandparents immigrated to the United States from Germany after World War I. Lauck fits the description of many neo-Nazi recruits—a social outcast as a youth, with a speech impediment, who became caught up in Hitler's teachings in his early teens. His activities (he also raises money for a military neo-Nazi group fighting in support of Croatia) were taken lightly at first, but today they have the eye of authorities in both the U.S. and Germany.

In 1972, at the age of nineteen, Lauck instituted his organization for the purpose of supporting neo-Nazi philosophies in Germany and, later, within the United States. Today, his publications and other neo-Nazi propaganda are distributed to groups in thirty countries. Indeed, the AO has become the world's largest supplier of Nazi propaganda. (While this material is illegal in Germany, the right to produce propaganda is protected by the Constitution of the United States.)

Hannelore Kohler of the German Information Center in New York told a Nebraska *World-Herald* bureau reporter in 1993 that Chancellor Helmut Kohl has made repeated attempts to emphasize to the United States how important it is to stop the publications, but United States authorities have rebuffed the requests on First Amendment grounds. Lauck, who scorns democracy, has made a good living under its protection.

Lauck's organization and the rest of the neo-Nazi movement alike have grown with the rise of anti-Semitism in Germany, the economic problems in every country he distributes to, and the spread of racism in general. The fall of the Berlin Wall, accented by German, French, and American problems with immigration, brought on a new growth of neo-Nazi recruits which caused membership to surge. The German government has estimated that as many as 43,000 German citizens support the neo-Nazis, while the Anti-Defamation League has put the number closer to 60,000.

The AO produces tabloids which preach racism and anti-Semitism in English, German, Swedish, Russian, Spanish, Dutch, Hungarian, French, Portuguese, and Italian. It also produces two "white power" television programs, which air in fifteen cities in the United States on cable television. The conflict between the production of hate material and the rights of free speech in Lauck's case, as with the conflict between the plotting of terrorist acts versus performing those acts in the case of the World Trade Center bombing, is a massive challenge to any democracy bent on fighting terrorism without stepping on individual rights.

Islamic Fundamentalists and State-Sponsored Terror

The fastest-growing religion in the world is Islam, and a major part of this growth is the Islamic Fundamentalist faction. In America, where we still have a basic belief in the separation of church and state, it is difficult to relate to the idea that the political leader of Iran is also the spiritual leader of Islamic worshipers globally. For American Catholics, such must seem akin to a pope also serving as U.S. president, medieval attitude and all.

The U.S. State Department's 1993 annual survey of terrorism calls Iran "the most dangerous state sponsor" and says that its leaders "view terrorism as a valid tool to accomplish the regime's political objectives, and acts of terrorism are approved at the highest levels of government in Iran." Iran's terror has been felt worldwide, from killings of opposition leaders in Iran, Germany, France, Ankara, and Rome, to the death decree (fatwah) issued on Salman Rushdie for statements made in his book *The Satanic Verses*.

When a *Time* reporter asked Iran's President Rafsanjani about Iran's support for the Hizballah terrorist group in Lebanon, Rafsanjani responded that the United States supports groups he considers to be terrorist, including the Mujahedin. A valid point, on a state level. But the World Trade Center bombing helps put the power of the Islamic Fundamentalists in perspective.

That story begins with a blind cleric, Sheik Omar Abdel-Rahman, operating out of a third-story mosque in Jersey City, New Jersey. (Rahman had earlier been arrested—but not convicted—for the 1990 assassination of Rabbi Meir Kahane, the radical founder of the Jewish Defense League.) Rahman's mosque was a gathering place for the men eventually arrested in connection with the bombing, all of whom had been seen at the trial of *another* member for the murder of Rabbi Kahane. Half the men involved in the bombing have become legal residents in the United States, but the others, *including* Sheik Rahman, not only got into the country through a mistake at customs, but have been illegal residents for as long as five years.

The State Department has tracked down leads that follow a money trail, a passport trail, and family ties from Iran to Egypt to Nicaragua to the United States. Most investigators are convinced that Iran supplied the bomb-plot funds to the followers of Rahman. They are *not* sure whether the World Trade Center was a target assigned by Iran, or if the group simply figured they had better blow up *something* in order to give the state sponsor its money's worth.

As Scott Appleby, of the Fundamentalism Project of the American Academy of Arts and Science, told *USA Today*, March 18, 1993, any act of terrorism "is a way of mobilizing recruits in cells and emboldening them to set off new chain reactions." This takes the uncontrolled action of the independent terrorist a step further—to where a worldwide message can be sent to cells, ordering them to erupt—without order, but with religious fervor.

Blackmail of unwilling terrorists is also common among Middle East countries, wherein they instruct Islamic residents of other countries to "answer the call" while their families, left behind in the home country, are held hostage.

What has become clear since the initial arrest of Rahman is that federal investigators, even at the time of his apprehension, did not fully appreciate the size and scope of Rahman's following in the United States, Egypt, and virtually throughout the Islamic fundamentalist world. His eventual trial would not only test principles of U.S. immigration policy, but also place federal authorities in a no-win situation: Convict Rahman and secure his status as a martyr in the extremist movement; fail to convict him and make him a hero.

While today we tend to think of terrorists as Mideast fanatics, terrorism worldwide is a relatively recent invention—and probably a tactic derived from Western culture.

The Balkan Terrorists

"These guys make Abu Nidal look like Mother Teresa." That's how Xavier Raufer, a French expert on the Balkans, summed up the history of terrorism within the former East-bloc countries for *Time* magazine in March 1993. (It was the murder of Archduke Francis Ferdinand and his wife in Sarajevo that set off World War I. The killer was a Serbian youth continuing a long history of a Balkan tendency to combine politics with terrorism.)

After the World Trade Center bombing, nineteen callers took responsibility for planting the bomb. One called their group the Serbian Liberation Front. Another represented Croation Militants. Another was with the Bosnian Muslims. As a matter of fact, all of these Balkan groups have long been well known for planting bombs and conducting other terrorist acts here and there in the hope of blaming such on an opposing side. They now are well known for attacks within the United States. For example:

December 1975: Croation nationalists plant a bomb in a luggage locker at New York's La Guardia Airport, killing eleven people and injuring
seventy-five.

Later in 1975: Croation hijackers divert a TWA airliner from New York
to Chicago, and then to Paris; and concurrently plant a bomb at New
York's Grand Central Terminal—this killing a police officer.

June 1980: Croat "Freedom Fighters" detonate a bomb inside the muse-
um at the Statue of Liberty.

From 1976 to 1980, Croats committed more than twenty acts of terror
inside the United States.

Terrorism comes from many different directions. In addition to the ones
listed above, there are the "academic" terrorists. For example, the Baader-
Meinhoff Gang in Germany had a large following among the German
intelligentsia, with donations and safe housing coming from thousands of
sympathizers.

In May 1986, *Scholastic Update* printed a piece, titled, "Terrorists Are
Criminals, Whatever Their Cause," which provided two definitions of terrorism:

> Terrorism is the threat or use of violence for political purposes, by
> individuals or groups, with the intent to shock or intimidate a target
> group wider than the immediate victims.
> —U.S. Central Intelligence Agency

> Terrorism is aimed at the people watching, not at the actual victims.
> Terrorism is theater.
> —Brian Jenkins
> U.S. expert on terrorism

The article went on to discuss differences between acts of terror and those
of war, stating that the criminals who call themselves "liberators" or
"freedom fighters" or "religious followers" all are in fact terrorists killing
certain people for the primary purpose of sending a psychological shock
to as many other people as possible. Regardless of how much the sane
individual agrees that terrorism is a despicable act of cowardice, these
very statements, and others like them, may be out of date. They assume
that the goals of terrorism have not changed, when in fact the trend in terrorism is to go *beyond* "theater." In the same article, Brian Jenkins concluded that "the prevention of terrorist attacks requires, first of all, an

understanding and awareness of this unconventional type of warfare." It is just as important to demonstrate that conventional views toward terrorism will soon be passé, and that by then terrorism will have become a valid war tactic in many areas of the world. We must understand those changes if we are going to prepare for them or—more importantly—discover ways to actually prevent terrorism. It is also important to understand that one man's freedom fighter is another man's terrorist.

CHAPTER 4

The Sleeping Giant

On December 7, 1941, the greatest terrorist attack in United States history took place when the Japanese bombed the U.S. naval base at Pearl Harbor, Hawaii. At least that was how the attack was perceived at the time by Americans huddled around their radios listening to President Franklin D. Roosevelt announce "a date which will live in infamy." The unprovoked attack not preceded by a declaration of war was considered a vicious, cowardly act against the democratic free world.

Researchers have since pieced together evidence that U.S. military and political leaders had ample warning that an attack was imminent. Some of those leaders simply refused to believe that such a bold attack was possible. Many historians suspect that others, including President Roosevelt, purposely ignored the evidence in hopes the attack would occur and give the United States an excuse and public support for entering World War II.

Once the attack on Pearl Harbor was a total success, the Japanese commander reportedly said soberly, "I fear we have only awakened a sleeping giant, and his reaction will be terrible."

Many counterterrorist experts agree that the United States is once again a sleeping giant, and that only another massive tragedy will wake us up to the reality of the terrorist threat. And part of that reality is that a terrorist threat is not necessarily limited to cosmetic explosions but includes also calamity that would pale the effects of the Pearl Harbor attack by comparison—politically, economically, and in measurements of human loss and despair.

The United States has been the foremost terrorist target since World War II, but now that it is the undisputed world leader, the chances of occurrences both abroad and at home have increased tremendously. Foreign ter-

64

rorists have learned that it is much more fruitful, and easier, to attack nations of influence abroad than to strike at elements within their own countries. A PLO faction gets much more exposure when it explodes a bomb in a New York synagogue than in an Israeli one, even though its primary aim might be to influence the outcome of its own *local* negotiations.

Another Government Misconception

Recent U.S. government reports and statements claim that the number of terrorist incidents are on a refreshing decline—although these same reports do admit that the *severity* of attacks has increased. In truth, the number of terrorist attacks has increased.

"Patterns of Global Terrorism: 1989," published by the U.S. State Department in April 1990, says: "The year 1989 saw a steep decline in the number of terrorist acts committed worldwide—one of the sharpest yearly drops we have recorded since the advent of modern terrorism in 1968." The report goes on to describe a 38 percent decline in terrorist incidents as compared to the 1988 figures, along with other significant drops in the number of people killed or wounded.

However, the Risk Assessment Information Service (RAIS), an independent research facility of Business Risks International, provides dramatically different statistics of world terrorist activities. According to RAIS, terrorist incidents in 1989 increased by 16 percent, along with a 10 percent increase in lethal attacks. RAIS also reported for that year that the number of attacks against U.S. business interests in particular took a sharp climb.

Why the 54 percent disparity between government statistics and private, independent industry statistics? Robert C. Quigley, executive vice president of Threat Research, Inc. and former chief of the F.B.I. Bomb Data Center, says the difference is a very dangerous problem of definition.

A key factor under the government definition is the "political motivation" behind violent acts, and therefore it becomes a subjective decision as to *which* violent acts are counted as terrorism. Under the RAIS definition, however, terrorism is any "unlawful use of force or violence against persons or property through a criminal act designed to intimidate or coerce a government, civilian population, or any segment thereof in furtherance of political or social objectives."

The problem with the government view, Quigley says, is that definitions shape statistics, and government statistics are misleading when assessing the risk of terrorism.

News reporting in the spring of 1993, after the World Trade Center bombing, is a good example. Practically every news reporter in the country ran to the government reports to get an angle on the terrorist threat, and to document stories with government statistics. Headlines announced reassuringly that terrorism was on the decline to millions of newspaper and magazine readers. Convenient graphs and pie charts reaffirmed the numbers. Virtually every political analyst and government official who had access to the official report repeated the theme. The result was a massive campaign of accidental misinformation. It sent a message to the country: Go back to sleep.

International businesses, as well as government officials, make decisions based on such reports. They decide whether or not to increase or "harden" (increase) security, implement new training programs, revise weapons dispersal, and change personnel procedures. These decisions, when based on misconceptions and faulty or misleading statistics, obviously can prove disastrous.

Such government statistics, which tend to soften reality and so lull the citizenry to sleep, may explain the results of a *USA Today* poll of businesses across the country, taken a few days after the World Trade Center bombing. For the most part, businesses were doing little or nothing to alter or improve their security. In fact, their main goal was to make certain no one overreacted to any perceived threat.

Ironically, just two months after the explosion, the FBI announced that it had uncovered a much broader plot: The World Trade Center was to have been merely the first of many similar targets throughout the United States, all of which would have been caught off guard had it not been for the lucky breaks that investigators realized in the case. The argument that the United States will become even more of a target, and indeed a target on its home turf, grows stronger every day.

One of the greatest reasons for terrorists to move their activities to direct targets within the United States is that it is becoming more difficult to attack Americans overseas. As security measures tighten at our foreign offices and at European and Asian airports, and as travelers and international business executives become more careful in their movements, it will be ever easier and safer to structure an attack *within* the U.S. for as long as domestic targets remain unprotected.

For terrorists who are looking to make headlines via disrupting a civilian population, the publicity of the World Trade Center explosion provides ample reason for similar efforts on U.S. soil. For just over $3,500 (the cost of building the unsophisticated bomb), the terrorist leaders who ordered the World Trade Center incident captured the nation's headlines for *months*. Every newspaper, every magazine, every television commentary, and every television news channel combined to provide the kind of coverage that would have cost an advertiser of even some pedestrian event hundreds of millions of dollars.

Had the same bomb exploded in any other country, the "fallout" therefrom would have been worth only a few inches of column space, plus only several minutes of electronic air time. If there is one thing all counterterrorist experts agree on, it is that terrorists will go where they get the most bang for their buck.

With each conflict around the world, the foreign vision of the United States as the "Ugly American" or the "Great Satan" continues to grow. It is partly a product of a superpower hate syndrome, increasingly emphasized since the Soviet Union collapsed, and especially now that the United States military is called upon to intervene in one "international" emergency after another.

The Afghan rebels we assisted in their war against the Soviets now have terrorist groups targeting U.S. and European interests! Three of the men arrested after the World Trade Center bombing, for example, had spent time with the Afghan freedom fighters. To them, the conflict had been an Islamic religious war, and the United States was no less an enemy than the Soviets.

Armenia, Bosnia, Serbia, Puerto Rico, the Philippines . . . the list of countries and territories with terrorist groups targeting U.S. interests seems endless. Even groups who are supposedly allied with the United States are a threat, when they stage an attack in hopes that it will be blamed on the other side.

In Somalia, six months after U.S. troops arrived on a peacekeeping mission, American aircraft started bombing arms caches in residential neighborhoods, as part of the United Nations commitment. The action in Somalia is an example of the difficulty inherent in using superpower warfare methods in a third world environment. In Panama, thousands of people were killed and injured when the United States launched a military attack designed to "get" Manuel Noriega—dead or alive. The mission was hailed as a complete success by the U.S. government, but at what cost in long-term foreign diplomacy? Other alternatives, including assassination, might have been more successful, less costly financially, and more effective in future relations—but completely illegal in today's current definitions of the moral conduct of nations.

The United States sends mixed messages to the world that cannot help but lead to a continued rise of terrorism. In Iran, at the same time we publicly excoriated their government for becoming the world's leader of state-sponsored terrorism, we sold them arms. And, prior to that, we supported a corrupt Shah who wanted everything except democracy for his country. In Palestine, Yasser Arafat, once seen as one of the world's most vicious criminals, now scoots up to negotiation tables with a $14 billion treasure chest. In Iraq, after the United States successfully helped build Saddam Hussein into one of the largest powers in the Middle East even as he brutalized the Kurdish people and exacted a reign of terror unheard of since Hitler, we attacked with a multibillion-dollar war.

The pattern goes back many years: After recruiting Ho Chi Minh to assist Allied efforts in World War II, we supported the creation of a corrupt South Vietnamese government. We worked closely with Manuel Noriega, perhaps even encouraging his connection with drug smuggling, while providing his troops with training, but then attacked his country in order to lay hands on him (or his dead body).

Multiply these examples manyfold and it is no wonder that the Ugly American image sticks in many regions of the world.

Mixed messages also go out in regard to our willingness to deal in tough ways with terrorists. Here in America they are protected by our own constitutional system: A criminal terrorist act is handled with the same excruciatingly slow process as is a murder trial. Years may go by without punishment. For terrorists who are willing to sacrifice their lives for a cause, or for their group, the fear of going to a United States prison is not all that fearsome, and in fact prolongs the effect of their single act—capturing headlines for perhaps decades as they are processed through the appeals system.

Terrorism *itself* is *not* illegal, *not* a crime, in the United States. Only the *acts* are, such as killing, and destroying property. The plotters from the Abu Nidal gang who were arrested in connection with the murder in St. Louis were *not* tried as terrorists. Their charge was racketeering—the type that no doubt leaves loopholes for a clever attorney (not only at the time of the trial but at the next series of parole or pardon hearings). Terrorists, therefore, are not treated *as* terrorists. Rather, they are treated as bank robbers, or charged with destruction of property, or for theft or murder—but not *as* terrorists.

The United States' track record in handling foreign groups confuses the issue even more. After tracking down the fugitive perpetrators of the December 21, 1988, PanAm explosion over Lockerbie, Scotland, we have yet to win their extradition. Similar cases abound—and in *all* cases the actual leaders behind the obscene acts have gone free, even though they have been identified.

While faulty foreign policy has for years had adverse economic, political, and diplomatic effects, the results abroad have been obscure, confusing issues easy for the public to ignore. Only now are we beginning to see how faulty foreign policy that has percolated through every administration since Roosevelt's may have a visible effect on the public right in our backyards.

Past Exported Expertise Comes Home to Terrorize

After World War II, the United States helped rebuild Japan—and now Japan is our largest economic competitor. We did the same for Germany and, in a smaller way, a host of other nations. We have taught nations how to feed themselves, and now the need for United States farm exports and industrial exports is much less than in even quite recent history. In many ways, for better or for worse, our willingness to share our expertise and visions have had effects we never imagined at the time of their first offering.

The same holds true for terrorism. In various conflicts around the world, from Cambodia to Afghanistan, Iraq to Bolivia, Nicaragua to Africa, the United States and its Western allies have brought previously untrained guerrilla forces to the heights of combat sophistication. We have even taught them how to overthrow governments.

This all ties in with a rise in the sophistication of terrorism, wherein the goal now becomes not to explode a pipe bomb, but to cripple the infrastructure of a country. Over the past fifty years especially, terrorists have either watched United States tactics in—or have actually been trained by Western experts in—how to effectively do just that. In South America and throughout the third world, we instructed "freedom fighters" in how to destroy electrical and water supplies to and within entire cities. We showed how effective and disruptive it is to cut off a nation's communication system. We trained rural peasants in ways to explode oil pipelines and pumping stations, and how to incinerate natural gas plants. In other words, we trained thousands of would-be terrorists in the psychological as well as the economic aspects of terrorism—not via mere cosmetic incidences, but through the destruction of the very inner workings of an entire country.

Some of this training was provided directly by the United States military to groups who were considered allies at the time. And a great deal of it was provided by ex-military personnel who took on mercenary roles—particularly after Vietnam. Now many of those former students are our enemies.

An Interview With a Terrorist

In 1988, when research for this book began, I met with a man who said he was a terrorist. His code name was "Jake." He considered himself a mercenary and an American patriot. At the time, it was doubly surprising to find such a man both in the United States and living in a small town (in Iowa). He was on crutches—due to a broken ankle he said he had received in a parachute jump into Angola just two weeks earlier.

A child's bicycle was propped in a snowdrift in the driveway to the split-level ranch house. In the basement, where he kept a small office, guns and ammunition were everywhere. Vivaldi was on the tape player. A copy of Shakespeare's sonnets was on the desk, next to some long-jacket rifle bullets. Everything about both the meeting and the man seemed incongruent to the point of the surreal.

Jake was about forty-five. He said he had been one of the last American soldiers to leave Vietnam on the day Saigon fell. He had also been one of the first American advisers to arrive in Vietnam almost twenty years earlier, a period he remembers with great fondness. He attributed his tendency to break ankles and bones to exposure to the chemical Agent Orange in Vietnam before the U.S. government's jungle defoliation program was banned.

Jake said he had been a member of the Phoenix Group, a division of CIA Special Forces in Vietnam specially trained for assassination. According to Jake, the Phoenix Group was disbanded when it became known that Americans were on their hit list, as well as North Vietcong "targets." Jake further stated that since leaving the military he had become a mercenary, sometimes working for the CIA but often for foreign countries. Some of his assignments had included training CIA and FBI agent recruits.

Said Jake: "I always tell them, if they are guarding a politician or diplomat, when they hear shots ring out, they should duck first, assess the situation, then make their move. But for Christ's sake, don't throw your body in front of the person you're guarding. It's a helluva lot easier and cheaper to replace a politician than it is a well-trained agent."

Jake explained two theories that can be applied to all facets of terrorism. The first was in regard to assassination: "If a halfway well-trained terrorist wants to kill someone, then that person is dead. The only reason an assassination fails is the terrorist's personal desire to extricate safely. He or she has to accept a less-than-adequate position to take a shot or place a bomb in order to escape after the fact. If the terrorist is willing to die or to be captured, then there is almost no way to keep the subject alive." This methodology, as will be detailed later, permeates most of our national-defense methods.

Jake's second theory was: "Anything can be ambushed. One person can ambush a group of people by attacking them in a narrow hallway. They bump into each other. They hit each other with their guns. They ram their rifle barrels into the wall. Maybe they even shoot each other. In any case, in the confusion, the one person can blow them all away.

"The same can be said for an entire platoon, a division, or an army. Or even an entire country. They are all susceptible to ambush with the same simple concept as trapping a bunch of guys in a narrow hallway. The playing field changes, but the rules are basically the same."

One of his more intriguing assignments, Jake said, had been to pick up three dead U.S. servicemen from Nicaragua and deposit them on the shores of Grenada on the day that U.S. forces invaded. According to Jake, the Bush administration wanted to avoid the problem of explaining why there were dead servicemen in a country where we supposedly had no troops at the time. From the shores of Grenada, the bodies could now be recorded as casualties of a sanctioned battle, and be shipped home to their families.

"Most of my buddies from Nam are somewhere around the globe, training guerrillas," Jake said. "Some are down in Georgia and South Carolina, doing the survivalist training thing, with military tactics built in. Others are in Africa and Afghanistan, and over in Asia.

"It's interesting, really, to see how each generation proliferates problems for the next. Take Vietnam. We beat the Germans in World War II. So where did most of Hitler's SS troops end up? In the French Foreign Legion. And where did these specially trained troops go? To Vietnam, where they got their asses kicked. So in comes the United States into the Vietnam conflict, and we develop our own brand of Special Forces. Then we're out of Vietnam, and these well-trained fighting men have nowhere to go. And, well, let's face it—they've been completely messed up now, right? They kill things. It's what they're good at. So now they are all over the world, teaching thousands of fanatics who really weren't much of a problem before how to be effective fighting troops."

According to Jake, ex-Phoenix Group members got together some years ago to discuss re-forming as a private mercenary group. Some had become involved with Aryan Nations or the Ku Klux Klan, and wanted to "be prepared" to save the country after the Nixon administration fell.

"The scary part about that was," Jake concluded, "that we almost did it. The only thing that stopped us was that we realized some of the leaders were so far gone, anything could happen. Like that American they found walking around the Nicaraguan airport who claimed he was with the CIA? The reason it caused such a stir was because he *was* with the CIA, and it was the first time I know of that the name 'Phoenix Group' was ever published.

"There's a code, kind of, that as long as we keep our mouths shut we won't get hassled by the CIA, and there's one action in particular that is our ace in the hole."

Jake later implied that the "ace in the hole" had something to do with the involvement of United States troops in the assassination of the president of South Vietnam—but then, Jake *was* being elusive.

Jake also said that the most disturbing part about the meeting of ex–Special Forces members was the large number who would have enjoyed implementing a plan to take over the United States, *just to see if they could do it*. Their experiences had convinced them that the country was not being run according to any of the democratic beliefs they had grown up with, so thoughts of allegiance to the country were confused—to the point where they could easily be convinced they were actually saving the country in the role of freedom fighters.

A few days later, during my interview with another ex–Special Forces member (who is now an insurance executive with a wife and five children), Jake's reportage was supported. In response to a question regarding his own interest in joining such a group, this veteran answered with a story.

"In one of my last actions in Vietnam, my buddies and I were trapped at the top of a small hill. Cong were coming up the hill at us from all sides. We'd been there maybe two days, outnumbered maybe ten to one, and we were running out of ammunition. Finally, to conserve ammunition, we would throw a grenade and they would all go scurrying. Then they would start climbing up again, and we would throw a bunch of dirt clogs, and they would go running again. We kept that up until we were down to the last grenade, then hand-to-hand combat. I think only three of us survived. I lost most of my friends on that hill. It was the last time I really felt alive. It's the highest trip you can imagine."

How formidable would the surviving members of the Phoenix Group have been had they re-formed after the war as a mercenary or extremist group? "We would have been unstoppable," Jake claimed. "Take fifty guys of our capabilities and it's amazing to think what we could do. Just in direct, physical action we could take over any city—wipe out the police force of any city in the first two hours. But that's just the surface stuff."

He pulled maps, charts, and books from a shelf, spread them across his desk, and proceeded to explain in detail how this small band of men could destroy the United States.

At the time of the interview it was only mildly disturbing to realize that Jake and many like him were sitting around plotting ways to attack governments and societies. It later became more frightening when researchers and scientists confirmed their theories, and federal agents agreed that ex–Special Forces members were prime recruiting targets of the extremist groups.

CHAPTER 5

The Spawning of a Terrorist Plot

A sophisticated terrorist plot against the United States would have one primary goal: to disrupt the civilian population. If this can be accomplished effectively, it is possible that the resultant chaos would allow the population itself to complete the destruction.

This is consistent with the general goal of almost every terrorist act: to convince the civilian population of a country it is no longer protected by its government. In doing so, terrorism strips away the legitimacy of government because, in the final analysis, most people would conclude that if a government is unable to protect them, then what good is it?

The past fifty years have seen created an attitude that government serves almost no other constructive purpose that justifies the outrageous national debt, personal income taxes, regulations, and exorbitant salaries and political expenditures of thousands of congressional staff members whose functions are largely questionable. The resultant public distrust of government becomes a primary target of the terrorist's psychological warfare.

Terrorists understand the psychology of their warfare very well. They have become masters of theater, manipulators of the media, and expert in anticipating actions of the populace.

Before unseating the Shah of Iran, the Ayatollah Khomeini flooded the cities and villages of Iran with hundreds of thousands of cassette tapes, so citizens could listen to his stormy threats to return to start his promised religious war. Throughout Desert Storm, Saddam Hussein adroitly timed his television appearances to give confidence to his people that he was still alive and very much in charge. In Iran and Lebanon, hostages were paraded in front of the world's cameras to take the negotiations from the secret rooms of executive offices to the full view of the public.

These foreign leaders of hostile countries and terrorist groups understand the American and European people well. They work with lobbyists who once were Washington political leaders, foreign diplomats, and policy insiders. They retain American New York and European public-relations firms and advertising experts. They read our newspapers and books, and watch satellite television. They retain American New York lawyers and bankers and investment advisers. They own property throughout Asia, Europe, South America, and North America. They negotiate deals with the world's largest international businesses, and collect royalties from them all. They are some of the world's richest individuals. In cases like BCCI and Iran-Contra, they have been on the fringes of some of the largest financial fraud scandals of the twentieth century.

In other words, as Jake pointed out in his terrorist scenario, as terrorist experts have warned (and, more to the point, as economists, physiologists, and political scientists have predicted), the leaders of subversive movements have the knowledge, intelligence, economic strength, and zealous desire to implement a plan designed to disrupt the United States itself. And they see signs that the United States is prime for attack.

Bringing On a "Natural" Revolution Through Low-Intensity Warfare

Until the American Revolution, it was difficult to imagine that the British Empire would shrink. The nation over which "the sun never sets" seemed destined to control the world—a concept which would have seemed ridiculous to the Romans when they first invaded the British Isles to find a backward people dwelling in hovels and grubbing roots for food.

Now the legacy of the British Empire is visible everywhere—in India, Kuwait, Hong Kong, Ireland, and Scotland, to name just a few remnants of the Empire that are in the news today. From the advantage of twenty-twenty historical hindsight, the Empire was destined to shrink to its present borders.

But even given its historical perspective, Great Britain tries to hold on to remnants. It has soldiers in Ireland. It conducted an all-out assault to protect the Falkland Islands from Argentina. It argues with Scots who petition for autonomy, while England itself is split almost equally over such subjects as the need for a monarchy at all and the exorbitant riches the country pays to descendants of a throne which serves a questionable purpose.

Ten years ago no one imagined the Soviet Union would cease to exist altogether as a political entity. It was actually easier to envision nuclear annihilation than to predict that the Eurasian superpower would self-destruct through natural causes. Today it has broken apart, with leaders of the various countries stuck in a potentially explosive argument between Old World communist doctrine and New World separatism. Even as politicians talk around the tables of Moscow, separatist movements are rising within each of their countries. And ethnic and religious groups who do not recognize the authority of the politicians arguing in Moscow are proceeding with their own agendas.

Germany is reunited, but the split between philosophical doctrines gapes ever wider in this country torn between allegiance to the global community and self-interest. Neo-Nazi sentiments long buried have come to the surface and mixed with the protectionist sentiments of conservatives who want to turn back the tide of immigrants that is flooding the country with economic calamity. As they stumble for solutions, a real danger exists that they will fall back on what they know—the kind of response that led them into World War I and World War II—rather than proceed to the unfamiliar territory of letting go of nationalism and lessening the powers of the nation-state.

Quebec is trying to split from Canada, and reinforcing demands that French be its official language. At the same time, the indigenous Indians are winning rights to massive land areas.

On July 23, 1993, Alaska filed a $29 billion lawsuit against the federal government of the United States, the largest state suit ever so filed. It charged that Alaska's statehood rights have been violated, in that various federal regulations deprived the state of the ability to earn a living from resources available in vast areas of its land. The suit was filed by the seventy-four-year-old Alaskan governor, Walter J. Hickel, who has lived in that state since 1940 and previously was its second governor, from 1966 to 1969.

Hickel won election to his present term of office on a secessionist platform that advocates Alaska's splitting off from the United States. He is known as one of the last of the old-time territorialists with political clout: He won 39 percent of the vote in a three-way race. But his election evoked long-term antagonism among some Alaskans. Although it is the largest state in the union, many believe it is treated like a distant colony. The suit asserts that federal regulations regarding state parks, wildlife refuges, and preserves not only deprive the 550,000 Alaskans from realizing an income from the vast tracts of land, but also overstep the understandings of its

statehood from back in 1959, when it came to be represented by the forty-ninth star on the U.S. flag.

In September of 1993, Hickel mysteriously disappeared from his Alaskan home. Many neighbors suspected that he had been assassinated by government agents because of his views—while others said they wouldn't be surprised if he just showed up one day, alive and well.

The world is going through a new phase, one of the few turning points of history, wherein nations who led the industrial period shaped world events, installed governments in foreign countries, and dictated policy in far reaches through massive armed forces, economic pressure, or both. But now the Industrial Revolution is over, and the only remnants are the political structures fighting fiercely to defend themselves.

Such historic events create opportunities for terrorists to actually accomplish their goals. They may find themselves unable to destabilize a stable situation, but if there is (as it were) a hole in the dike, they can make it wide enough for the currents of the times to do their work. If there is a crack in the foundation, they can insert a bomb to crack it further. The United States' political system—not the features of democracy and principles of freedom and individual rights, but the cold war belief in massive armies, and the industrial belief in central government for the masses—may in fact be the largest example of a system about to explode.

Indeed, now that the United States has won the cold war, it sometimes seems that we were simply left holding the bag as the last survivor of an age gone by. From Vietnam to Serbia and Somalia, the United States is looked upon by members of the United Nations and NATO to provide the modern military strength to fight ancient ethnic battles wherein a small military target hides at the center of a civilian population. Peacekeeping forces are sent, fired upon, and then supported by more troops—who in effect become another of the occupied nation's internal armed tribes.

It is difficult to identify a historical situation in which military invasion by a foreign power altered the long-term natural course of internal conflicts. At best, such courses have been stalled for only a short time.

In the mind of the "democratic fundamentalist," the end result of future turmoil will likely be positive, with a return to the rights of the individual and the decentralization of government. But in the meantime, the next phase of global evolution may not be so pleasant as we redefine such terms as "strength" and "leadership" and "power."

Signs of the cracks in the United States' foundation are no less important than those that led to the breakup of the Soviet Union. In California,

for example, a movement to split the state into three parts has reached the legislature level, a concession to more inflammatory movements that have sprung up from time to time over the years, suggesting actual secession from the country.

Texas Monthly magazine proposed in April 1979, the concept of Texas's disassociating itself from the United States and reattaching itself to Mexico, to form a gigantic, oil-rich nation called Texico. The article was only partly in jest in arguing that Mexico relates more to the needs of Texas than does Washington.

Demographic analysts watch the apartheid movement in South Africa as the black majority takes control from the white minority. The South African experience could well provide a barometer for the United States, where projections of whites becoming a minority are pegged at within the first half of the 21st century. In North America, whites may not only become a minority to blacks, but to Hispanics as well.

For the same reason, social analysts watch California deal with its current problems—projecting that the state's conundrums of today will be reflected in the country's troubles of tomorrow. The riots, the collapse of the welfare system, a broke government, the immigration numbers and border crossings, the environmental issues of Los Angeles, the flight of the wealthy, secession movements, urban poverty, youth gangs, racial tension—California provides a mirror in which nationwide reactions and consequences may be imaged.

In the meantime, just as Texas sees itself as a territory not properly reimbursed for oil and gas sent to the upper states, smaller states see themselves as subservient to the more populous ones. The less populated states wrestle with the issues of water, agricultural production, and mineral resources all going to serve their more fully occupied neighbor states.

Native Americans want lands declared to sovereign nation status, not just reservation status, and they want other private lands converted to Indian ownership.

Farmers being driven off their lands have a hatred for both banks and Washington politics, mindful of the early 1930s Great Depression era. Some have joined rural militaristic groups, or have called upon the LaRouche group for controversial legal assistance they could not find elsewhere—a group that mixes anti-Jew and anti-government sentiments to explain economic woes, and charges a fee to farmers to submit lawsuits that never win but tie up the courts in a kind of paper revolt.

Taxes keep climbing while politicians find themselves stuck with a welfare society they cannot figure out how to abandon. Instead, they deepen

the problem with various forms of national health care, rather than attack the problems of health care with proactive solutions.

A class war is in the making over issues of welfare, immigration, Social Security, Medicare, income taxes, and business taxes, a war which will be heightened by only a slight worsening of the economy.

Children are being arrested in classes for carrying guns to public schools that pump out graduates who never got an education. They look to basketball stars and rock stars for inspiration they do not get in school or at home.

Foreign tourists are being murdered on our streets while criminals are being released from overcrowded prisons. Serial killers and mass mur–der–suicides in post offices, office places, and fast-food restaurants have become so commonplace that they are hardly news anymore.

All of this nation's internal strife and division is fodder for the terrorist, and invites psychological war.

So, what do observers *see* when they look at the strife of the United States? They see a country not mentally prepared for a war that lasts longer than a few days. They see riots in the streets because of racial, eth-nic, and economic divisions. They see a civilian population that can erupt after something as simple as an NBA basketball championship to cause millions of dollars of damage to a city during a victory party. They see a country where youth gangs control entire neighborhoods in which drugs are freely peddled.

A country where established religions are having trouble maintaining their legitimacy, millions of citizens turning instead to cults, semicults, and subversive elements for support. A country where child abuse is epi-demic. A country in debt, with unemployment skyrocketing in some areas and a welfare system collapsing after creating a welfare society.

Even a slight decrease in the economic scale of the country sends acts of racism to new heights.

Observers also watch while cities are being looted after electrical black-outs and hurricane disasters—and the crowd reaction is entered into their own predictive analysis of what would occur if they were to create a "con-trolled" disaster.

From the political point of view, they see a system wherein the two major political parties no longer have the respect of the citizens, who view Democrats and Republicans alike as self-interest groups, as reflected in the U.S. voter statistics—the lowest in the free world.

In short, they see a nation prime for psychological warfare. Psychological warfare is a prime factor in the newly emerging low-intensive warfare (LIW) methods of the future. But psychological warfare itself is not a modern invention. Its basic principles were laid down in the second half of the sixth century B.C., during the Chou dynasty, by Chinese military strategist Sun Tsu. In his treatise on war, *Ping Ta*, which he prepared for a dynastic ruler, his principal thesis was: "The highest art of warfare lies in breaking the enemy's resistance even before he has been brought to battle."

This twenty-six-hundred-year-old observation sums up the final goal of today's sophisticated terrorists. They understand strategy and tactics. They know the physical and moral weaknesses of a country, and they know how to exploit them. And if they are clever, they can implement their plan without ever facing our military.

Because of their willingness to commit insane acts, terrorists and the "rogue" countries are currently in control of these changing events. "Low-intensity warfare" is a term coined by our military strategists, but it is a reactionary term. It implies that the military recognizes that the marching armies of the past are *indeed* of the past. But it was the terrorists and rogue countries that gave the world that definition.

The Danger of Hardening

The most obvious response to the terrorist threat is that we should harden our security, our political stance, our moral position, and the complex webs of our infrastructure. But there are dangers here, too. If they become hardened, they also become brittle.

CHAPTER 6

Domestic Terrorist Groups

We tend to be preoccupied with international terrorism. The tragic and senseless loss of life on several viciously downed airliners, and the image of religious fanatics sneaking around on perverted missions, have captivated us.

History supports, however, that *national* terrorism (the type performed by groups within their own countries) actually has been the greater threat on a worldwide scale, whether you are using a misery index or an economic index to measure the impact. In the United States particularly, we now have the growing problem of seeing through the gray shadows between the definitions of national versus international terrorism. (Did the World Trade Center bombing fall within the category of international terrorism? Most of the villains were naturalized U.S. citizens!)

To the terrorist victim it really doesn't make a lot of difference who planted the bomb—but in dealing with trends, one of the more fruitful exercises might well be to predict that foreign, state-sponsored terrorist activities to be carried out in the United States will be most successful if they interact with those of the subversive elements already here and familiar with the turf.

Our experience to date with homegrown subversive elements also points to some of the more intriguing issues we will have to face in the future.

In the arrests of the second group of terrorists connected with the World Trade Center bombing, we had an introduction to this concept that foreign plotters would work with domestic subversives. One of those arrested was an American-born Black Muslim who was a member of a Black Muslim Islamic fundamentalist group known as the Fuqra. He was brought into the World Trade Center plot to supply the materials for the bomb itself.

81

The Fuqra

Most Americans had never heard of the Fuqra prior to the spring of 1993, even though the group's beginnings date back to 1962. With very little attention from the news media, the Fuqra has grown to over three thousand members over the past three decades. Many of the members are black Vietnam veterans brought in to train recruits in the effective use of weapons and sabotage.

In the 1930s, W. D. Fard, a fabric salesman in Detroit, Michigan, founded the Black Muslims—a natural title for an organization of African-Americans who converted to the Muslim faith, or Islam. Fard mysteriously disappeared in 1935, and Elijah Muhammad, an automobile worker who was born Elijah Poole, took over the leadership. Muhammad preached separation of the races, and the formation of an all-black state or territory within the United States. He favored all-black schools and encouraged black-owned businesses as the key to black self-sufficiency. His separatist beliefs also separated his Black Muslim group from other Muslim organizations.

Elijah Muhammad successfully recruited young blacks to his version of Islam, and his most successful recruiting places were the jails and prisons. The group was particularly effective in recruiting members during the turbulent late fifties and sixties. His most famous convert, Malcolm X, was recruited in prison during this time, and Malcolm went on to become his most important recruiter through speeches and writings. After visiting Mecca, Malcolm left the Black Muslims in 1964 and converted to traditional Islam, a move for which Elijah allegedly ordered Malcolm's assassination which was carried out in 1965.

By 1970, the number of Black Muslims nationwide, which had peaked at about 250,000, started to decline, and the followers split into rival groups. On one side was Elijah Muhammad's soft-spoken son, Imam Warith Deen Muhammad; on the other was fiery Louis Farrakhan.

Imam Muhammad rejected his father's ideas of separatism and preached orthodox Islam, American beliefs, and self-reliance. His American Muslim Mission had one hundred thousand members, and accepted whites.

Farrakhan preached black supremacy and separatism. He claimed to be Elijah Muhammad's legitimate heir after Elijah died in 1975, but Elijah's second son, Wallace Muhammad, became the official leader until he stepped down in 1978, placing the leadership in the hands of a ten-member council.

Wazir Ali Muhammad, today's head of the Nation of Islam, Inc., formerly known as the Black Muslims, claims to know nothing about the Fuqra terrorist group other than what he reads in the newspapers.

The birth of Fuqra traces back to Brooklyn in 1980 and a charismatic mystic from Pakistan, Sheik Mubarik Ali Jilani Hasmi. Jilani began preaching at the most influential black American mosque in the borough, then returned to his home in Lahore, Pakistan. He now makes periodic visits to the United States, and Fuqra members send him money. U.S. intelligence officials say that Fuqra members regularly travel to Lahore for religious indoctrination and terrorist training.

It is suspected that Pakistan uses Fuqra for state-sponsored terrorism because the organization seems to operate freely in that country, without any government interference.

Sudanese instructors (Sudan was the country of origin claimed by many of the World Trade Center villains in their entry visas) reportedly provided the training to Fuqra members in Pakistan. Fuqra members are also reportedly being used to funnel assistance to Kashmiri separatists in India, Pakistan's main rival.

Jilani persuaded American Fuqra members to join the Afghani guerrillas during their war against the Soviet Union—also a claim made by the terrorists arrested in New York. (One State Department official told a *Newsday* reporter that, for the insurgents, making the transition from hating the Soviet Union to American or Egyptian targets was not all that difficult. "To them, they [Westerners] are all evil and have to be resisted by force.")

Husain Abdullah, the head of a Brooklyn security firm and one of the early organizers of Fuqra in the United States, denies that the sect engages in terrorism. It is widely known, however, that they have a number of rural "retreats" spotted across the United States—particularly in upstate New York, and in the Colorado Rockies, the deserts of California, and the back country of South Carolina.

Abdullah claims that the government is setting up Fuqra for another Waco incident, "to create a blueprint to destroy us." However, authorities from almost every pertinent agency in the United States and Canada believe that Fuqra has been behind dozens of bombings and assassinations over the past ten years. Most of these attacks have been against Islamic targets that incur Fuqra's wrath and fall victim to its vow to "purify their Muslim religion by force or violence."

In October 1992, a combined force of law-enforcement officials had one of their biggest breaks in penetrating the activities of the Fuqra. On

Thursday, October 8, a heavily armed SWAT team, along with an assortment of 60 officers from local, state, federal, and Canadian agencies, stormed the group's 101-acre compound in the Rocky Mountains outside of Buena Vista, Colorado. The stated legal charge was racketeering tied to a $355,000 scam in which the group collected false disability benefits from Colorado's workers' compensation plan.

The compound had been a dilapidated shack on vacated mining property near Trout Creek Pass in Chaffee County. There were a number of mining shafts on the property, and in two of the cave-like drill passes agents found a cache of weapons, including several AK-47 Soviet assault rifles. In addition, agents found two men, two women, and twenty-one children living on the property. The men were arrested and charged. The women, both pregnant, were thought to be the mothers of the twenty-one children as well. (This phenomenon of reproduction, according to Islamic terrorist experts, was in keeping with the preachings of the Fuqra—to "breed the Black Muslim leadership into the White House.")

Four other men were arrested in concurrent raids, and the official agency forces involved expanded to 150 in Colorado Springs and at the compound in Pennsylvania.

This was not the first raid at the Colorado compound. Two years earlier, a similar force had raided it in search of stolen property and also found a cache of firearms and ammunition; and at a storage locker they found pipe bombs, handguns, silencers, bomb-making instructions, thirty pounds of explosives, and military training manuals. During that 1990 raid they also found papers which indicated a number of planned assassinations and bombings. One of Fuqra's targets was Sheik Khalifa, a controversial cleric in Tucson, Arizona. The Sheik did not seem surprised to learn, when the FBI contacted him, that the Fuqra were planning to kill him, and one week later he was found stabbed to death in his mosque.

The papers in the FBI's possession contained some chilling passages in reference to the plot to assassinate Sheik Khalifa. Careful instructions said that since police patrolling in the area of the mosque was heavy, "Dispatching the subject should be in the quietest method feasible: knife, garrotte. . . ." It also warned that "He may not be there" at the anticipated time, so, "As we wait, everyone who comes must be eliminated until he shows up."

Assistant Attorney General Doug Wamsley told the *Arizona Daily Star*, "They were to be herded off into a room and told the mosque was being robbed, and then the people were to be killed." Luckily for worshipers, no one showed up to interrupt the murder, and the Sheik was on schedule for his death.

The Fuqra are also suspected in a rash of other murders and attempted destructions:

1979: San Diego—Hare Krishna temple
1982: Queens, NY—Islamic-Iranian temple
1983: Tempe, AZ—Islamic Cultural Center
      Portland, OR—Hotel Rajneesh is bombed
      Canton, MI—Dr. Mozaffar Ahmad assassinated
      Detroit, MI—Ahmadiyya Center firebombed
1984: Philadelphia—Hare Krishna temple firebombed
      Seattle, WA—Vedanta Society temple bombed
            —Integral Yoga Society bombed
      Kansas City—Vedanta temple bomb attempt
      Seattle, WA—Vedanta member attacked
      Denver, CO—Hare Krishna temple firebombed
      Overland Park, KS—Hindu physician kidnapped (never found)
      Tacoma, WA—Three immigrants from India shot to death
1985: Leetsdale, CO—Power station firebombed
      Houston, TX—Islamic mosque attacked
      Rockford, IL—Vat Thothikalam Lao attacked
            —Laotian Temple attacked
1986: Bethany, WV—Hare Krishna member injured
1988: Augusta, GA—Humana Hospital doctor murdered
1990: Tucson, AZ—Sheik Khalifa murdered
      Quincy, MA—Islamic Center attacked
1991: San Diego—Islamic Cultural Center attacked

These are just a few of the actions which officials are certain involved Fuqra members. A number of other radical groups also spun off of the Black Muslims. The leader of one of these, a Florida sect known as the Yahweh group, was sentenced to life in prison in 1992 for ordering the deaths of fourteen "white devils" and wayward disciples.

The goal of the Fuqra group and a number of former Black Muslim groups is to take over the United States by means of a purified Islamic population. From a rhetorical point of view, there is no law against this. Nor is it illegal to attempt to breed your way into power—sexual and marital laws aside. But the Fuqra's success in carrying out some of their plans, their possible connections with state-sponsored terrorism, and what they might be up to next, all constitute cause for concern.

One of the reasons why Fuqra criminal suspects have been difficult to capture over the years is their practice of dividing into small cells so that no front-line member—or even any local commune leader—knows what the other cells are planning. Thus if they are captured and questioned, singularly or in any combination, they have no solid, coordinatable information to offer to the officials.

One estimate puts the number of Islamic worshipers now living in the United States at just over four million and (especially if based on the trend of Islamic expansion over the past ten years) probably growing fast. U.S. government officials are worried that a racist backlash will develop against Muslims if more attacks inside the United States are carried out in the name of the Islamic holy war—and they are quick to point out that of the four million Islamic residents, less than one-tenth of 1 percent are Fuqra members. One official has said that, yes, all Islamic worshipers are basically Islamic Fundamentalists because they all believe in literal interpretations, but that just a small percentage believe in violence also—so, there *is* a difference between basic fundamentalism and militant fundamentalism: violence.

But people have a natural fear of the unknown, and Islam itself has always seemed an especially mysterious unknown to most Westerners— especially Americans. So the point might be better made by looking at the separatist groups in the United States who are comprised of white, Anglo-Saxon heritage.

The Christian Identity Movement

In 1984, an ill-fated attempt to violently take over the United States government by a white supremacist group called "The Order" involved a small number of people with a large number of sympathizers. The attempt revealed common patterns of revolt, and recent developments show that the movement not only goes on today but recently has gained momentum. Federal experts who eventually testified at a conspiracy trial agreed that the attempt by white supremacists came within just a few days of causing the death by poison of over 400,000 residents in Chicago and New York. The group was tied to a much larger federation of white separatist sympathizers known as the Christian Identity Church.

Few indeed understand that the white supremacist movement has moved to new fronts which are much more dangerous than the antiblack attitudes of the Ku Klux Klan even back in the fifties and sixties. The hate propaganda has been expanded to include Jews, Jewish sympathizers, homosexuals, the United States government, and anyone who does not agree with the supremacists. The hundreds of groups themselves have a complex overlapping of white supremacy versus white separatism, and a mixed dialogue of individual rights, tax protest, the right to bear arms, Hitler worship, government interference, and preparation for Armageddon.

All of these groups—The Aryan Nations, The Order, The Posse Comitatus, the Ku Klux Klan, The American Nazi Party, the Aryan Brotherhood, the Arizona Patriots, the Confederate Strike Force Skinheads, the White Student Union, the SS Action Group (there are over 130 of these organizations, large and small, operating in every state in the union)—have found a common connection in the Christian Identity Church, which raises their hate teachings to a dangerous and sometimes fanatical religious status.

This volatile mix of hate, politics, armed confrontation, economics, and religion can be traced back to two books, *Identification of the British Nation With Lost Israel*, and *The Turner Diaries*, that apparently form the basis of what now amounts to a loosely knit religion of most of the white supremacist and white separatist organizations.

The 1871 book, *Identification of the British Nation With Lost Israel*, by Edward Hine, concluded that the people described in the Bible as Israelites actually left the Middle East about 700 B.C. and moved north through the Caucasus Mountains and settled in the British Isles. Therefore, Hine proposed, Caucasians are the true Jews, and today's "false Jews" are actually a Mongolian Turkish race called Kazars.

Since publication of that book, the Christian Identity Church has turned the above theory into a religious tenet and mixed it in with animosities stemming from both the Deep South and the Depression era—from which evolved a blend of Christian fundamentalism stirred with hatred for the blacks and Jews. The burning crosses of the KKK were a symbol of their identity with the Christian Identity movement.

Combining hatred with scripture is not even that new to the United States. In 1704, predominantly Protestant Maryland enacted legislature called "An Act to Prevent the Growth of Popery," which levied a heavy fine on Catholics who attended masses.

In 1834, Samuel F. B. Morse, inventor of the telegraph, gave twelve anti-Catholic speeches in New York in which he warned that the Pope was about to send hordes of Catholics to the United States, to establish a "Romish Kingdom" in the Mississippi Valley.

The American Party, in 1856, won 21 percent of the vote with former president Millard Fillmore as its candidate. The primary support for the party was the Identity movement.

It was in the early 1900s, during a marked increase in immigration from Russia and Europe, that Jews were added to the target list of the Identity movement. This quickly evolved into three themes: Jews were taking over the financial operation of the United States, blacks were instruments of the Jews, and the government had become a Jewish weapon. The U.S. government was now called ZOG—the Zionist Occupational Government.

The KKK reached its peak during the Depression, and its rebirth after World War II was stymied first by postwar economic stability and then by a government crackdown on them in the fifties and sixties. The demise of the KKK, and the rise of a generally more liberal attitude toward blacks, disenchanted a lot of members and sympathizers—all prime targets for a new phase of the Identity movement.

They did not have long to wait to be hit. Dr. Wesley Swift, a leading Southern Depression-era white supremacist and KKK organizer, moved to California after World War II and formed the Church of Jesus Christ–Christian, also known as Aryan Nations.

Leadership of the church was taken over by Richard G. Butler, a California aeronautical engineer, in 1970. After a publicized demonstration march resulted in the loss of jobs for many of his members, he moved the Aryan Nations headquarters, along with most of its membership, to an idyllic twenty-acre spot at Hayden Lake, Idaho, at the edge of Coeur d'Alene and the magnificent national forest of the same name.

Idaho was chosen—and particularly this area of the Idaho panhandle just eighty miles from the Canadian border—because it had the lowest percentage of both black and Jewish residents in the United States. It was from this spot that Aryan Nations would build its campaign to create an all-white enclave in the U.S. encompassing Idaho, Washington, Oregon, and parts of Colorado.

Aryan Nations, with its strong ties to the Christian Identity Movement, would attract thousands of members and sympathizers from all of the other organizations of similar bent—the Posse Comitatus tax protesters, skinheads, American Nazis—with the Christian Identity movement, or sometimes called the Christian Identity Church, as "the glue that binds us together."

The plan was working to a large degree. Members and their families were moving into small towns in Idaho and voting themselves into select positions. This success was spurred on by the economic problems in the Midwest in the mid-eighties, reflected not only in the numbers of sympathizers actually moving to Idaho, but also in the growth of membership throughout the country, and even in a temporary reemergence of strength and visibility by the KKK.

In the late 1970s and early 1980s, thousands of farmers and employees nationally were left suddenly bankrupt as land values plummeted and manufacturing plants closed. The disenchanted—particularly the tax protesters of the Posse Comitatus—found solace in the fiery sermons of the traveling preachers from the Christian Identity Church and its various offshoots.

An earlier surge of supporters had occurred in the seventies, tied to the 1973 Arab oil embargo, when the sudden fear of economic collapse spurred on an increase in survivalist thought. This movement was again spiked by the 1979 oil crisis. That crisis, along with the then-recent failure of the U.S. to win the Vietnam War, caused many to conclude that the government was no longer capable of protecting them. Scores of these survivalist individuals and groups, along with the tax protesters and Vietnam veterans, became neighbors of the supremacists and separatists in rural Idaho and Michigan, and in other remote areas. While a great percentage of the fringe element would argue that they do not now support the Hitlerite attitudes of the more extreme supremacists, they do find common bonds and sympathy with the overall attitudes.

Although Aryan Nations and sympathetic groups preached a disgusting blend of hate and dissidence, their actions through the seventies and early eighties proved primarily legal. In 1985, however, a year after an explosion of violence suddenly swept the movement, an FBI official said that investigators were surprised by the violent actions of 1984. They had been keeping close watch on the goings-on in Idaho, and had concluded that the groups were nonviolent.

What happened is representative of the danger implicit within any organization that relies on impending doom to keep its membership list active: Sooner or later, something *has* to happen to prove that the fears are real, even if it takes the creation of a self-imposed Armageddon. Or—from the fanatical believer's point of view—it suddenly becomes clear that now is the time to defend oneself.

The deliverer of the overt action against ZOG was Robert J. Mathews. From among the rhetoricians of the McCarthy era in the 1950s, Robert Mathews was influenced by two men: Robert DePugh, whose Minutemen collected an arsenal of weapons and survivalist gear in preparation for the impending war against communists; and Robert Welch, founder of the John Birch Society.

At the tender age of eleven, Mathews had become a member of the John Birch Society, to the disapproval of his father but the blessings of his mother—who saw it as a wholesome alternative to the "hippie" culture.

He was still a teenager when he joined his first paramilitary group, the Sons of Liberty, made up of fellow Mormon gun enthusiasts. Their uniting themes would echo again in the themes of Mathews's Silent Brotherhood and The Order: societal collapse due to communist infiltrators in the government, particularly the Internal Revenue Service; the ills born of the Jewish control of the media; and a return to the original U.S. constitutional government.

Mathews, who had flirted with the idea of attending West Point, was also influenced by fellow Mormon Marvin Cooley, who taught resistance to the income tax. Gradually Mathews's animosity shifted from Russia to his own country.

Mathews's conservative lifestyle was well-accepted by his Mormon neighbors, and (again) against his father's wishes he was baptized in the Mormon Temple at Mesa, Arizona. According to Kevin Flynn and Gary Gerhardt (who wrote a book featuring Mathews, *The Silent Brotherhood: Inside America's Racist Underground*), Mathews had "moved beyond simple anticommunism. He was forming a more complete conservative philosophy and now had a religion to go with it."

After being convicted of tax evasion, Mathews moved to Idaho and met Butler. He embraced the Aryan Nations and the plan to create "The Inland Empire" for whites only. He also embraced the Christian Identity Church and the belief that the white race was doomed unless somebody did something about it.

This is where the second book comes in: *The Turner Diaries*, by William Pierce of Arlington, Virginia. It's a pamphlet, really, and revered as almost holy among many of the Christian Identity movement. It is a fictional account of how white supremacists successfully launch a campaign to take over the United States by killing Jews, destroying FBI headquarters, and implementing a nuclear attack on Israel.

While a great deal of the Aryan Nations propaganda was nothing more than talk, sprinkled with a lot of hate and military-preparedness training (which culminated each year at an annual Aryan Nations Congress four-day picnic at Hayden Lake), Mathews ached to put the plans into action. He had created a small cell within the Aryan Nations which he called "The Order," or (otherwise) "The Silent Brotherhood."

Mathews' charismatic personality succeeded in bringing together and uniting members of the disparate groups, and at the summer Aryan Nations Congress of 1983, a handful of men agreed to join the armed struggle that Mathews had envisioned—almost a carbon copy of the plan in *The Turner Diaries*. (It was at the 1983 Congress which members of terrorist groups from Europe, particularly Germany, also attended.)

The plan was to finance The Order through armored-car robberies and bank holdups, kill Jews and government officials, and to wreak havoc on the population to such an extent that the government would be forced to recognize the supremacist view.

In 1984, The Order netted almost $5 million from two armored-car robberies in Seattle, Washington, and Ukiah, California. They also bombed a Jewish synagogue in Boise, Idaho, and kicked off a national counterfeit-money-laundering scheme designed to (but of course didn't) cripple the economy.

In June 1984, Mathews and four other men machine-gunned Denver talk-show host Alan Berg in his driveway. Berg's outspoken rage against the white supremacists had made him a number one target on their hate list.

While The Order was in the Northwest robbing Brinks armored cars and plotting the assassination of international financier Baron Philipp de Rothschild, other factions were striking out from the Arkansas Ozarks—stalking officials, slaying Jews, and planning to poison water supplies.

Mathews was eventually surrounded by federal agents on a small island near Seattle, and died in the ensuing gun battle.

By 1987, forty-six supremacists and separatists had been convicted of over one hundred crimes tied to sedition charges. One of the charges against the Arkansas group, who had two hundred pounds of cyanide in their possession, was the intent to poison the city water supplies of Chicago, New York, and Washington, D.C. Expert testimony at the trial confirmed that, had they carried out the plan, at least four hundred thousand would have died.

Since the 1984 plot of The Order, there have been a number of cases involving FBI agents having to surround a farmhouse, an apartment, or a compound to lay siege to yet another terrorist, or terrorist group, refusing to surrender. But, as the head of the Aryan Nations said of Mathews's death, "He is now a martyr to the sympathizers and their mailbox is full of letters from people worldwide asking how to join The Order."

A recent case indicates that the degree of discontent and dissident sympathy has not diminished. On July 8, 1993, white separatist Randy Weaver was found innocent of killing a federal marshal in a shootout wherein over one hundred agents surrounded Weaver's cabin to arrest him for failure to appear in court. Weaver's wife and son were killed by sniper bullets during the eleven-day siege. At the time of this writing, Weaver was deciding whether he would press charges against the government for their deaths.

The trial could prove a landmark for white separatists and tax protesters. Defense attorney Gerry Spence, who successfully turned the issues around to put the federal government on trial, said the Idaho jury had sent a simple message to federal officers: "You are our servants. We are not your slaves." His statement was echoed by the thousands of sympathizers who had converged on Idaho from all across the United States and Canada during the eight-week trial and twenty-day jury deliberation, the longest in Idaho's history.

Five days into that trial, the siege of the Koresh camp in Waco, Texas, came to its violent end. And even though Weaver was found not guilty months later, the government has still not made it clear whether the Waco compound's inhabitants broke any laws, or were merely suspected of breaking laws on the first day of the siege.

Of course, for every hate group there is an "I'll hate you back" group. The Jewish extremists have fought back from time to time via the Jewish Defenders, the United Jewish Underground, and the more familiar Jewish Defense League. Here again, traditional Jewish organizations distance themselves from these groups.

Other groups have taken action on U.S. soil even though their complaints have been of an international nature: the Red Guerrillas Resistance; the New African Freedom Fighters; the United Freedom Front; the May 19th Communist Organization; the Organization for the Puerto Rican Revolution; the Omega-7 anti-Castro group of Cuban exiles; the Provisional Irish Republican Army; and the Irish National Liberation Army. It is expected that these types of "sympathizer" groups tied to international causes will expand rapidly in the post–cold war atmosphere of confusion and realignment.

The recent history of dissent in America brings challenges to the forefront which will have to be dealt with on a broader scale in the future. There is a real danger that the people who revolt against government laws will simply be rewarded with delay by getting more such laws passed. Idaho, which is proud of the independence of its people but does not want to be known as a hate haven, has since passed "hate laws" which have been duplicated in other states. (The Mormon Church was instrumental in supporting passage of these laws.) While such laws seem reasonable, they do bring into question whether a national danger will create national laws—which conflict with the very democratic principles they were intended to protect.

Some hate groups seem to have little by way of ideological basis, however, and are simply driven by hate. When eight members of the Fourth Reich Skinheads were arrested in Los Angeles on July 15, 1993, they had just completed plans to start a race war. Their initial target was to be the congregation of the First African Methodist Episcopal Church, one of the largest and most prominent black churches in South-Central Los Angeles. They had also planned to assassinate Rodney King, the victim of the 1991 Los Angeles police beatings (whose trial had kicked off the race riot of 1992), along with other prominent black figures across the country, plus selected Jewish leaders.

In a series of coordinated raids in Orange and Los Angeles counties, police discovered machine guns, mega-pipe bombs, ammunition, and mounds of neo-Nazi propaganda and hate material. As with the arrests of the New York bomb plotters, the FBI had benefited by using an inside informant who had penetrated the local neo-Nazi groups several years before. Apparently throwing around a great deal of government-supplied money, the undercover agent worked to gain the group's trust. He supplied beer, steaks, and cash, bailed out young supremacists who had been arrested in Canada, and even convinced the group to let him store some of the weapons to be used to start the racial war they predicted.

At the time of the arrests, the supremacist organizations had just completed a check on the flamboyant undercover agent, and were about to expose him to the local groups. Only a rift between the two national groups, the White Aryan Resistance and the Church of the Creator, delayed action.

In addition to the leader, who was a sandwich-shop manager, the arrested included minors, a flight engineer for Continental airlines, and an accountant for a real-estate firm. But only the leader was actually charged with plotting to attack the church. The other members, due to legal restrictions, were charged only with illegal-weapons violations. These same restrictions would be used by the defense, which would claim that the group was baited—and that even the idea for starting the racial war was brought to them by the undercover agent. Even though the group seemed motivated by hate, this defense was the type that might very well allow them to go free of any serious punishment.

White supremacist activities, and even their tendencies, bring into question the fragility of democracy—as well as the repetition of trends.

For example:

Do the Aryan Nations simply represent the surface of a bubbling pot of racism and dissatisfaction? Who and what are behind the Christian groups accused of taking over the Republican Party reelection campaign of George Bush?

Why did David Duke, with his views toward white supremacy and racism, do so well politically?

Is Rush Limbaugh, who presents his "like it is" views through innuendo- and satire-laden reportage over a leading radio show, on a TV program, and in a pair of best-selling, record-breaking books, but an airy outlet for a frustrated conservative group of millions? Or is he, in a broader sense, the voice of a bewildered group of millions looking for someone to bring sense to their lives? If so, perhaps there is a serious gap of trusted authority—not because of Rush Limbaugh, but because the public cannot find something other than a television personality to fill the gap.

Kahane—U.S. Domestic Terrorists Export Violence

On February 25, 1994, Dr. Baruch Goldstein entered a holy site in Hebron, on the Israeli Occupied West Bank, killed 29 Palestinians and wounded more than 90 others. Goldstein's attack was an assault against the fragile and controversial Israeli and Palestinian negotiations, but as Goldstein's background was revealed the assault quickly became an example of how a U.S. hate group can export violence to another country. The Hebron massacre also completed a vicious circle comprised of the World Trade Center bombing defendants, the blind cleric Sheik Omar Abdel Rahman and the other Arab extremists charged in the conspiracy to attack the United Nations, and the Jewish Defense League (JDL). The connecting link was Rabbi Meir Kahane, who had been assassinated four years earlier.

Kahane was an American-born Jew who in the sixties had failed in various attempts to become a world figure as a Jewish right-wing radical. Then he founded the JDL and embraced a typical terrorist mentality. In 1971 Kahane told Michael T. Kaufman, a reporter for the *New York Times*, "We have no great funds, no great influence, so the answer is simple: to do outrageous things." As Kaufman said in March 1994, also in the *New York Times*, in a recollection of that meeting twenty-three years earlier, "It was a formula he used for the rest of his life, one that led to his being killed, one that is still being used by his followers."

Kahane's JDL more or less became the Jewish counterpart to Abu Nidal's AO: the JDL declared itself an enemy of anyone (Arab or Jew) who took a moderate position on the Israeli-Palestinian peace process. While the JDL's influence never gained political strength in the U.S., Kahane's extremist attitude found a following among the various right-wing factions in Israel after he immigrated there in 1971. The Israeli group spawned by Kahane was called Kach, which means "this is the way." The Israeli government paid little attention to Kahane's two groups until 1984, when Kahane won a seat in the Parliament. Four years later, on the eve of the next election, Kahane's organization was banned from the ballot as racist. That ban was upheld again in 1992.

Kahane's influence with extremist Jews grew throughout the 1980s in both Israel and the U.S., and his bitter actions toward Arabs culminated in his assassination in 1990. An Arab immigrant, El Sayyid A. Nosair, was acquitted of the murder but was sentenced on related weapons charges. He was a follower of Sheik Rahman, who was suspected of ordering the killing, and most of the perpetrators of the World Trade Center bombing and the follow-up conspiracy plot were friends of Nosair, some of them in attendance at small street demonstrations that took place during the trial. Even though Nosair was still in prison in 1993, he was suspected of helping to plan the United Nations bombing conspiracy.

Kahane's death inspired a spin-off of the original Kach. This group of younger Jewish extremists in both Israel and the U.S. calls itself the Kahane Chai, or "Kahane Lives." The group has grown to over ten thousand members in the U.S., according to Mike Guzofsky, associate director of the Brooklyn-based United States branch of Kahane Chai.

Although Dr. Goldstein had been a member of the Kach almost since its inception and had a known history of anti-Arab extremist attitudes (including refusal to provide medical assistance to Arabs wounded in battle), the Israeli government had no physical evidence to prosecute either Goldstein or the group—until the Hebron massacre. On March 13, 1994, the Israeli government outlawed Kach and Kahane Chai, branding them terrorist organizations on the same level as the Arab Hamas militants. Israel's antiterrorist laws, which had in the past been used only against Arabs, were expanded to include "the establishment of a theocracy in the biblical Land of Israel and the violent expulsion of Arabs from that land."

The Israeli law now places the U.S. in a similar position as it has had with the Germans: activities and organizations that are illegal in Israel and Germany are not illegal in the U.S. At the very least, in regard to fundraising and propagandizing, the U.S. serves as a safe house for these organizations, and possibly for the terrorists themselves.

CHAPTER 7

Ease of Access—To Materials, to American Shores, to Sensitive Facilities

There is no need to spend many pages revealing the ease of access terrorists have to weapons and materials, our American shores, and to our sensitive facilities. While documentation of these subjects is extensive, the argument against them is not.

A quick look at the daily newspapers reveals the crux of this reality.

No one doubts that anyone seeking a weapon or explosive device of any kind could not find it today in the United States. That this extends to uranium, plutonium, and other materials needed to build a nuclear bomb is also a surprise to absolutely no one. Hundreds of pounds of the material is on the open market from previously Soviet nations, and hundreds of pounds disappear annually from United States military and civilian stockpiles. Only a small fraction of what has been stolen is needed to create a devastating bomb.

But we do not have to get into the sophistication of building a nuclear bomb to make the point. Material for the bomb that blew a one-hundred-foot hole through six stories of the World Trade Center was available at local stores. The "witches brew," as the FBI called the bomb mixture discovered a few days later in a plot to blow up the United Nations building, was a barrel of fertilizer mixed with fuel oil. It was missing only a small detonator device at the time of the FBI raid to stop the next series of attacks.

Most of the weapons preferred by terrorists are not only available in the United States—they are also legal to carry or otherwise transport herein, too. This fact muddles one of the gray areas surrounding the Waco cult. The same may be said for the fact that in Texas it is almost as easy to obtain a license to deal in arms as it is to get a driver's license. And, as a licensed arms *dealer*, the leeway for stockpiling firearms and munitions is even broader. Actually, restricting terrorists to otherwise legal weapons is hardly confining, since the primary requirements that terrorists insist on in the arms that they purchase around the world are reliability and simplicity of use—and such conditions are easily met, especially in the United States.

Accessibility to powerful weapons on a global scale is even more of a concern, due to the sophistication of those being marketed freely among terrorist cells, rebel groups, and terrorist-sponsored countries. The Stinger antiaircraft missiles are at the forefront of this dilemma.

The Stinger was one of the more useful inventions of recent times in terms of low-intensity warfare. It is thought to be the weapon that made the difference in breaking the back of the Soviets in the Soviet-Afghan rebel war. During the early years of that war, Afghan rebels hiding in the remote valleys and mountain enclaves were helpless against attack by Soviet fighter planes and helicopters. Not only could the Soviet-backed government seek out and destroy the rebel camps and arsenals at will, but also they could do so without submitting their ground troops to the massive casualties experienced by the Americans during the Vietnam War.

Suddenly, in 1986, the war planes and helicopters were being blown out of the sky, and a long convoy filled with body bags and wounded soldiers started returning to the Soviet Union. The economic cost of the war increased tremendously, along with the demoralization of both the soldiers who had been transported to Afghanistan for what they thought would be a short skirmish, and the long-suffering civilian populations in the East-bloc countries.

From 1986 to 1989, a $3 billion CIA covert operation to support the Afghan rebels secretly sent almost one thousand Stinger missiles to the rebel front, through connections with the Pakistani government. The Stinger, which finds its target via a homing device that senses and locks on to an aircraft's engine heat, is capable of destroying an aircraft from a range of seven miles or more. It is lightweight, highly accurate, and considered the best of its kind. It can be carried on one shoulder, and fired from almost any position by a single person.

But three hundred of the deadly Stingers are missing and unaccounted for. And the CIA fears that the weapons will fall into terrorist hands, for use against the United States. The CIA eventually offered $10 million to the rebels, in a bid to reclaim the Stingers, but the stakes were raised by Iran. In July 1993 the CIA asked for an additional $55 million, to be able to continue the bidding, but even that seemed likely to prove too small a gesture when compared to what Iran or other terrorist sponsor-states doubtless would be willing to pay. The Afghans are cash-starved after years of war, and their main sources of income are heroin—and weapons sales.

Complicating the problem is that the CIA must rely on the Pakistani intelligence agency to help retrieve the missiles, since the latter distributed them in the first place. And complicating the problem still further is that the Pakistani government favored a rebel leader who was the most anti-American (and thus received most of the deliveries). That leader, Gulbuddin Hekmatyar, who is now Prime Minister due to his superior arsenal, has maintained close ties with Iran throughout the Afghan–USSR war years.

It is almost certain that Iran, North Korea, or some militant Islamic group will win any close bid, and it is questionable whether *any* amount of money from the Americans will be enough to obtain the weapons. The rebels, known as the mujahedeen, or holy warriors, are more or less allied with the Islamic Jihad holy war led and sponsored by Iran. Four of the men arrested in the World Trade Center bombing and the related plot to attack other targets in New York were mujahedeen rebels.

A 1993 *New York Times* report on Afghanistan said, "Travelers from more than 40 Islamic countries go there to learn from the rebels who stared down the Soviets." David Whipple, a former CIA national intelligence officer for counterterrorism, said in that article, "Some of the same people who are actual or potential terrorists in this country are former guerrilla fighters in Afghanistan."

These immigrants to the United States who have maintained their connections for weapons may also have kept their connections in drug trafficking. The eleventh suspect to be arrested (on July 23, 1993) in the plot to bomb targets in New York—Matarawy Mohammad Said Saleh—also had a record for drug dealing. Once again, the same drug distribution routes which come from overseas and spread across the nation internally can also be used for weapons distribution. Stinger missiles, automatic weapons, plastic explosives—there is little doubt that if someone wanted to buy them in this country, getting them would be a relatively simple exercise.

On a similar note, no one denies that U.S. borders are the most porous anywhere, with literally millions of illegal aliens entering across them annually from every part of the world. They come by water on the Atlantic and Pacific coasts and the Gulf of Mexico, and by land from the vast stretches of unguarded territory bordering Mexico and Canada.

If they come through legal channels, then the numbers are increased by over twenty-one million people processed annually by the Bureau of Immigration and Naturalization. Should they choose to outstay their temporary visa, it might be years before they are accidentally discovered. The Bureau admits that it is so overworked that it is lucky to actually review even 5 percent of the applicants—*including* those requesting asylum—who are given a card and asked to show up at some later date for a hearing.

Our system for dealing with temporary visas is different from those procedures in most other countries. In Great Britain and the European nations, visitors must make periodic personal visits to an immigration office, or face deportation. Although American travelers abroad accept these restrictions as normal and unobtrusive, to inflict the same requirements on visitors to the United States conflicts with our principles of democracy, and constitutes an invasion of privacy.

In other words, foreign terrorists who are not already here can come in anytime, anywhere they choose. In fact, it is probable that an armed battalion in full uniform of a foreign country could cross the Canadian border and reach Chicago before anyone took it seriously. And if that same battalion bothered to disguise their uniforms and trucks as a National Guard unit, they wouldn't be paid heed at all until they decided to reveal themselves.

That terrorists would also have easy access to most of our government facilities is also accepted, and that they would have access to *all* of our public utilities is a given—since most of these latter facilities have no security whatsoever (at most, security would amount to nothing more than the stereotypical retired cop on duty who also acts as receptionist). The January 25, 1993 deaths of CIA agents *at CIA headquarters*, perpetrated by a foreign taxi-cab driver, point out this reality. Consider also the disgruntled employee who recently crashed a car through the main entrance to the Three Mile Island nuclear reactor.

In his book *The Fourth World War*, Count De Merenches is astounded that the United States might allow a potential foreign army to move freely about the streets of our largest and most sensitive areas, communications systems at the ready for coordinating attacks. He was talking about our legions of taxi cabs—which are so common in our major cities that they have the advantage of seeming to be invisible. And, as anyone who has tried to explain directions to a taxi driver in New York or Washington, D.C., has discovered, a great percentage of the drivers *are* recent immigrants from foreign countries.

The targets of future terrorist attacks will fall into three categories.

First will be the cosmetic targets—the "public message" category. These will include famous structures like the World Trade Center and the Statue of Liberty, well-known department stores, and prominent landmarks in the target city or area.

Second will be nonmilitary government targets, including for example the United Nations building, the Supreme Court, the White House, and (on a more localized basis) state-capital buildings, Internal Revenue offices, and FBI headquarters.

In many ways the vulnerability of this category of target is due to similar attitudes brought on by our democratic beliefs. Just as an individual can speak against the government in this country without stepping over the line, until taking an overt related action, or can own a gun without breaking the law, until committing a crime with it, our internal-security defenses are designed to *catch* criminals—not to stop them *before* a crime is carried out.

When leading antiterrorist experts are asked what stops a van from pulling up in front of the White House and firing a shoulder-held Stinger missile, the answer is that the saboteur would never escape. The answer is *not* that the attack would be stopped before the damage was done.

The White House has an elaborate system of surveillance devices, and those decorative potted plants and gates are carefully placed and anchored to prevent entry by an armored vehicle. But very little of the White House security would stop the use of a slightly higher level of modern technology and weaponry. It is even questionable whether a terrorist with modern explosives would be caught at security if he or she tried to enter disguised as a member of one of the White House tour groups.

A similar scenario could be proposed for virtually every nonmilitary government target, including those that presumably enjoy superior (if not impregnable) security.

The basic goal of terrorists in each of these first two categories respectively is simply (1) to taunt authorities, and (2) to cause havoc in the most public manner possible. These goals are part of what terrorists consider their psychological war. If citizens lose confidence in government and feel they are not protected by government, then government itself begins to lose authority.

Many targets are also chosen because they are relatively free of risk. The attacks give credibility to members of a group, or of other cells—or they may simply demonstrate to foreign investors that they are getting their money's worth.

Even assuming that the experts are correct in stating that an attacker would not escape after hitting a target like the White House, that gives little solace when the attacker is a religious fanatic who doesn't necessarily care whether or not he or she escapes.

Jake, the former Special Forces member who met with me, gave two interesting examples of the weakness of our security systems. He had been hired by the government to test the security of various government buildings that had supposedly been hardened due to direct threats. One of these was in Miami. Its occupants had cause to believe that the Cuban Omega-7 group would retaliate against them for one or another reason.

Making matters worse for Jake, the office that had hired him had sent a memorandum to the commander in charge, informing him that a test would be conducted within the next few days. The commander, in turn, forwarded a similar memorandum to the officer in charge of security. They had everything except Jake's picture pinned to the bulletin board.

Nine days later, Jake got out of a taxi cab in front of the building. It was raining.

Security in the building had been tightened so as to direct all foot traffic through one set of double doors at the top of long, granite steps leading up to the building from the sidewalk. All of the men entering the building were dressed in suits, while Jake had shown up in a baggy pair of pants and a sweatshirt.

After surveying the outside of the entrance area for a couple of minutes, Jake ran to catch up to an umbrella-toting middle-aged man in a dark suit who was halfway up the stairs. The man responded to Jake's friendly hello, and they proceeded under the protection of the umbrella. Inside the double doors was a small lobby leading to the elevators and the interior hallway. These were protected by a security desk, and two armed guards on either side of the entrance to the hallway. The guard at the desk said good morning to the middle-aged man he had seen coming and going at the building for many years, and the man and his apparent friend, Jake, proceeded into the hallway past the guards.

At the interior lobby, Jake left the side of the middle-aged man and asked another employee for directions to the commander's office. He was directed up an escalator to the second floor. It fed him into a quiet corridor which led to a cluster of offices at the end, this area featuring (and apparently guarded by) the desks of three secretaries. As Jake arrived, one of the secretaries was about to take in a silver tray of coffee and dough-nuts, obviously for the commander.

Jake informed the secretary of his embarrassment for being late for a private meeting with the commander—would she let him carry in the tray, as a way of making amends? Moments later, the lid was lifted off the tray, in front of the commander. He looked up at his secretary, astonished. On top of the doughnuts was what appeared to be a live (explodable, but not primed) grenade.

"Bang! You're dead!" said Jake.

Jake's penetration of the tightened security, finding the commander's office, and entering with a live grenade, had taken a total of two and a half minutes.

A few months later, in a similar security test in Philadelphia, here's what happened to Jake: Because the security guard obviously took inor-dinate pleasure in exercising his authority, Jake concluded that there was no peaceful means by which he was going to get into *that* building. An hour later, Jake stood across the street and watched as a small sports car pulled up to the curb and a beautiful young lady climbed out, adjusting her short skirt on the way to the front door. The security guard beamed as he held the door open for her. And so did Jake. His accomplice had success-fully gained entrance to the building.

According to Jake, women make some of the best terrorists in the world—especially in the United States, where (in general) men have been taught to be respectful of "the weaker sex." Police report that this defer-ence is one of the most subtle but potentially explosive root causes of dan-ger in their handling of domestic disputes. To illustrate an entirely feasible example: a call comes in, saying that shots have been fired in an apartment building. The police go there, unhesitatingly (per such emergencies) break down the door, barge into the living room, and immediately train their guns on the only person they see. Then they notice that he's bleeding pro-fusely—even as he apologetically tries to explain why a woman suddenly is standing behind them, a faintly smoking gun in her hand.

The *third* category of targets of future terrorist attacks will be much more strategic: They will be designed to interrupt traffic flow. Targets might include traffic bridges and tunnels, both of which can easily be blown by day or night. As in the case of the tunnels in New York, where the security guards refused to go to work in June when they heard on the radio that someone might try to bomb the tubes, any security guards on duty would be only a minor inconvenience.

Military targets would probably be excluded, unless the terrorists were trying to make a specific point of protest against a specific act by one of the military departments. They might also be attacked for a diversion, but otherwise there would be little strategic value in bothering with military targets because they would be only a small obstacle.

The most important targets would have to do with energy sources and the public utilities: gas, oil, electricity, water, and nuclear plants. It is here that the United States is most vulnerable to massive damage and long-term consequences. And these targets are the subjects of the next part of this book.

Part II

PHYSICAL TARGETS

CHAPTER 8

The Vulnerable National Infrastructure

When the outline for this book was written many months prior to the World Trade Center explosion, it predicted initial terrorist targets. First on the list was the World Trade Center. Second and third on the list were New York City's Holland and Lincoln tunnels. It was frightening indeed to see the predictions realized even before this book was written. More frightening still was to learn that the targets were even more vulnerable than had been assumed. However, no amount of screaming or publicity at the time would have been sufficient to awaken the bureaucracies to what seemed so inevitable.

But this is not an unusual dilemma. In 1981, I told several different audiences of direct marketers and insurance company executives that the computer giant IBM would either cease to exist within twelve years or find itself in bankruptcy struggling to reorganize. The purpose of the statement was to warn all of IBM's client companies that if they continued to develop "Baby Blues" (IBM clones) within their own organization, they would inherit IBM's problems by default, either on a companywide basis or, at the very least, within their multimillion-dollar computer departments. Numb stares from the audience, and some chuckles, finally drove the subject underground.

IBM's problems finally came to their predictable Armageddon in 1993, hitting the press at about the same time as the World Trade Center bombing. And by July 1993, a few days after the second group of Muslim terrorists was arrested, financial "experts" were predicting that as many as seventy thousand IBM employees would be in effect fired—forced out of the company or into early retirement.

It didn't take clairvoyance or a high degree of computer expertise to foresee problems for IBM and centralized computer systems in general. In fact, here was a classic case of experts who couldn't see the forest for the trees and allowed its calamity to evolve. We are now at a similar point with regard to terrorism—only in this case our vulnerability to it is a subject that must not be driven underground.

Energy and National Security

We are presently in a situation where one person could incinerate an entire city, and a small group of terrorists could endanger both the nation's and the world's oil supply. But energy sources are not the only parts of our system which have fallen prey to the old-world mentality of centralization. The same weaknesses exist in almost every phase of modern distribution, including food and water supplies. But while each of these distribution systems has built-in weaknesses, the problem of fault tolerance is exacerbated by the fact that the different distribution systems are also reliant on each other: There is no food if there is no gas, no gas if there is no electricity, and so forth.

Part of the reason for these infrastructure problems is the evolution of our industrial society over the past two hundred years—the change from an agrarian society, in which 90 percent of our population was rural, to an industrially based society wherein only 2 percent of our population was rural. The trend became that of centralizing everything—government, distribution systems, even production sources—to serve a mass society. But the Industrial Revolution is now closing, and almost everything that has become familiar must change to fit a new mentality. Many of our present systems make no more sense than the building of high-rises to house the poor.

Just as the military must reorganize itself to fit a new age, and just as government must redefine itself to fit a new future of diverse cultures, our energy and resource distribution systems must rid themselves of the massive networks which can be brought down by terrorists at any of thousands of vulnerable choke points. Energy sources top the list of priorities because they are vulnerable and their disruption can easily lead to a cascading, total calamity.

People remember the oil crisis in the early 1970s, when long lines of cars waited for gas, and prices quickly soared by over 120 percent. This rise was caused by a drop in the world oil supply of a mere 2 percent. Even though it was later discovered that some oil companies had secretly stockpiled oil in tankers held offshore, it was the first time that Western countries were forced to realize or admit publicly their dependence on foreign oil. While the crisis did kick off some research and development of alternative energy sources, we soon allowed ourselves to be lulled back to the old system, and as recently as 1991 the world held its breath again in fear that oil from the Mideast would be cut off, or fall into the hands of the dictator Saddam Hussein.

The destruction, or perhaps even the disruption, of energy supplies could bring on the loss of millions of jobs virtually overnight, the starvation of hundreds of thousands, and to at least some extent an environmental catastrophe. And there is another reason why energy sources should be a top priority on our national-defense list: They are so simple to destroy, as shown in the next four chapters, that it is ridiculous to even imagine that they are not at the top of the list of terrorist targets.

As one Department of Defense official explained in the wake of the World Trade Center bombing, the terrorist strives to get the most bang for his buck by achieving the most efficient kill ratio. He can spend five thousand dollars and explode a bomb in the World Trade Center. Or he can spend one dollar on a bullet and wipe out the electricity to an entire city. Or maybe kill millions of people with a small vial of inexpensive but lethal chemicals. If the option is left open, sooner or later the terrorist will respond.

CHAPTER 9

The Explosive Mixture of Terrorism and Liquid Gas

According to a General Accounting Office (GAO) report, in 1977, "Successful sabotage of an LEG [liquefied energy gas] facility in an urban area could cause a catastrophe. We found that security precautions and physical barriers at LEG facilities are generally not adequate to deter even an untrained saboteur. None of the LEG storage areas we examined are impervious to sabotage, and most are highly vulnerable."

Liquefied energy gas (LEG) is the generic term to describe both liquid *natural* gas (LNG) and liquid *petroleum* gas (LPG).

Even though the energy content of a single LNG transport tanker (ship) is equivalent to that of fifty-five Hiroshima-size atomic bombs, very little has been done to assure that LNG shipments are protected from sabotage as they come and go through the ports of some of our major cities. Regardless of the government's own reports and warnings, LNG tankers lumber into the hearts of city harbors, and these cities are in danger of being leveled on any given day.

LNG was created as a means to ship huge amounts of natural gas from overseas. Its processing starts at a gigantic, billion-dollar liquefication refrigerator wherein natural gas is chilled and condensed at a temperature of $-260°F$. It is colorless and odorless. It goes into the tankers as LNG, at a compressed volume 620 times smaller than the original gas. The tankers are specially insulated cryogenic vessels which carry the LNG to similarly insulated cryogenic storage tanks. The LNG is then piped to a nearby gasification plant, where it is boiled back into gas for distribution to customers via pipeline.

In addition to the overseas tankers, approximately sixty small plants in North America also liquefy domestic gas as a convenient way to store local LNG supplies for peak use during winter demands.

Whereas oil contains more energy than does LNG, the liquid natural gas is actually more hazardous. Burning oil does not spread far over either water or land. LNG, on the other hand, is less than half as dense as water, so a single cubic meter of LNG weighs just over half a ton. One cubic meter of spilled LNG rapidly boils into approximately 620 cubic meters of natural gas, which mixes with the air—a mixture of between 5 and 14 percent is flammable.

A single cubic meter of spilled LNG can make up to 12,400 cubic meters of flammable gas-air mixture.

If the extremely cold liquid *is* spilled, it will boil to gas in about five minutes, but it will still be heavier than air and will drift along the land or water surface—as far as three miles from the spill site—until it reaches an ignition point. This would take ten to twenty minutes, and, depending on the air current, the plume could actually extend as far as twelve miles over a longer period of time. Once ignited, the resulting fireball would burn everything within its area and start subsequent fires as far as two miles farther away. Such a fireball could engulf a city with the ferocity of the Hiroshima atom bomb many times over—and there is no known equipment that could put out a very large LNG fire.

Another problem with LNG and its extreme cold is that even a small leak, whether started accidentally or purposely, would cause most metals to become brittle and break. All of the tankers, the liquefication and gasification plants, and the insulated storage tanks are in danger of accidents caused by minor leaks outside the special storage membranes. The trucks that carry LNG across the nation on our highways and interstates—through crowded as well as open areas—are just as susceptible to leaks as are the tankers, or even more so—and they are definitely even more susceptible to sabotage.

The fallibility of the humongous tankers is cause for great concern by (among others) their insurors. Lloyds of London has had to pay hundreds of millions of dollars because of construction faults and cracked insulation structures, as well as tanker beachings. *All* of the tankers could be *easily* sabotaged because they allow access below the cargo area, and the turning of a couple of pressure valves could cause the load to self-destruct by overpressurization of the fragile cargo.

As disturbing as all of this is regarding LNG tankers, more troublesome is the realization that they are probably the most protected and secure vessels in the entire energy distribution network.

LNG storage tanks and terminals are located across the globe; forty-five are in the United States alone, each holding potentially disastrous amounts of the expansive material. There have been accidents and near-disasters in Tokyo harbor, just outside London, and in Algeria and Boston. These terminals and their storage plants have repeatedly failed to pass inspection by the Government Accounting Office (GAO). Here's why: Like so much of the rest of the U.S. distribution system, all of our terminals and tanks are built aboveground, easily accessible to either short-range or long-range attack, and surrounded by containment tanks that tend to be insufficient to contain *any* serious spill. In Japan, the tanks are buried below ground, where containment of a spill is more likely. The GAO's conclusion is that access to any of the U.S. LNG storage facilities would be easy for even an untrained saboteur.

In the eyes of a terrorist, those familiar LNG trucks you see on the roads are valuable "bombs on wheels" which can be swiped, then moved, largely or even totally unnoticed, to any location of their choosing.

The Destruction of Boston

Of all the cities in the world, Boston is the most susceptible to destruction due to the vagaries of LNG transportation. Recently some citizens there realized how fragile their protection is from LNG natural disasters or accidents, and filed suits against the Everett Distrigas Company, petitioning the city to halt the transport of LNG through the center of town. But even Boston residents apparently have no idea of how susceptible they are to intentional sabotage, because the tankers still are unloading in the close harbor, storage remains kept aboveground and in direct line with the airport's traffic lanes, and trucks continue to roll through the streets—and across the most vulnerable part of the city, including the ideal terrorist spot.

Some Northeast states have long had a love–hate relationship with the maritime industry, which in modern times became virtually equated with the oil industry. In parts of those states it is not unusual to see a gigantic storage tank practically in the middle of an otherwise typical residential neighborhood—and lobster boats scurrying to get out of the way of tankers churning up a nearby river. In many cases, the willingness of the locals to put up with such gigantic eyesores has been rewarded by lifelong property-tax reductions or abatements—the economic value of which in fact grows during hard economic times there.

Because of this sort of arrangement, it has for a long time not been all that unusual for a city like Boston to allow one of the nation's largest LNG storage facilities to be built just minutes from its downtown. But—as the headlines now regularly report—the public finally is awakening to today's nasty realities, even if local government has yet to shake off the effects of comfortable somnolence.

As many as ninety LNG trucks a day leave the Everett Distrigas terminal. Most of these travel the elevated Southeast Expressway, which passes over the entrances to the Sumner and Callahan tunnels connecting Boston to Logan International Airport across the bay. Because these tractor-trailer trucks are subject to all of the normal hazards of highway traffic, they are involved in many accidents. The probability of eventual disaster along the expressway and (as a result) elsewhere is obvious.

The LNG trucks also are subject to sabotage or hijacking. Even if the vehicles were rerouted, it would still be an easy matter for a terrorist to commandeer one and drive it to any location of choice. If the location were the ramp above the Callahan and Sumner tunnels, a small puncture or valve release would allow the contents of the heavier-than-air LNG to flow downward. As the GAO has reported: "The forty cubic meters of LNG in one truck, vaporized and mixed with air into flammable proportions, are enough to fill more than one hundred and ten miles of six-foot sewer line, or sixteen miles of sixteen-foot-diameter subway system."

The resultant explosion throughout the city of Boston would of course be catastrophic—but the damage would go beyond the direct effects of the LNG explosion itself. *Indirect* explosions caused by methane backup in the sewer lines across the breadth of the city would be a nightmare, not only in the downtown office district but in the suburbs as well.

In Louisville, Kentucky, a 1981 sewer explosion involving only sewer gas tore up *miles* of streets. And in 1992, a similar catastrophe occurred in Mexico City. For these reasons, each time a smart city employee anywhere enters any part of a sewer system, he first tests the enclosed area for methane buildup. And these were *natural* disasters *not* involving the LNG additive!

An example of the potential domino effect of an explosion in any part of a city's distribution system occurred in St. Paul, Minnesota, on July 22, 1993. A city crew working on minor repairs to a sewer in that town's Dayton's Bluff neighborhood accidentally punctured a small hole in a natural-gas line. A high volume of gas was sent rushing into a neighboring apartment building, and a few minutes later, at 8:53 on a Thursday morning, an explosion reported as sounding like a sonic boom flattened two buildings and set fire to a third.

The blast and the resultant fireball killed two people and injured twelve. More people would have been killed or injured had it not been for the efforts of the city crew workers, who risked their lives to evacuate the building—and, too, had the explosion occurred just an hour or so earlier, before many of the local residents left for work.

But it would be misleading to imply that other cities are not also at risk. The risk goes wherever a truck can travel. This is made even more evident when you look at the facts surrounding the more familiar liquid petroleum gas (LPG), which can be even more hazardous.

Liquid Petroleum Gas (LPG) (Butane or Propane)

Unlike LNG, LPG is shipped in liquid form, as propane or butane. You see tanks of it everywhere—in trailer parks, and larger ones (those big white tanks) outside of farm homes. It is a far older and more familiar fuel than LNG, but it is *less regulated* and *more hazardous*.

Most LPG is transported through over seventy thousand miles of pipeline, within sixteen thousand pressurized railroad cars, and via twenty-five thousand pressurized trucks. Small, aboveground storage tanks, each a target, feed the transports; vehicles and the storage tanks themselves are fed by LPG underground storage tanks usually kept in salt domes or caverns.

The LPG transports are more dangerous than the LNG ones for a number of reasons. First, they are pressurized, not chilled; and, since they do not require insulation, the tanks are single-walled rather than (as are the LNG tanks) double-walled. In other words, they are easily punctured and destroyed. An LPG load also causes extremely high pressures when exposed to heat, and is more likely to explode when exposed to fire.

Because of the number of LPG transports, they are involved in thousands of accidents each year, some causing serious damage and numerous deaths. Fireballs from just one railroad carload of LPG have attained a radius of over one thousand feet, and the fireball from a single truck can reach a radius of over two hundred feet—more if the truck is actually propelled by the explosion. Ironically, trucks and rail cars carrying LPG travel daily through cities and towns which, due to safety concerns, do not allow LPG storage—even though the trucks and rail cars are more likely to explode.

Sabotage to moving trains and trucks across the United States is not uncommon, and they are prime targets for tampering when they sit for many hours (and sometimes days) at truck yards or rail yards.

Unlike LNG, LPG not only is heavier than air when it is released, but also remains so much longer. This means that it can spread much farther across the surface, or deeper into subway or sewer systems. It also ignites at just a 2 to 9 percent air mixture. Even a *small* LPG leak can be dangerous!

LPG storage and transport facilities units are, indeed, everywhere, and we have not paid much attention to where we have located these LPG facilities with regard to what they sit beside. A major LPG receiving terminal near Los Angeles Harbor sits near the Palos Verdes earthquake fault, a U.S. Navy fuel depot and tank farm on the one side and a dense residential area on the other. In turn, LPG tankers are coming and going in the vicinity, bringing with them their own possibility of igniting an LPG holocaust.

In 1981, a crash of an FB-111 aircraft came close to demonstrating the worst of all possible LPG worlds. Near Newington, New Hampshire, the plane crashed close to the second-largest LPG/LNG tank farm in New England, which sat next to the huge fuel depot of Pease Air Force Base—which is only a couple of miles from Portsmouth and another half mile from the nuclear submarine base. The domino effect of any subsequent worst-case scenario explosion would actually have had the potential of wiping out the entire eastern seaboard, simply because the flash point or devastation radius of each facility was not taken into consideration when they were designed and situated.

This same problem of LPG storage near sensitive areas exists in virtually every city and every government facility—if not posed by the actual storage plants, then by the trucks that pass by nuclear plants, office buildings, government agencies, and residential areas at all hours of the day. LEG and LNG transports and facilities give terrorists the opportunity to destroy or harm these targets without firing a shot, without spending a cent, and probably without being discovered.

CHAPTER 10

Gas and Oil as Terrorist Targets

While the thousands of liquid natural gas and liquid petroleum gas tankers, tanks, and trucks provide ample terrorist targets, the anticipated effects of a single incident are primarily local—each target representing the destruction of a single neighborhood, city, or specific government facility. A slight expansion of this plot (targeting the primary gas and oil reserves and distribution systems within the United States) expands the ranks of the potential victims to include every citizen of the nation.

Like no other commodity, oil exemplifies a number of factors regarding energy vulnerability, from the euphoric statements regarding the world as a global community to the testy frustration that industrial nations feel in having become totally dependent on oil and the third world dictators who control it.

The 1973 and 1979 oil crises demonstrated how quickly prices of oil could skyrocket, and how quickly "shortages" could develop, this combination causing long lines at the pumps and hyperventilated inflation in the United States and Europe. Through complex negotiations and economic considerations by OPEC countries, the 1981 OPEC decision to regulate oil costs transferred over $50 billion back to the industrial world in 1986 alone, ending the economic crisis and stimulating a prolonged growth of wealth by driving down inflation. Such was the scare that the United States began a program of holding six hundred million barrels of oil in reserve, ready to either fill necessary volumes or to flood the market in order to correct price fluctuations.

But just as the economic crisis was ending in 1987, the Iran-Iraq war extended for the first time into the international arena. Iran successfully broke through into Iraqi territory bordering Kuwait, and because Kuwait was assisting Iraq, Iran launched missile attacks on Kuwaiti oil fields. Complicating the situation was the discovery by Kuwait that the Bush administration had lied to them. While vowing not to trade arms with third world nations, it was suddenly revealed, the United States was secretly sending weapons, including missiles, to Iran in exchange for hostages— even though the U.S. was supporting Iraq in the war.

This situation was complicated further when the war suddenly took a turn that put Iraq on the offensive. Iran responded by starting a "tanker war," sinking ships from third world countries that were trying to make the oil run to Kuwait. Fearing that the Russians would take advantage of the situation, the United States took the lead in protecting the tankers. It was imperative that it protect the flow of oil from the Mideast, and keep Russia from gaining a substantial increase of influence in the region.

By 1988, Iraq was winning the war and Iran's economy was in a shambles, with the United States patroling Iran shores in the gulf. Ironically, when the U.S. destroyer *Vincennes* accidentally mistook an Iranian Airbus for a fighter aircraft and shot it down, killing 290 civilians, Iran took that as a sign not that the United States had made a mistake but that it was now ready to enter the fight with earnest. Within four weeks, Iran was negotiating a ceasefire—which Iraq soon accepted.

Two years later, Iraq invaded Kuwait, and the concept that oil-producing countries and oil-consuming countries could (or had to) get along due to mutual self-interest was fading fast. Suddenly Iraq, the world's largest purchaser of arms and the only Mideast country not to hide its hatred of the West, was about to become the world's largest holder of oil.

George Bush summed up the dangers: "Our jobs, our way of life, our own freedom and the freedom of friendly countries around the world would all suffer if control of the world's great oil reserves fell in the hands of Saddam Hussein."

Such is the dependence of the industrial world on oil. The irony is that the United States has left itself in a position where it could be drowning in oil but unable to get to it.

A Nation Without Oil

Some say there has never been a war that was not fought primarily for business reasons, regardless of the rhetoric with which it was insulated. From the first discovery of oil in Pennsylvania to the creation of petroleum billionaires and giant refining conglomerates, and to the rise to power of the "black gold"–rich Mideast countries, oil has been the lifeblood of the continuing Industrial Revolution. Virtually every aspect of civilization has been transformed by the discovery, refinement, and distribution of oil. Every person alive has lived in the age of oil, and that age will continue, driven by both need and greed, until that particular resource runs out or is shut off.

If oil were suddenly denied us, our entire petroleum-based way of life would soon end. There would be no automobiles and no jobs. No food. Millions of people would be crowding around polluted rivers and streams in quest of water itself because the systems which deliver water would not work. The resultant economic collapse and political and social chaos is almost unimaginable. So too it is almost unbelievable that the United States, the most industrialized nation in the world, has left itself in a position where its oil *could* be turned off overnight—without further access to either foreign *or* domestic oil. And that this could be accomplished, almost as a whim, by a small band of terrorists. This weakness is further enhanced by the realization that Islamic extremists, who claim they do not hate the people of the West but want only to destroy the evil monster capitalism, could do so with an eruption of biblical—indeed, of Cecil B. DeMille—proportions.

Cut Off From Foreign Oil

The West has good reason to be concerned about the discontinuation of petroleum-based supplies from the Middle East. Oil facilities have become a common target of warring countries as well as of saboteurs, because no one understands better the value of oil than do the Arab states. This is why, when Iran attacked Iraq, it fired missiles at the oil fields of Kuwait. And why, when Iraq attacked Iran, Iraq attempted to destroy the oil fields first, a move in reply to which Iran responded with attacks on Iraqi oil transports. Later, Iraq destroyed the oil wells of Kuwait when it retreated under Desert Storm pressures.

The history of terrorist attacks on oil and energy installations for the past twenty years parallels the wars between and among countries. Explosive ruination of oil fields in Kuwait, Saudi Arabia, Syria, and Libya—as well as similar attacks on both oil supplies and transports throughout South America, the Middle East, Asia, and Europe, occur frequently. Tankers have been destroyed or crippled by missiles, bombs, and underwater mines. Tanker crews have been seized and robbed of their valuables by petty thieves, and even oil tankers have been captured by pirates and held ransom.

The fragile network of the oil supply system throughout the Mideast is held together by seven thousand miles of aboveground pipe, most of which passes through hostile territory plagued by either ground disputes or religious differences. It has been broken (and not repairable) for as long as one hundred days at different periods—so regularly in fact that such damage to it is now seldom considered news at all.

In the 1960s, the first goal of an insurgent group against a government was to seize control of the radio and communication stations. Today, when attacking an industrial country, it is the oil supply first.

Cut Off From Oil Platforms

The oil platforms are a prime terrorist target. They are understandably easier to destroy than are the oil ships at sea, and the response time from present security agencies would be, in most cases, a matter of hours. Platforms in the North Sea and the Gulf of Mexico would be helpless in case of terrorist attack, and with each explosion the companies behind the wells would be affected economically. Platforms have exploded for any number of reasons—from sabotage to shipping accidents to faulty construction or inadequate repairs.

Fragile Storage Tanks

Storage tanks have been elephantinely visible targets of terrorists, and the United States has not been immune from attacks on them. A St. Paul, Minnesota, oil tank farm was bombed in 1970, and storage tanks in California were bombed in 1975. In 1980, six American Nazis were captured prior to completion of their plans to destroy gasoline tank farms and natural-gas pipelines in North Carolina. This type of storage tank usually is protected by only a chain-link fence bearing a sign which makes certain that anyone who cares to know what they contain is adequately informed. But they also provide a convenient map for terrorists.

Even though recognizing these tanks' vulnerability, the United States government couldn't seem to adjust centralized policies merely to face new realities, and proceeded with its prearranged national energy defense plan by stockpiling the aforementioned 600 million reserve barrels of oil in a centralized location—where it could be at the very least rendered useless, and quite possibly totally destroyed.

Oil Refineries

The Office of Technology Assessment has reported that the destruction of seventy-seven of the largest U.S. oil refineries would cut off two-thirds of the U.S. oil supply and "shatter the U.S. economy." This was its warning in a 1979 report designed to simulate a nuclear attack against the United States. Because not much has changed in U.S. policy with regard to the location or security of sensitive refineries since that report was issued, it is interesting to examine the same vulnerability in light of terrorism today.

Refineries tend to be located near the places where oil is extracted, and so they are clustered together in Texas, Louisiana, Alaska, and California, with over half in Texas alone. (Oil is not worth much in this country until it is refined, so refineries are the indispensable spokes of the oil distribution wheel.) Not only are the refineries situated uncomfortably close to each other, or at least conveniently close to each other, but the many byproduct plants tend to be clustered in the same vicinity—including petrochemical plants, rubber and synthetic production plants, and fertilizer plants, along with the storage plants themselves and the transport trains, ships, and truck yards.

It would not take a nuclear bomb to explode a refinery, as was proposed in the 1979 study. That could be done with three or four sticks of dynamite, or a trained saboteur could pull it off just by turning the right valve. The pressurized and highly explosive hydrocarbons could be ignited by any one of over two hundred vulnerable spots in the typical oil refinery.

At the same time, if the terrorist goal was simply to end the oil production of a refinery and not necessarily explode it, there are any number of ways to make the refinery inoperative to the point where oil output would be cut to zero for anywhere from three months to a year. Replacement parts for the more complex workings of refineries are not readily available, and if a few of the facilities were similarly damaged at the same time, the down period could be extended for many more months.

Since the warning to government officials that oil refineries are vulnerable to destruction, they have proceeded to make them even *more* vulnerable! Plants have been enlarged, rather than dispersed, and they are still located in areas subject to floods, earthquakes, tornadoes, and hurricanes. Refineries have increased their production of lighter products, which require more highly explosive hydrogen and more critical controls sensitive to detonation. The plants can't operate without electricity, and so have tended to depend heavily on purchased sources of it, as well as to rely on fragile computerized power control systems of the faulty IBM mainframe variety. Economic considerations have led to a series of other aggravated vulnerabilities, including fewer skilled workers on-site, a reduction in spare parts, increased storage capacity, flimsy construction, and larger terminals.

If terrorists refer themselves to the right maps at (for example) a public library, they can carefully select a small group of refineries—each of which (again) usually is protected by stereotypical retired cops—and follow through to create havoc with economic consequences not seen in the United States since the Great Depression.

Natural-gas processing plants are similarly vulnerable, and even more concentrated, in Louisiana and Texas. A single strike in Louisiana (which produces a fourth of the nation's total energy needs) could end natural-gas delivery to the eastern seaboard for as long as one and a half years. Any alternate routing of supplies to that approximately one-third of the nation's population could be easily cut off.

Pipelines

There is enough oil pipeline crisscrossing the United States to encircle the globe fourteen times. And almost every inch of it is subject to small-group terrorist sabotage. In other words—without touching a refinery, a pumping station, a single tank or storage farm; without attacking a single tanker or truck transport; without even knowing where the 600-million-barrel national oil reserve is located—a mere handful of terrorists could deprive the nation of oil for an indefinite period of time. According to no less an authority than the Government Accounting Office, damage to just a minor portion of these lines would cause an energy shortage more harmful than the 1973 Arab oil embargo.

The most complicated and intricate of all U.S. oil pipeline systems is the Colonial Pipeline, which runs from Texas to New Jersey. Fed by multiple source points, it supplies almost three hundred marketing terminals along its route, from which more than thirty shippers distribute over one hundred product variations. All this is done via almost four thousand miles of pipe whose flow is powered by eighty-four pumping stations using enough electricity yearly to power the equivalent of the entire upper northeastern states for an entire month. It took ten supply companies just to keep up with the initial demand for valves.

"[These lines were] constructed and are operated with almost no regard to their vulnerability to persons who might desire to interfere with this vital movement of fuel," a government study reported six years after completion of the pipeline in 1977. Thus it is clear that at least some insiders knew, early on, that there was good reason to assume that these pipelines were in constant danger of sabotage. In fact, from almost the first day of the world's first oil pipeline, in the Pennsylvania oil fields in 1865, sabotage occurred—in that case, on the part of disgruntled union members. Bombings have more recently occurred in a Shell pipeline in California, along the Trans-Alaska Pipeline, and at pumping stations and cooling towers in Kentucky and Louisiana—along with over thirty bombing attempts of various pipeline installations in the United States.

Some of the most sensitive areas of the control systems of both the Colonial and Capline systems have been vandalized by juveniles who have climbed over presumably protective chain-link fences to do so—or simply walked right into the open control centers!

One of the most exposed areas of the pipeline systems is water crossings, of which there are hundreds. At the river or stream the pipeline either spans the crossing or is suspended from a bridge. And a bridge is one of the easiest of all terrorist targets—as demonstrated by the number that are blown almost weekly in countries having a terrorist problem.

In one location in particular, the faulty design of the pipeline system could allow a terrorist to accomplish a number of goals with one blow. Since two of the major pipelines intersect and loop over the Mississippi River, just one explosion could both end oil flow through two of the country's most critical pipelines, and stop traffic flow across the crucial bridge—as well as the barge traffic on the river—for many weeks. These sensitive intersecting points are clearly shown on maps available to the general public.

Of course the Trans-Alaska Pipeline, because of its remote locations and the hundreds of miles wherealong it is exposed aboveground, is subject to attack at almost every mile of its course. It crosses a number of rivers, three mountain ranges, five seismic areas, and four glaciers—and both government and industry studies indicate that it is virtually impossible to protect.

Small explosive devices commonly available are enough to blow *any* of these pipelines. In the case of the Arctic pipelines, it wouldn't even be necessary to actually blow up the line: Because of the extreme cold, a terrorist would accomplish the goal simply by slowing down the flow of oil—which soon would freeze and turn into a tube of gel hundreds of miles long.

The good news about this situation is that while pipelines themselves are extremely vulnerable, they are the easiest items in the entire distribution system to repair. The bad news is that this is *not* true of the pumping stations. Damage to a series of stations—or of just *one* required to conduct a high lift—would be most devastating. These stations are powered by extremely sensitive, large, and costly engines and equipment. They are not stock items, and it can take months to receive replacement parts. They mainly sit unprotected in locations where they are needed to assure efficient oil flow.

The same vulnerabilities also exist for the thousands of miles of pipelines that carry either natural gas or petroleum gas, with however the added problem that a break or leak *also* creates an *explosive* mixture. As with the pumping stations of the oil lines, the most vulnerable function of the gas lines is the compressor stations, which provide a similar function and are spaced every forty to two hundred miles along the routes. Yet another problem with the compressor stations is their reliance on gas from the line itself to power them—thus utilizing a large percentage of national energy consumption, and forcing them to malfunction whenever there is a depressurization *anywhere along the line*.

Entire networks of the gas pipelines rely on extensive computer communications fed into a central processing center. A simple disruption in the communications quickly renders the center inoperable.

As with LNG and LPG, stopping the flow of energy is not the only danger when it comes to oil. Because of the pressurization of most of the systems, it can actually be more harmful to increase flow or pressure—particularly in the case of gas lines which proceed from each city gate and into the millions of residences themselves. Fires and explosions across any city would be the expected result.

The extreme delicacy of the oil and gas distribution systems is accented by one of the industries' major problems: theft. Spiking of oil lines, and tapping gas lines, are common occurrences, as is the stealing of tanker and truck shipments. And the same simple technology that goes into a common theft can be used for sabotage.

The frightening vulnerability of our entire oil and gas distribution systems seems remarkably naive in today's climate. It is difficult to imagine an entire industry being so aware of the potential for a complete collapse of national security, but proceeding to exacerbate the problem with each expansion. That degree of difficulty pales, however, when you look at our electrical system.

CHAPTER 11

The Electric Grid

All of the hundreds of thousands of miles of electrical transmission lines that cross America are subject to terrorism.

"However caused, a massive power-grid failure would be slow and difficult to repair, would gravely endanger national security, and would leave lasting economic and political scars," Amory B. and L. Hunter Lovins report in their book *Brittle Power*. "It is not pleasant to have in the back of one's mind that the next time the lights blink out, they may take an exceedingly long time to come back on again," they continue.

In fact, the lights could be out for many moons if certain equipment had to be replaced—equipment for which the delivery time is as long as eighteen months.

A July 1993 fire at a plant in Tokyo destroyed the company that manufactured half of the world's supply of sensitive material required to make computer chip components. If such a disaster occurred in any foreign plant manufacturing any of a number of the sophisticated materials or components required for U.S. electrical systems, power here could be shut off indefinitely. Or at least long enough for subsequent political and social disasters to develop.

Of all the terrorist acts around the world, attacking electrical transmission is the most common. It is extremely easy to shut off the lights of a city in order to (for example) make a point, or disrupt the citizenry on election night—and the effect is instantaneous.

The United States, due to the tremendous size of its transmission system, is less flexible than the systems of most small countries—more centralized and more subject to failure of complete grid systems. The Lovins reported that, "With careful selection of targets and of their most vulnerable times (peak loads), it would not be beyond the ability of some technically astute groups to halt most or all of the electrical supply in any of America's . . . grid regions." Or to shut down all four of the grids at the same time.

The United States' power system is divided into four electrical grids supplying Texas, the eastern states, the midwestern states, and the northwestern states. These are all interconnected in Nebraska. A unique aspect of the electrical grids, as with communication grids, is that most built-in, computerized security is designed to anticipate no more than two disruptions concurrently. In other words, if a primary line went down, the grid would ideally shut off power to a specific section while it rerouted electricity around the problem area. If it ran into two such problems however, the grid is designed to shut down altogether.

Sometimes the loss of electricity to major cities and broad sections of the country is due to equipment failure, a natural disaster, operator error, vandalism, or (as in at least one case) a small cat that was incinerated when it wandered into a sensitive area of a power station and shut the station down.

Electrical lines are the most accessible to saboteurs. It is not unusual for three hundred insulators to be shot off in one day by pranksters and hunters, for example. And those thin wires also can be cut by bullets—given a real marksman (such as a terrorist). But whereas insulators and wires can be easily replaced, most other items in the electrical grid system cannot. For example, if *any* rifleman shot up the transformers, for example, it could take up to a year or more for replacements to arrive from overseas suppliers. In just one night a relative handful of mere pranksters could bring our national system to its knees, let alone a group of terrorists acting with malicious intent. And yet you often find these transformer farms, large and small, totally unprotected.

Electrical components are costlier and even more difficult to replace than their counterparts in the oil and gas systems. And, according to the Department of Defense, one bullet from a relatively small-caliber rifle would be all it would take to cause a leak in a transformer and send it into a meltdown, wherein it would self-destruct.

The hundreds of hydroelectric dams that provide a portion of our electric supply are relatively secure from any attack which would cause the dams themselves to break. Yet—and now this begins to sound too familiar—a single bullet into a transformer at the base of a dam could render the facility inoperative.

But it is the nine hundred or so thermal plants (steam-raising) that are most susceptible to attack, and most desirable to terrorists because they supply in excess of 80 percent of the nation's electricity. These installations dominate the nation's four grids, not only because of the power they supply but because of the power they use, requiring constant gas and cooling-water supplies as well as explicitly accurate computer and communications linkage. If any one of these components is interrupted, the thermal plant shuts down.

Unlike as with the oil and gas systems, there is no major storage of electric energy once it has been generated—so availability (and therefore usage) stops almost immediately upon generator shutdown. Electrical transmission also must be precise—flowing at precisely sixty cycles per second over three parallel lines. Damage to equipment will ensue if this stability factor is not synchronized in all parts of the grid. Response to any fluctuation (unlike that in the oil and gas systems, wherein there might be a few minutes—or even hours—to respond to an aberration) must be immediate. Any correction in any such electrical system must be accomplished with lightning-like speed.

This sort of systemic sensitivity is in a way its own worst enemy in that it leaves every aspect of the electrical grid open (even to terrorism)—and that means thousands of miles of transmission lines, plus switchgear, switches, transformers, generators, voltage-reducing transformers, computers, and communications networks.

An experience at Grand Coulee Dam (Columbia River, Washington), one of the world's largest hydroelectric plants, demonstrates the sensitivity of the process. This dam has sixty-one-foot rotors in its three electric generators which must be turned several times per hour—by hand, if necessary—to avoid warping. One day, a disgruntled employee was able to damage many of the coils beyond repair with just a simple hand tool.

All of the energy from all of the thermal plants and hydroelectric plants and other such sources is basically compressed into relatively few but almost endlessly long systems of transmission lines. In most states some portions of these lines have been downed occasionally by saboteurs of whatever description. In Minnesota, disgruntled farmers kept FBI agents befuddled for almost five months in 1979 and 1980 while toppling one transmission tower after another, causing over $7 million in damage. In 1981, a trash fire at the Utah State Prison caused an arcing at the switchyard next door—blacking out all of Utah and parts of Idaho and Wyoming, and leaving over 1.5 million people in the dark.

Although there was a hundred-thousand-dollar reward for information leading to the arrest of vandals in the Minnesota incident, the reward has never been claimed.

Transmission and distribution substations are frequent sabotage targets, although their individual loss serves to black out only a limited area for a limited time. But they are popular with terrorists because they can be taken out as easily as driving down the road with a gun out the window. There have been many attacks on substations in the United States, causing millions of dollars of damage. Small bombs have destroyed substations in Arizona, New Mexico, and Colorado. A series of bombings against power supplies in Oregon in 1974 caused the government to order a massive manhunt and to consider calling in the National Guard and cutting back on power usage.

Bombings in general in the United States have risen as high as two thousand per year, according to FBI statistics. Averaging out the peaks of specific campaigns against public *utilities*, however, the number of bombings directed at public utility companies has been approximately ten per year over the last fifteen years.

Thirty Million People Blacked Out

It happened in July 1977, when New York's main electric power grid operated by Consolidated Edison plunged the city and much of the northeast into darkness. Birth rates soared nine months later. The outage was reportedly caused by a combination of natural disasters and system inefficiencies, but demonstrates how vulnerable the electric grid system can be to a different kind of terrorism—a kind of reverse terrorism. The outage and equipment damage were not caused by a system shutdown, but by a massive power surge.

This blackout, and the confusion and inconvenience it caused to residents, was traceable all the way back to two lightning bolts. The rest of the story is largely an example of why complex systems fail—ranging from operator error to equipment faults. It is also, however, an example of how these systems can be brought down not by interrupting power supply, but by creating surges, or by convincing the complex computer sensors that they "think" there is a surge.

A fluctuation above or below the sixty-cycles-per-second synchronized pulse can knock an entire grid out of whack. Its various protective devices kick into action, not knowing they are getting false signals, and the resultant flow of energy to narrow corridors of the working system can cause extensive damage to the sensitive and expensive equipment all down the line. In 1965, for example, New York experienced a similar blackout. Bottom-line reportage claimed that the problem had begun at a transmission tower in Canada.

The U.S. Energy Research and Development Administration's 1976 warning is still valid:

"Today's electric energy system in the United States is one of the most complex technical systems in existence. Unlike most other industries, the individual components do not operate independently but are tied together in an interactive system covering most of the continental United States, wherein deliberate or inadvertent control actions taken at one location can within seconds affect the operation of plants and users hundreds of miles distant. . . . There will be problems [in the future] of great importance which will be quite different from today's problems, and the conceptual tools and underlying theory required for their effective solution have not yet been developed."

As with the petroleum industry, one of the most vulnerable parts of the electric system is the control and communications systems themselves. They are not only subject to similar failures, which kick off internal grid system failures, but they are also subject to technological terrorism. For example, a small pocket magnet placed near a computer can render an entire system of any size inoperable. Or, a computer hacker with a laptop can gain access to communications systems anywhere in the world and manipulate their entire electrical wherewithal at will—flipping switches, shutting down generators, creating surge signals—virtually taking control of national security.

Gas and electricity are the common denominators of the world's energy system. Without them, entire countries would virtually cease to operate. In fact, the absence of electricity alone would deprive most people of gas, too—since gas pumps no longer have hand cranks. Long lines would form in front of full tanks of fuel with pumps nobody could get to operate. Too, electricity drives many of the generators and control centers of the oil distribution system as well as of the communications systems. Subways would stop. Elevators would be inoperable. Food in cold-storage facilities would start to rot. Most industries and offices would be unable to conduct business. And so on.

Without gas and electricity, given today's complex distribution system, there is no movement.

CHAPTER 12

Nuclear Energy

Never mind that humans are the only species on Earth with the capability of designing technology that could end all life on the planet. These God-given talents allowed terrific leaps forward into both the Industrial Age and the Nuclear Age, and the results have forever changed the world.

There are people watching television via satellite today who remember a world without automobiles. A great-grandmother in Denver can call a great-granddaughter in Paris almost instantaneously, to coordinate a meeting at an airport the next day. And they can now see each other "live" from thousands of miles apart while they talk via videophone. As they go about their daily lives, these people—like most others everywhere—don't stop to think about the miraculous capabilities they now have at their fingertips, or the fact that those and the many other inventions they take for granted grew out of the necessities of a changing world in the mid–nineteenth century. (Miracles of modern mankind have become so commonplace that few people can tell you when the last space shot took place, or give the names of the astronauts aboard.) Since necessity is indeed the mother of invention, with a little bit of luck the same talents that gave humankind the ability to create awesome scientific achievements will also allow intelligent people to figure out how to survive their own more problematical conditions of the mind.

From an historical point of view, we are moving at record speed toward making oil, gas, *and* nuclear energy obsolete, with advancements in wind, solar and hydropower techniques and battery-operated articles, even though at present things seem to be moving at a snail's pace for environmentalists and antinuclear groups alike.

129

A futurist would shake his or her head at the third world countries that are trying so hard to catch up to the energy technologies of the industrialized world. They are pinning their hopes on oil- and gas-driven systems which are already becoming obsolete. They also see nuclear power as a way to leapfrog their country into the twenty-first century.

In reality, the jump to nuclear is a leap to obscurity, for the development of the nuclear industry is the result of a mind-set left over from the oil and gas mentality. At best, nuclear energy is a temporary stopgap designed to continue the fallacy of centralized energy systems. Whether you look at the nuclear industry from an economic, political, or environmental point of view, it can in reality only be viewed as either a roadblock or a stepping-stone along the path to the energy resources of the future.

An unfortunate byproduct of this dalliance with nuclear energy is the proliferation of nuclear weapons and other nuclear capabilities. But the spread of nuclear weaponry is not nearly so dangerous as the spread of nuclear expertise.

Just as saboteurs successfully dismantled the first oil pipeline laid in Pennsylvania back in the 1800s, nuclear energy plants have also been a target of terrorists (and others) almost since the first day of plant operation. The more-or-less successful attacks and the near-miss missions against nuclear complexes total in the thousands. Plants have been gone after not only by terrorists but also by foreign powers, environmentalists, disgruntled employees, and psychologically disturbed outsiders. Given all these, plus the hundreds of accidents and failures due to all sorts of other causes (including human error and natural disasters), it is absolutely remarkable how few radioactive releases have occurred. However, as we move into a new age of terrorism, it can be expected that attacks on nuclear sources will increase—and it would be foolish to assume that none of these will prove devastatingly successful.

Nuclear energy plants themselves, as well as nuclear byproducts, as targets of terrorism may well speed along the advancement toward more diverse energy resources. They have been favorite targets of terrorists on a worldwide scale—and are one of the few target-description subjects about which it can be said that an explosive device with a timer which can fit in your pocket could kick off a target-site reaction large enough to devastate an entire city, or make thousands upon thousands of acres of land uninhabitable for a number of lifetimes.

Like most other utilities designed in the United States, nuclear energy systems were designed with the idea in mind that we live in an ideal society wherein natural disasters, manmade disasters, accidents, and human error all will conveniently bypass these vulnerable objects. In fact, our security, via both physical and technical protection, is not designed to withstand *any* type of "direct hit" above analysts' predetermined minimum level of probability by inside intruders, outside attackers, or other external pressures.

The Three Mile Island reactor keeps popping up as an example. In 1993, a lone man drove his car through the front gate there and crashed into the center building of the plant itself. Authorities were quick to point out that, had the intruder even been carrying a conventional bomb, instead of being empty-handed, the facility probably would have been able to withstand the impact. But what if the intruder had carried an unconventional bomb—such as a small nuclear one? Such a scenario is entirely feasible—and such an attack would be devastating, to say the least. The materials necessary for building such a bomb, and the worldwide talent pool in many industrial and third world countries alike able to build it (and more) make this kind of possibility likelier than ever.

But this was not the first such incident at Three Mile Island. In 1976 a disturbed employee drove a car onto the site, scaled a chain-link fence, entered a sensitive area of the facility, and departed—all without replied-to detection. Some time later, a local newspaper reporter got a job as a security guard at the complex, and soon the utility tried to get an injunction against the paper to stop his follow-up feature story. The utility's justification for the injunction was that a report detailing the inner workings of the complex would be a serious threat to the facility and the public alike. This statement was indeed profound—but it did not (and does not) bode well, considering the hundreds of security guards who leave nuclear facilities each year, voluntarily or involuntarily.

In the early morning hours of March 28, 1979, Three Mile Island Unit 2 experienced a near meltdown of its inner core. The first major nuclear accident in the United States, its effects were exceeded only by those of the 1985 Chernobyl accident in the Soviet Union. The Three Mile Island accident effectively put the brakes on what had been a rapid advancement of the nuclear power industry, demonstrating for the first time that we had created an industry we knew little about—and that plants were being operated by personnel not skilled enough to handle unusual problems. Two years later, it was discovered that two shift managers at Three Mile Island had cheated on their licensing exams. The managers were fired and thirty other employees had to be retested.

In 1988, scientists at Three Mile Island were still hoping to complete the bulk of the cleanup operations, with researchers still taking samples from the core for analysis.

A 1990 publication for Applied Research and Public Policy reported that Three Mile Island was a classic example of bureaucratic bungling: "Anger, denial, blame and, finally, acceptance—the classic responses to tragedy—depict the way the U.S. nuclear industry responded to the Three Mile Island accident. Acceptance means that the industry has finally accepted that a nuclear accident can, in fact, happen."

From Three Mile Island's original technical and human problems that resulted in a near-meltdown in the late 1970s to the incident of the gate-crasher in the 1990s, the facility continues to serve as an example of how weakly protected nuclear complexes are, and how lackadaisical the plant owners, supervisors, and government commissions are with regard to the extremely hazardous conditions that could result from a failure at any of the hundreds of locations around the country.

A subtle yet major difference between past and current experiences at Three Mile Island has slowly become more noticeable: The 1970s problem captured headlines for weeks—but the 1990s one was so mentioned only briefly.

A German report titled "Aufgetretene Unfaelle Mit Kernschaeden" ("Past Accidents With Core Degradation") (in thermal reactors) noted in 1987 that a major result of the Three Mile Island and Chernobyl disasters was "Less attention was devoted to a number of accidents in civilian and military reactors."

Other disasters? We don't often hear *at all* about nuclear accidents, so we assume that there are extremely few of them. However, in the same year as the German report, the journal *Nuclear Technology* published an article which dealt with the risks of post-nuclear evacuations of civilians. It detailed 320 nuclear accidents—in the United States—which required evacuations of civilian residential neighborhoods:

"While timely evacuation has the potential to save many lives, there is a finite risk associated with the act of evacuation itself. From a detailed questionnaire, data were obtained on 320 past evacuation events that took place in the United States from 1972 to 1985 to quantify risks associated with evacuations. It is found that risks associated with evacuation of a 16 kilometer radius to be approximately 100 times greater than the risks associated with a 3.2 kilometer radius evacuation."

Three hundred and twenty nuclear accidents serious enough to cause evacuation—and the general public is basically unaware of all but three or four of them!

Just as we no longer quite remember the names of astronauts, we have almost forgotten the dangers of nuclear radiation. And while it may have been unhealthy to live with the paranoid fear of nuclear attack that consumed people for so many years, it may now be even more unhealthy for the public not to be aware of what is going on in the nuclear world—and to accept that ignorance as normal. Too, we have left nuclear responsibility in the hands of politicians and utility companies who—in the backs of our minds—we suspect will likely base their decisions and actions pertinent thereto on whatever is most politically or economically expedient. The same frustration we have with politicians who keep screwing up the national debt is buried with regard to their involement with nuclear energy, however, simply because the consequences are too awesome to think about. The fact is that this situation is in effect one of the major flaws in our security dike—wherein there are plenty more cracks waiting for terrorists to widen.

Some experts say that one of the biggest problems with the advancement of modern technology is this: We are creating systems so complex, with so many different functions either directly or indirectly dependent on each other, that it has become impossible for scientists, operators, and examiners alike to foresee what might go wrong. In other words, we're faced with a high-tech version of Murphy's First Law: "If anything can go wrong, it will." But in this case, solutions to unexpected problems will have to be solved as they arise, and sometimes at emergency speed. The nuclear systems are held up as a leading example of this reality—as well as an example of extreme consequences.

An extension of this fragile balance of high-tech power and awesome risk is the recognition that a terrorist would not have to attack a nuclear plant in the traditional sense in order to cause serious problems.

Given the Three Mile Island track record, which to *some* extent eventually is repeated at almost every other nuclear plant, a terrorist individual or group could enter a nuclear complex quite easily. The security force encountered would (unlike the brave defenders in fictional movies or books) very likely be similar to the security guards in the Holland and Lincoln tunnels in New York who refused to report to their stations when they heard there was a terrorist warning.

There have been periods when as many as ten attacks per month have been carried out on nuclear targets in Europe. Israeli agents have been accused of assassinating the top Iraqi nuclear expert while he was visiting Paris. Nuclear facilities, and at times their employees too, have been taken hostage and held for ransom. Some employees have been executed. Armed assaults have been carried out in Spain and Italy, and bomb attacks have taken place in a widespread sweep of targets related to a specific utility company in both countries.

In the United States, the visitors' center at the Trojan reactor in Oregon was bombed in 1971. Electronic controls have been badly damaged by simple bombs, as was the case of the two that exploded at the Stanford Linear Accelerator in 1971. Unexploded bombs were discovered at the Point Beach reactor in Wisconsin in 1970, and the Illinois Institute of Technology reactor in 1969. Someone was arrested in 1976 for attempting to steal materials for the purpose of blowing up a nuclear power plant.

Operation and management of the nuclear industry are subject to the same foibles and human frailties as are those of other industries. For example, a supervisor with personal economic problems, or an otherwise disgruntled employee, could activate problems far worse than a random bomb. The following several paragraphs illustrate these points.

At the Indian Point Two reactor in New York, a 1971 fire set in an outer building that contained control panels, cables, and pumps did almost $10 million in damage. The arsonist was a mechanic and maintenance man at the plant. Seven other reactors reported suspicious fires found to be set by worker sabotage: the Zion reactor in Illinois; Quad Cities in Illinois; Peach Bottom in Pennsylvania; Fort St. Vrain in Colorado; Trojan in Oregon; Browns Ferry in Alabama; and the Beaver Valley plant in Pennsylvania.

Florida Power and Light experienced one hundred incidents of sabotage damaging off-site equipment during a single strike.

General Electric's Knolls Atomic Power Laboratory in New York has been subject to arson, along with several U.S. nuclear research facilities and reprocessing plants.

At the Surrey reactor in Virginia, two workers were so dismayed by the lack of security at the nuclear facility that they did over $1 million in damage to the plant, to bring the problem to public attention.

A night watchman was wounded by an intruder at the Vermont Yankee reactor. In 1972, the New York University reactor building was broken into. A year later, so was the reactor's fresh-fuel storage building. Theft attempts of enriched uranium took place in two subsequent years at the Erwin, Tennessee, plant, and ten thousand dollars' worth of plutonium was stolen at the Kerr McGee plant in Oklahoma by employees.

In 1980, security guards admitted an ex-employee who showed them a long-out-of-date security pass. They held the gate open for him as he drove off in a truck stolen from a high-security area of the Savannah River plutonium production plant.

A U.S. bomb-design center, the Lawrence Livermore Laboratory, never saw a ton of lead shielding disappear within the space of one year. In 1978, the FBI arrested a man who had arranged to sell nuclear warheads to members of the Mafia. He had claimed that the devices would come from the nuclear submarine base, although the validity of his contacts were never confirmed.

The government's own test teams have successfully penetrated nuclear facilities without detection, and a number of politicians, reporters, and ordinary citizens have carried weapons into high-security areas just to prove they could.

At the General Electric Fuel Processing Plant in Wilmington, North Carolina, an employee stole two sixty-six-pound drums of low-enriched uranium via the trunk of his car. His aim was to extort one hundred thousand dollars from the company or he would expose them to public embarrassment.

In January 1986, a worker at the Sequoyah Fuels Corporation's Sequoyah facility in Oklahoma died when a cylinder of uranium hexafluoride ruptured while it was being heated in a steam chest. He expired because he inhaled hydrogen fluoride fumes which resulted from a reaction caused when the contents were mixed with airborne moisture.

On December 9, 1986, the Unit Two reactor at the Virginia Electric and Power Company Surry Power Station tripped, causing a main feed line to rupture. Water flushed from the line and engulfed personnel in the area. Several workers were injured and four were killed.

Twenty truckloads of contaminated tools and materials were extracted from the ground and stolen from the radioactive waste dump in Beatty, Nevada.

Highly enriched uranium, enough for a dozen nuclear bombs each large enough to devastate a large city, was stolen from the Apollo, Pennsylvania plant.

There have also been numerous accounts of harmful uses of stolen radioactive materials, from laced drinks at universities to radioactive dust sprinkled over seats to contaminate train passengers—and, as in the case of a Tulsa, Oklahoma, nuclear plant employee, death of the thief due to radiation.

When we think of terrorist attacks on nuclear facilities, we usually imagine an armed attack on those large plants where the reactors are kept—possibly even a missile strike of some kind. However, just as with the electrical, gas, and oil distribution systems, the most fragile targets of the nuclear industry are not the reactors themselves, but their dependence on alternative power sources and energy sources to avoid both over- and underpressurization. As previously mentioned, either can result in the desired catastrophe, and can be accomplished without anyone's ever entering the facility itself. For example, deprive a nuclear system of the feeder water, or the electrical power from its generators, and you have the makings of a nuclear disaster.

Both external electrical grid outages in areas serving nuclear reactors, and internal plant electrical outages, are common. It is remarkable that to date both have not happened at the same time. But it would be a simple matter for an individual to arrange for precisely that. At most plants, even those where the reactors are reasonably secure, the generators sit in a shack-like building nearby. These could be knocked out by either close-up small-arms fire, or a shoulder-held rocket from quite a distance. And the visible power transmission lines could be taken out even more easily.

In fact, as the above examples more than hint at, *every* aspect of the nuclear distribution cycle is subject to terrorist attack. From the reactor and all of the supporting facilities required by the reactor complex, to the reprocessing plants and the waste-disposal systems and dump sites, terrorists have learned that each represents a radioactive risk which can be exploited.

Nuclear systems and the risks they represent also capsulize the brittleness of all the U.S. energy distribution systems. This point is best made when you consider the requirement for extreme personnel expertise at each nuclear facility.

All records of accident and sabotage experiences, as well as government studies, conclude that a major difference between a serious accident and a catastrophe is the personnel inside the nuclear complex who have the ability to contain whatever problem arises. This necessity would not represent such a severe problem if the nuclear facility were self-contained. But it can be affected by any combination of a number of external causes.

A terrorist group could overtake the facility itself, as has happened in Europe. If the facility is unmanned, a few turns of the controls could easily send the reactor into a self-destruct mode. Even if the terrorists fled the scene with any captives, they could use explosives to destroy the control room and/or block the entrance. If they simply vacated, the type of expertise needed to take over controls effectively would not be readily available, in most instances.

Oil, gas, and electrical grid outages also cripple a facility if the on-site generator is knocked out. In such a case, the facility could quickly move to an emergency status wherein personnel would be forced to vacate the controls.

An LNG gas-tanker truck driven through the front gate could be the explosive agent needed to blow the facility. Or an overturned LNG truck a few miles upwind, or even a liquid-fertilizer truck with a plume cloud headed in the right direction, could cause emergency evacuation procedures.

In the worst-possible-case scenario, if meltdown did occur, then events internally and externally alike would be both uncontrollable and unstoppable. Everything from that point forward—economically, politically, socially, and physically—would happen on a massive scale. An encouraging note (and somewhat darkly humorous): in March 1994 it was finally suggested that we pass legislation which insists that nuclear plants be protected from car bombs.

It is difficult to imagine any single event being more destructive than a nuclear disaster in a populated area. But that possibility exists in the minds of some people anyway. One of the methods that terrorists would likely take advantage of to neutralize the personnel in a nuclear facility that might be used for such a purpose would more than likely involve chemical or biological weapons. And on a much broader scale these are indeed predicted to be the weapons of choice for the future.

CHAPTER 13

Jurassic Park
and Biological
Warfare

In 1347 in the Crimea, the Tartars held siege to Caffa, which was occupied by Genoese defenders. The Tartars eventually catapulted their dead over the walls protecting the city and infected Caffa with bubonic plague, to spread the disease throughout the population. The ploy was so effective that the Genoese inadvertently carried the disease back to Italy.

Chemical and biological warfare are sprinkled throughout the history of human conflict. In the early settler days of the Old West, Indians would poison water holes to deprive soldiers, settlers, and their animals of precious drink in the middle of the hot plains or deserts. Russia claimed that the Germans spread typhus among civilians and troops alike during World War II. The Japanese operated a biological weapons factory from 1936 to 1945. They developed an anthrax bomb and experimented with cholera and typhoid. They used over two thousand prisoners of war as guinea pigs, and China claims that the Japanese spread the diseases in eleven cities, causing over seven hundred deaths.

North Korea said that the United States spread plague in 1951; and China claimed that anthrax, cholera, and plague had been used by the U.S. against its northeastern provinces. Though the United States denied the claim, serious questions remained. It became known that the U.S. *was* involved in a biological weapons program after World War II, and reports have come to the surface that we *were* prepared to use the new "weapons" being developed. It is not difficult to imagine what military leaders might have planned in the climate of the "Red Scare" and the fear of communism during the early years of the cold war.

Orson Welles's fictional pre-Halloween radio-show adaptation "[The] War of the Worlds" (October 30, 1938) spread panic nationwide as millions of people convinced themselves that New Jersey—and by extension the United States—was being attacked by Martians—even though the program was punctuated by what was tantamount to "commercial breaks" stating that it was only—repeat *only*—a dramatization. Joseph McCarthy accomplished an even greater reaction in his falsified campaign to convince Americans that the nation was riddled with communist traitors.

It was this same fear that propelled the superpower arms race up until 1992—and, now that Soviet records are available, it is being shown that this, too, was very much the product of overworked imaginations and misleading military analysis.

The attitude toward nuclear weapons development—to maintain a parity with the Soviets by producing more weapons with more deadly range and effect—was applied to almost every division of military preparation, and it was this parity issue that allowed it all to be justified under the name of national defense. In short, the best defense was a good offense, and the only way to assure an eventual peace was to demonstrate to the opposing side that the only other option was mutual annihilation. (In many ways, the United States applied this theory to chemical and biological agents also, exploding into the biological weapons arena in much the same manner as it did the space exploration program.)

At the conclusion of World War II, the United States recruited both German and Japanese scientists who had developed the chemical and biological weapons for Hitler, the Jewish death camps, and the gruesome exploratory camps in Manchuria. Just as we promoted to our own space program the same scientists who had successfully created unmanned rockets meant to destroy London, we promoted the doctors and scientists who created the deadly diseases and mass-extermination gases of our former enemies.

In the scientific, medical, and psychological fields, the inhumane experiments that these practitioners performed on their victims were invaluable in taking a large number of theories into practical application. Researchers in democratic societies shouted their abhorrence of the torture which took place under the Nazi regime, but they rushed to capture the results. This same experience by some of the German and Japanese doctors and scientists who were either directly or indirectly responsible for millions of deaths not only saved them from being tried and executed as war criminals, but catapulted them to the top positions in our emerging technological industries.

With these attitudes toward the evolution of ever more efficient methods of killing, it is a small wonder that over the course of six hundred years or so we have figured out how to stop tossing diseased bodies over a wall in order to infect our enemies, but instead have learned how to accomplish the same feat with a small vial of liquid or a short spray of aerosol.

A steady progression of scientific discovery has paralleled the development of even more awesome weapons. A moral conflict has always existed along the fine line between scientific achievement for the good of mankind and its contradictory usages for military power. We are most aware of this phenomenon with regard to the discovery of atomic power and its almost immediate manifestation at Hiroshima and Nagasaki. This moral conflict is particularly true, and even more complex, in the world of chemical and biological advancement.

Just as the atomic discoveries of the 1940s changed the latter half of the twentieth century, genetic research and DNA breakthroughs have moved to a fascinating new level of progress—although along with this progress comes the increased threat of new strains and forms of biological warfare and terrorism.

Dinosaurs and Germ Warfare

"We have found the secret of life!" That was biologist Francis Crick's excited announcement to his partner, James Watson, back in 1953 when he ran from his research laboratory to find his partner in a pub in Cambridge, England. And he was not exaggerating. Watson and Crick had discovered the structure of DNA.

Within just four years of that discovery the scientific community had learned how DNA transmits instructions to cells; how chromosomes determine genetic function; how to synthesize a cell; how to fuse cells from different species; how to isolate, map, and synthesize a gene—how to actually change the heredity of a cell. And now genetic scientists or biologists have the capability of creating entirely new forms of life, to the point where they could very well eclipse the foundations of evolution itself by creating a completely artificial new life form.

Author Michael Crichton based his best-selling novel *Jurassic Park* on the recent advances of DNA research and the theoretical possibility that a duplicate of any animal, including a thirty-million-year-old dinosaur, could be reproduced from a single DNA blood cell. Mosquitos which had bitten the dinosaur, carried off its blood, and then become encased in tree sap were preserved over the millennium in a petrified medium called amber.

This concept is based on recent scientific discoveries—and now there is some new archeological or biological announcement almost monthly that appears to change the way we will look at evolution in both the distant past and the near future. In 1992, for instance, one group of bioscientists announced that they were analyzing air which had been trapped in amber in order to ascertain atmospheric conditions prevalent millions of years ago. They hoped to unravel such mysteries as why huge dinosaurs could survive with such small lungs, and to discover what sudden changes in the climate or atmosphere caused the rapid disappearance of so many species during the same period.

Biological scientists argue among themselves just where genetic research can lead. One group insists that while the hypothesis put forth in Crichton's book is theoretically valid, it is beyond our current technological capabilities to substantiate. Others agree, but insist that if research continues at its current pace, it would be foolish to predict limitations.

AIDS research may well *result in* the next genuinely historic breakthrough in medical science. If successful, scientists will, for the first time in history, be able to tame a virus—an entity that can change between "dead" crystalline and "living" pathogenic forms. This will present a gigantic moral dilemma—possibly even more tremendous than that springing from the development of atomic energy—because scientists will be able not only to cure viruses, but to create strains that have not previously existed.

Medical science has been instrumental in the development of biological weapons because research into understanding and curing a disease often means the development, countering, and controlling of the bacteria that produce the disease. In other words, you can't cure a disease until you have learned how to create it. And past patterns show that once we *can* create a disease, someone is willing to package and distribute it for economic or political gain.

The difference between a plague (epidemic disease) and a biological weapon is only in the manner and purpose in which it is "delivered." The World Health Organization (WHO) defines biological weapons as those that rely on the results of infectious multiplication within the target organism. These weapons deliver microorganisms (bacteria, viruses, rickettsiae, fungi, and protozoa) or toxins (poisonous chemicals from organic matter) derived from living organisms, to produce deadly or debilitating disease among humans, animals, or plants.

A number of bacterial diseases are capable of being used as weapons—among them Venezuelan equine encephalitis, typhus, Rocky Mountain spotted fever, Q fever, anthrax, brucellosis, plague, and typhoid.

Natural toxins also have biological weapons potential. These are bacteria that kill by releasing toxic chemicals within the living host. A prime example is clostridium botulinum, better known as botulism, which takes six to eight hours to affect humans.

How well would these weapons work?

When military experts testified in the 1984 case against white supremacists who were about to dump two hundred gallons of cyanide into the water supply of either Chicago, New York, or Washington, D.C., the experts predicted that at least four hundred thousand persons would have been killed in any one of those cities.

A World Health Organization report indicates that if anthrax were sprayed over a city of five million, over one hundred thousand would die, and one hundred and fifty thousand would be incapacitated. Likewise, according to the same report, if botulism were dumped in a city water supply in sufficient amounts, almost 60 percent of the residents would receive a lethal dose.

Military biological scientists around the world continue to develop biological weapons even more lethal. According to a 1991 report from *Jane's Defense*, effective operational limits (desired for military use) require lethal agents to cause at least 25–50 percent fatalities in field operations, while incapacitating agents need only a 20–30 percent accuracy.

Methods of dissemination of biological weapons are usually carriers (such as insects, fleas, mosquitos, and rats). The most effective methods of delivery would be aerosol spray released from an aircraft, and contamination of the land or water.

From the terrorist point of view, the greatest reason for using biological weapons is the possibility of creating an epidemic—particularly in an area where the disease has not previously existed and where the enemy is ill-prepared to respond with inoculations.

Another likelihood, rife with both physical *and* economic consequences, is the possibility that animals would be attacked by the infective agents, with no immediate sign of foul play. Cattle are susceptible to a number of diseases, including Q fever, anthrax, Rift Valley fever, and foot-and-mouth disease. Pigs are vulnerable to African equine fever and foot-and-mouth. Chickens and turkeys, sheep, goats, horses, and other animals have their own strains of plague and diseases. For all practical purposes, once an animal population has been exposed to any of a variety of diseases, the only way to contain it is to slaughter them all.

It is not unreasonable to believe that a majority of the United States' ability to produce meat and grain alike could be threatened by a relatively simple plot to attack food-producing industries. The world economic impact of such an event would be catastrophic, comparable only to some of the worst famines of the past.

Since early in the 1980s, the United States has directed air attacks against suspected chemical and biological weapons factories in Iraq and Libya, and CIA Director William H. Webster said in an August, 1990 issue of the *International Defence Review*, that at least twenty countries have an active biological weapons program. These include many third world countries, among them states known to sponsor terrorism. Webster confirmed that such weapons are being developed throughout the Mideast, including in Egypt, Syria, Iran, Iraq, and Israel.

Even though biological weapons are called "the poor man's nuclear bomb," due to the relative ease and low cost of producing such weapons to create massive numbers of deaths, the United States is probably the leader in developing chemical and biological weapons—all under the guise of national defense. The Biological Weapons Convention of 1972, which has been ratified by 110 countries, prohibited the development, production, and stockpiling of biological and toxin weapons. But there was therein a huge loophole, in that research was not banned—leaving a thin line between offensive development and defensive research. So we, too, take advantage, of course.

The United States has conducted research on anthrax, dysentery, brucellosis, glanders, plague, and tularemia, all this at Fort Detrick, Maryland, and at the Dugway Proving Ground in Utah. Any attempts to conceal the research at the Maryland site have been exposed by a number of accidents that have resulted in staff members' becoming infected by at least one of the diseases at one time or another.

In 1985 the USSR and other critics of the U.S. program were upset that American labs were working on the genetic engineering of a new influenza virus. This obviously implied the development of an offensive biological weapon and, under pressure, the program was presumably scaled down. Ironically, this was the same year in which the Reagan administration won its case to persuade Congress of the need for new chemical weapons. Thus, funds for development of a new and improved U.S. chemical weapons stockpile were approved on December 19, 1985.

A 1988 *Jane's Defense* review summed up the reality of the situation: "Officially the United States and its NATO allies are committed to abolishing chemical weapons. These weapons, considered reprehensible and inhumane, rely on disruption and paralysis of the body's functions for effect and are likely to cause more civilian than military casualties in wartime. They are, in NATO terms, weapons of mass destruction. Most nations, having adhered to the Geneva Protocol of 1925, have pledged not to use them. Only the United States, among NATO members, has maintained a chemical arsenal, although France is understood to have a limited capability."

The primary case for the Reagan administration's chemical rearmament program was the common one: to counter Soviet superiority in the field. The Soviets were slightly ahead of the United States in chemical and biological weapons development, and in Afghanistan they had demonstrated a willingness to use them. The argument was that only a respected United States stockpile could deter Soviet first use of such weapons, and that eventually the comparable stockpiles could lead to a mutual disarmament.

In another interesting twist, the Soviets wanted to talk about designing a nonproliferation treaty to keep chemical and biological weapons development from spreading to other countries—but the United States wasn't interested.

Today, while there is much concern about what will become of the former Soviet Union nuclear weaponry, there has not been a great deal of public information released regarding what has (or will) become of the huge stockpiles of chemical and biological weapons. The danger of these materials falling into terrorist hands is great, as well as is the danger of the materials not being properly stored. Residents of the East-bloc countries are at risk from simple accidents and various forms of unintentional spillage, as are most residents throughout Europe.

Since the mustard-gas attacks in the trench warfare of World War I, the West has not had much direct experience with chemical weapons. Highly toxic mustard gas is still stored in huge quantities in the United States, as well as in the former Soviet countries, but most of today's chemical warfare agents come in the form of liquid or solid aerosols. The most highly toxic lethal agents are Sarin (GB), Tabun, VX, and Soman, all of which cause death within either minutes or hours, depending on the dosage and the entry route into the body—usually respiratory or skin contact.

Next come the lethal agents of the pre–World War II period: the blood destroyers hydrogen cyanide and cyanogen chloride, and the lung irritant phosgene.

The lethal agents are followed in order of toxicity by the incapacitating and hallucinatory agents. These are not favored by the military, however, because although they are the most readily available, they are among the most difficult to handle.

Up until 1985, most of the United States' chemical warfare stockpile was considered obsolete by the military. Under the aforementioned 1985 directive, the huge stockpile of chemicals and aging weapons designed to carry them has gradually been reduced, and is expected to be totally replaced by 1997 in favor of materiel more compatible with the latest military tools for delivery.

For the military, as well as for terrorists who would attempt to use chemical or biological weaponry, one of the biggest problems has traditionally been the transporting and storing of the dangerous chemicals. This problem has also been solved by innovative military and biological scientists via the introduction of *binary* weapons whose warheads utilize compartmentalized containers that keep the separated components of the deadly payload harmless until they are ready to be combined into lethal form at or after the time of firing.

These weapons are designed for both short- and long-range attacks, and their components vary, based on the desired effect. If it is assumed that friendly troops will want to move into an area quickly after an attack, then the toxins used must be those that will have a low persistency factor. For the longer-range targets, however, toxins can be used that can infect any given area for a longer number of hours, or even for many days.

The large amount of aging chemical weaponry in the U.S. arsenal has caused a massive attempt to destroy the stockpile in order to make room for its new, more reliable replacements. Incineration was chosen as the ideal method, and it has been in use at the Rocky Mountain Arsenal in Colorado for over twenty years. The Toole Army Depot in Utah has also been in use since 1979, employing the Chemical Stockpile Disposal System. There was also a major stockpile of chemical weapons on the Johnston Atoll in the Pacific Ocean. The destroying plant there has become a prototype for full-scale destruction facilities which will be set up in eight locations throughout the United States.

Studies of military history have shown that if one side was without an adequate supply of retaliatory chemical weapons, the other side would have a propensity to use them. Conversely, if there was little to gain from the use, chances are that they would not be used at all. This helps explain why Hitler never ordered the use of toxic chemicals in battle throughout World War II.

Prior to the breakup of the Soviet Union, a major concern was that a third country would utilize chemical weapons, negating the standoff between the two superpowers but resulting in massive death among either the United States' or the Soviet Union's civilian populations. Military experts agreed that, in the growing climate of terrorism, this was a not trivial problem which needed to be addressed.

The point was better made earlier, in a National Security Paper by Senator John Tower, then chairman of the Armed Services Committee. Upon completion of the study, the paper concluded: "Unfortunately, the containment of biological weapons development is impossible and its threat remains very real." The same can be said of chemical weapons development and deployment.

A further report said of biological weapons: "The other problem is the relative ease with which modern weapons can be made. It would be perfectly possible to produce the key binary components in a secluded corner of a variety of chemical installations, such as those manufacturing bulk pharmaceutical products or pesticides. The same applies to conventional agents, but with increased risks."

With terrorists and other nontraditional adversaries now the primary enemy, these points become even more sobering. Not only do we have enemies who have little to risk in utilizing these hideous weapons, but we can be more certain that they will be used by desperate opponents who do indeed view them as the poor man's nuclear bomb.

One of the military objections to the use of chemical and biological weapons has in recent times been the fact that they would cause more harm to a civilian population than to a military force. This certainly is more of a deterrent than it was when Winston Churchill threatened to counter *any* German chemical attack with chemical attacks against *every* German city.

The United States' experience with Agent Orange, a chemical herbicide defoliant, provided an example where chemical warfare can not only harm the enemy and the civilian population, but our own troops as well. From 1962 to 1971, over 11.2 million gallons of Agent Orange were sprayed over the jungles of South Vietnam, along with 8 million gallons of other herbicides.

Although the National Cancer Institute waited until 1969 to report that the pesticides and herbicides used in Vietnam were potentially harmful, it was to take another two years before the Nixon administration would ban their use—and Vietnam veterans have been waiting ever since for the government to own up to its mistake. However, at long last a July 1993 report from the Institute of Medicine (an arm of the National Academy of Sciences) said they had proof that Agent Orange caused at least three different kinds of cancer, and two skin diseases—respectively: soft-tissue sarcoma, non–Hodgkin's lymphoma, and Hodgkin's disease; and chloracne and porphyria cutanea tarda. The report, based on an overview study of two thousand herbicide studies, paves the way for veterans to qualify for the permanent disability and medical benefits approved by the Bush administration in 1991 for Agent Orange victims.

Dow Chemical, one of eleven manufacturers of Agent Orange, and Monsanto, a producer of herbicides, *still* argue that there is no sure proof that herbicides cause illness—even though, in an ironic twist, Elmo Zumwalt III, son of a retired Navy admiral who had ordered the spraying of Agent Orange, died of Hodgkin's disease in 1988, after serving in Vietnam. And he was but one of many toward whom the chemical companies felt no final responsibility.

But this sort of knowledge makes only more obvious what could actually be accomplished by chemical and biological weapons if the civilian population *were* the primary target.

A 1985 Senate committee hearing was shocked by the testimony of retired Gen. Frederick Kroesen, who had led an in-depth study of chemical warfare for the U.S. Institute for Defense Analysis (the three questions were asked by a committee member):

"Are you saying that the Alliance has no agreed-upon strategy for how to respond to chemical attacks?

"Are you saying that the political representatives of NATO members, meeting in joint NATO councils, have not yet discussed the best way for the Alliance to meet the chemical threat?

"Are you saying there is no agreed-upon set of tactics for how to fight a chemical war, as well as no agreed-upon set of offensive or defensive chemical stockpile requirements?"

"Yes," General Kroesen responded. "I believe we were saying all of those things. . . ."

One hundred and sixty million dollars was approved for chemical warfare development in the following year, and then another $200 million in the next year.

If the Senate committee was shocked then by the lack of U.S. and NATO chemical weapons planning, wait until they find out about our total vulnerability to chemical warfare on the domestic side now! Let's take a look at a few examples of what we face.

The destructive possibilities of a single individual standing atop a tall building in (say) New York with a lethal spray is almost unimaginable—in light of the fact that a government report indicates that a toxic aerosol sprayed one-mile *off the coast of California* could result in as many as five hundred thousand deaths.

Most government studies in the past have assumed that protection would have to be manifested against a foreign (overseas) attack supported primarily by conventional weapons and troops. Few studies have addressed the domestic issue—or considered that a small group of people, or even one individual, could covertly kill millions of people without even worrying about being detected.

Every city's water treatment plant in the United States is an unprotected target. Americans have nothing to compare to the devastation of such an attack. Perhaps the Des Moines, Iowa, flood in the summer of 1993 would provide some insight into the hardship of living without water for many days. But Des Moines' floodwater hadn't poisoned the populace from the start.

Also in midsummer 1993, New York City got a taste of what it would be like to discover that the city's water supply had been contaminated, when a bacterial infestation mysteriously survived more than three times the dose of chlorine usually used to assure safety in tap water for the millions of residents and workers. What truly frightened the analysts was how the case emphasized that a foreign agent can enter the water supply undetected. The City takes 12,000 water tests annually which are analyzed by a laboratory, along with extra tests in the warm summer months. The July tests revealed that water samples from two of New York's reservoirs had tested positive for coliform bacteria. This is not an unusual result, since there are thousands of different strains of coliform bacteria, the most common of which is found in human and animal intestines and feces—but even harmless amounts ring the alarm bells, because their presence often points to the existence of more dangerous varieties. Some forms, like Escherichia coli 0157:H7 (e. coli), *can* cause serious problems. That was the bacterial agent in the earlier 1993 outbreak in the Pacific Northwest linked to undercooked Jack in the Box hamburgers.

After tests from the New York reservoirs remained positive for three consecutive days, a water alert warning was issued for two districts in Manhattan—the Greenwich Village–Chelsea area, and the neighborhood near the South Street Seaport. The contamination was not strong enough to harm most people, but it had the possibility of killing babies, the elderly, and persons with AIDS or with other ailments that reduced the effectiveness of their immune systems.

"We're not dealing with a Milwaukee situation here," a New York State health commissioner said, referring to a city water contamination problem in Wisconsin earlier in the year when a waterborne parasite made tens of thousands of people sick, and water had to be transported in for the city residents for days.

What puzzled inspectors most was that the water coming from its sources, almost all of it originating from the Delaware and Catskill reservoir systems, was normal—and that samples from ten of the twelve inner-city plants were normal. It did not seem likely that the contamination was caused by a leak, because the water is delivered under heavy pressure, and so any break in the pipes usually results in a leak out, not a leak in. Most unnerving was the fact that the city, state, and federal agencies all were stumped about the cause and strength of the contamination. And, without any answers, they were unable to predict whether or not the contamination would spread.

After a week of carting water to lines of waiting residents in the Chelsea area, the Environmental Protection Agency announced that it had found signs of contamination throughout the New York City water system, from East Tremont in the Bronx down to lower Manhattan and on out to Little Neck, Queens, and even the distant Tottenville area of Staten Island.

During the warm summer months, the city pumps between 1.5 billion and 2 billion gallons of water a day. Earlier in the year, it had quickly identified other contaminants in the 6,000 miles of water systems: Both were tied to improper chlorination, and valve settings which had allowed water to stagnate.

While sabotage was ruled out in the investigation, one supervisor refused to give details on the location of the twelve water reservoirs located throughout the city. "Anonymity is the only protection we have," he told a reporter.

By early August, environmental officials reported that they thought the cause of the bacterial contamination had come from sea gull droppings in a reservoir in Yonkers. The city has budgeted $177 million to *cover* that reservoir in the future, including the cost of a reflecting pool meant to avoid changing the appearance of the area (because the reservoir is visible from the Gov. Thomas E. Dewey Thruway).

Contamination of city water treatment plants by natural causes is not uncommon, and the cures are expensive. The experiences have given residents a feel for the frustration and inconvenience of being without water—but these experiences could not approach the added hardship (not to mention the horrors) of half the population lying dead in the streets during the same period. And this *is* the possible result of chemical and biological warfare. And the possibility from which we have no known protection.

In September 1993, the U.S. government concluded that mysterious illnesses suffered by hundreds of participants in the Persian Gulf War apparently were caused by still-unknown biological or chemical agents used by Iraq.

CHAPTER 14

The Vulnerability of Computer Intelligence and Communications

The inexorable links among all of the nation's distribution systems are the nation's computer and communications networks.

Computers and telecommunications have become so ingrained in our society that much of our government, industry, military, and national defense would be seriously disrupted or cease to function if either of these systems failed for even a few hours or days.

From a conspiratorial outlook, the U.S. government's deepest, darkest secret for almost fifty years has been the total vulnerability of these systems. While society moved into the information age, it did so with systems that can be destroyed almost at will, or utilized to send the country (and thus much of the world) into a fifty-year depression which at least this country might not survive. The negligence of those responsible has left us needlessly exposed—not only to one or another foreign superpower, but also to any small group of lunatics bent on creating havoc.

From a pragmatic point of view, however, there was no deep, dark secret—just a deep, dark *weakness*—that the enemy camp has not yet chosen to exploit. Government, industry, and the military, all using millions of computers and other data-processing systems, simply followed a familiar trail of developing advanced technology which can be used either to gradually improve humankind or to send us into a self-destruct mode with startling immediacy.

It is precisely for these reasons that both the United States and the Soviet Union had plans to knock out the other's communications and computer systems as one of their first acts in the event of war. Both knew that a small nuclear explosion released approximately sixty miles over the center of the United States would permanently destroy the communications and computer operations of the lower forty-eight states. The Soviets had a similar first-strike plan for the invasion of Europe.

The electromagnetic pulse (EMP) of a nuclear explosion travels at about one hundred times the speed of lightning. Although so brief, it is a powerful field which reaches its full intensity in about ten billionths of a second. It can be stopped only by specially designed cabinets and equipment. Its peak strength may be six million watts per square meter, or about six thousand times the peak density of sunlight. A single blast would have a radius of approximately fourteen hundred miles.

A similar effect would occur if a nuclear blast happened at a lower altitude (say from the top of a tall building), but the radius of the affected area would be reduced accordingly.

We tend to think of nuclear blasts in terms of the physical devastation unleashed on Hiroshima on August 6, 1945—a large city flattened, with tens of thousands of people killed and many thousands of survivors exposed to crippling or mortal doses of radiation. But the realization that nuclear technology is one of our inventions that can wipe out most of our other technology is perhaps even more important in the overview.

To quote directly from *Brittle Power*, "Any metal object—power lines, telephone lines, wires, instrument cabinets—would pick up the pulse like an antenna, focusing its energy into any delicate electronic circuitry in the area. The result: instantaneous, simultaneous failure of all unhardened electrical and electronic systems, including electric grid and pipeline controls, telephones, and other telecommunications except fiber optics. Most power grid controls would be damaged functionally or operationally (erased computer memory). Power lines would act as long antennas, collecting the pulse over great distances. The induced surges—as high as thirty thousand megawatts—could damage insulators and transformer windings, and would probably burn out many end-use devices that happened to be operative from line voltage at the time."

In other words, because of EMP, anything that relies on the electrical distribution system is in danger of being damaged or knocked out completely. This includes power plants which would not only be in danger of shutting down, but would be in the even greater danger of running out of control. Even though utility companies are aware of these possibilities, with each expansion they expand the problem, partly because of outdated design trends, but mostly because the cost of protecting the electrical grids would be astronomical.

Solid state electronic devices are particularly vulnerable to EMP whether or not they are connected to an electrical source. Solid state ignition systems in automobiles and trucks, including police vehicles, would be rendered useless. But these solid state units are widely used in nuclear plants throughout the country with the very real danger that a cascading tragedy of nuclear core meltdowns would occur, endangering broad areas of local populations. The result of simultaneous meltdowns would be devastating to the point that there might not be much of a country left since most of the reactors are located near heavy population centers.

Virtually every part of society with electronic reliance could be permanently or temporarily disabled, including the electronic ignitions in most vehicles, both civilian and military.

But this is the extreme example, important here only to point out that the United States has no civil preparedness plan to deal with such a situation, and most countries have not even considered the possibility. There are more common ways to accomplish the same effects—methods which are just as likely to be employed by terrorists—for which we also have no civil response plan.

Cutting off communication alone to the various nerve centers of our energy system would be enough to bring the systems down. Conversely, cutting off electrical power to the systems would bring most of them down.

The computer and communications control centers themselves are subject to sabotage, and even those systems that installed off-site backup systems did so with the trade-off that they offered yet another series of transmissions which could be intercepted, and another part of the control system which could be entered.

But physical access to computer and communications centers in the traditional way is itself becoming obsolete. According to many computer experts, the next great American Pearl Harbor will be terrorists' *technological* attacks on our computer and information systems.

"Why plant a bomb in an airplane when you can bring a country to a standstill by sabotaging the computers that run its banking, communications and air traffic systems?" That's the question Winn Schwartau, a computer terrorist expert, posed to Congress during a 1991 hearing on the vulnerability of our nation's computer systems, as reported by the magazine, *Edge Publishing*.

"Our computers are so poorly protected they can essentially be considered defenseless," Schwartau told Congress. "An electronic Pearl Harbor is waiting to happen."

This danger involves more than the stealing of information, or even the distortion or destruction of information. Our computers are so intricately interwoven throughout our energy and defense systems, they can be used to activate all of the physical destruction of a thousand terrorist attacks, or even a nuclear attack.

Through even a laptop computer the nuclear EMP blast effect can be emulated and transmitted to a local nuclear plant, or any other sensitive facility. This would have the same result, at a mere fraction of the cost, of a nuclear explosion. This emulated signal could be used in a number of ways at a number of different facilities.

The telephone system regulates its millions of miles of lines through a low voltage charge sent through the lines, the same low voltage that causes the companies to warn against talking on the telephone while in the bathtub. The consistency of this signal tells the computer sensors whether everything is working properly.

A computer-emulated signal can send a false surcharge—a signal over the same lines—which can be sent from any telephone in the country, or possibly from an overseas telephone connection. This false signal would send the telephone system into an automatic shutdown, with switching stations closing according to their preprogrammed assignment to protect the line. The same automatic efforts to reroute telephone signals would be further exasperated.

An obvious physical threat to the hundreds of thousands of computer centers, as well as the hundreds of communications control centers, around the country is their penetration by saboteurs. No computer center in existence can honestly say it is safeguarded from intentional destruction by attack from either an outside group or even one internal employee. Likewise, no communications network is protected from what until now has more or less been an unforeseen possibility.

Obviously, telephone lines can even be cut yet quickly repaired. But telephone control or switching centers can be knocked out rather easily—and, although the telephone system is able to reroute the disruption of one center, the disruption of just two or three central computer centers would be devastating to the entire network. This tactic is common to guerrillas and terrorists alike. At the beginning of any military conflict or internal coup, the first goal is either to take over the enemy's communications systems, or to destroy them.

After twelve years of civil war, El Salvador is finally concentrating on getting its shattered telephone system operating again. Out of 308 telephone company offices throughout that country, 42 were destroyed. Today they have built the system back up to provide 2.5 telephones per one hundred people, the lowest percentage in the Western Hemisphere. Telephone switching stations and hydroelectric dams had been dynamited, causing massive power outages and telephone downtime.

Telephone switching stations which are scattered about U.S. cities are crucial to our communications network. They are squeezed in at any number of unprotected locations. In 1992, a failed AT&T switching station in New York City put both Wall Street and the New York Stock Exchange out of business for an entire day, with an estimated loss of billions of dollars in trading value. The failure resulted in 4.5 million blocked domestic long-distance calls, nearly 500,000 interrupted international calls, and the loss of 80 percent of the Federal Aviation Administration's circuits. A similar failure on November 5, 1991, in Boston resulted in a 60 percent loss of calls in that area.

Sprint Communications, one of AT&T's competitors, was quick to run an advertisement which promised "All the basics you get from AT&T. Except the outages. And downtime!" AT&T was most embarrassed by the event, but what seemed absent from all reports about the incident was that the same thing could happen to *every* switching station in the country, and that Wall Street could very well have been shut down for *weeks*, had the cause of failure been intentional. This was alluded to in a follow-up lawsuit by AT&T: Sprint was forced to modify the advertisement when AT&T proved that Sprint was also subject to outages and downtime.

But the most effective use of the computer and communications systems as terrorist tools would not come from crashing the systems. On the contrary, it would come from using the systems for an even greater calamity.

Security Management Magazine looked at these possibilities from a business point of view. An article written by R. D. Ginn, European managing director of Continuity Planning Associates, said experience shows that a growing number of disasters are manmade and deliberate. And a recent survey in the United Kingdom showed that more than 60 percent of computer disasters could have been avoided—making the point that the cheapest form of disaster recovery is preventing the disaster from happening in the first place.

One international company examined by Ginn had a worldwide network of over ten thousand terminals processing on-line applications. A large portion of the information contained in the computer system was not manmade; it was information that was a product of the computer itself. Personnel had never seen the information, and there was no paper trail for redeveloping the data. If this internally generated information was lost, it would be lost forever. That company estimated that if its computers were down "for more than twenty minutes it would have a devastating and costly effect," Ginn reported.

Industrywide statistics mirrored the fears of the company as well. If a disaster from *any* cause creates downtime of most companies' computer systems which lasts for only four to five days, the companies' efficiency is reduced by 50 percent. By the eleventh day, it is down to just 9 percent.

Since no company can operate successfully at a 9 percent efficiency, massive layoffs of employees are usually the first reaction to this internal destruction of a company's ability to function.

Another report cited by the article showed that of all businesses that suffered a disaster to their computer centers, most survived less than one and a half years. After five years, 93 percent of those companies that had experienced computer disasters failed to exist.

With these facts in mind, the following story about a computer hacker—or what was at first thought to be a computer hacker—drives home the susceptibility of our nation's systems to what some call "intelligent terrorists."

In August 1986, the Lawrence Berkeley Laboratory (LBL) noticed that their systems had been visited by a computer hacker. It was first brought to their attention when the computer reported an accounting error: A new account had been created without a corresponding billing address. It must be immediately made clear that, across the computer industry, companies receive thousands of indications annually that either they have been entered, or someone had attempted to enter their computer systems. Most of these indicators are ignored, however, because it is almost impossible to track an intruder.

In this case, however, LBL also received a notice from the National Computer Security Center that someone from LBL had used *its* computer to try to break into one of *their* computers through a MILNET connection. MILNET is the military computer network giving access to hundreds of computer systems within the military and private industry, including a number of research laboratories working for the government.

LBL's first reaction was the common one: Remove the errant account. But they noticed that the problem remained. Not only had the intruder managed to retain access to their computer system—he had successfully assigned himself "system-manager" status. This basically gave him control of the system itself, with all the implied abilities to retrieve data, move it, change it, delete it, or distort it.

This is not an uncommon problem. In the past, computer hackers or "phone phreaks" have been viewed as somewhat inconsequential nuisances by the public, but in fact they cost the telephone and computer companies billions of dollars each year. They also demonstrate that the same systems they utilize successfully are open to terrorists with more sinister motives. In one recent example, a large company discovered that their systems had been intruded upon, and made an attempt to refuse the hacker's further access. The intruder responded with a threat to shut down their computers altogether if they tried that again, and demanded millions of dollars in protection money if the company wanted to stay in business and avoid the embarrassment of letting its clients know that their information was not secure.

LBL decided to take a different approach. Knowing that the intruder was using their computer to reach other computers, they decided to allow him access while they printed out and traced all of his actions.

It started out almost as a game, with the personnel at LBL assuming that they eventually might catch some student at the nearby university playing with a friend's computer from a dorm room. However, it soon became apparent that, rather than just playing around, the intruder was using LBL as a hub to reach many other computers, including military and defense contractor locations and research laboratories. LBL then began what they thought would be a rather simple exercise, which however continued for almost a year as they watched the intruder access almost 450 other computer sites.

LBL's published report on the project describes itself as a research institute with few military contracts and no classified research, unlike an LBL sister-research center which does have extensive military and classified files but was not intruded upon. LBL's computer environment was typical of that of a university: widely distributed, and accessible from a number of locations.

It was difficult to maintain secrecy during the invasions, knowing that the intruder held system-manager privileges. They had to avoid sending electronic messages, knowing that the hacker would read their network messages from time to time, and even access the systems inside several computer security companies. They also knew that the intruder was sophisticated enough to note whether their attempts to trace him caused any undue lag time—so they printed his various messages and commands on line printers and recorders. They captured every keystroke the invader made, and kept a detailed logbook summarizing his traffic, the traces, and rising suspicions, as well as LBL's interaction with law-enforcement officials and representatives from the other companies that the intruder had attempted to access.

In the world of phone phreaks, it is customary for the intruders to dig through the systems: to access the most sensitive areas of company management and, in the case of electronic mail messaging, to invade the most sensitive personal areas as they read the mail from one employee to the next. Sometimes they leave messages, just to let the invaded company know they were there. Among ardent phone phreaks there is a code that they will not alter or disrupt resident data in any way—although there *have* been a number of costly mishaps, in addition to intentional acts of sabotage.

Using the system backwards, LBL kept all messages about the intruder off of all electronic communication devices, and planted false messages to make the intruder feel more secure. As they monitored the intruder, they also discovered hundreds of other unauthorized attempts to break into systems.

When LBL noted an intrusion of another computer, either they or the FBI would contact the victim company. In most cases those companies would immediately disable the intruder or deny him access—moves which also would reveal that he had been detected at those other computer sites. From the intruder's point of view, only LBL had failed to identify him. In reality, only LBL *did* identify him.

The intruder's route arrived from a typical access communications port, which meant it could have originated from anywhere in the world. An initial trace led to a nearby dial-up Tymnet port in Oakland, California. LBL reported that they then received a court order allowing them to trace the calls to a dial-out modem belonging to a defense contractor in McLean, Virginia. "In essence, their LAN allowed any user to dial out from their modem pool and even provided a last-number-redial capability for those who did not know access codes for remote systems." In other words, the caller did not even have to use the code-breaking software that is available to enable phone phreaks to call sequence numbers until they find access. The redial service simply led him to whatever contact he wanted.

Having found the defense contractor site, LBL could now complete a histogram of the caller's activities—which, they discovered, had been going on for many months *prior* to the time they discovered him, all at the expense of the defense contractor. The telephone bills indicated a number of short calls, to all around the United States, whereby the caller collected lists of telephone numbers and then buzzed them via modem. He would summarily attempt to log in, using common account names and passwords, most often at military bases where the intrusion had been noted but ignored.

After the intruder was denied access to the defense contractor, he continued to enter LBL's system through other routes. LBL credits the outstanding cooperation of Tymnet in enabling them to trace calls to points in Germany, where he entered university and public dial-up modems and gained system-manager status at a university in Bremen. He disabled their accounting program, and used their port links to connect to other modems around the world.

By this time, the trackers had acquired four computer port locations from which to gain a logistical accounting of the intruder's source: LBL, the university in Bremen, Tymnet, and the German Bundespost were quadrangulated to attempt to gain a fix. LBL began a measurement of network delay times and determined that the intruder was calling from overseas, not across the street from a college dorm, as they had originally suspected. This tied to both the physical-network trails and to the German passwords that were often used.

The researchers at LBL needed to keep the intruder on the line long enough for an extensive trace to be completed in Germany. They therefore created a totally fictitious file made available only to the intruder from Germany regarding the "Star Wars" plans, as they were called by President Reagan, and included the invitation to subscribe for further documentation by mail. A few weeks later, the intruder came across this irresistible file and spent more than an hour reading it, even as telephone technicians managed to finish the trace.

With the trace completed and the location turned over to authorities in Germany and the FBI in the U.S., LBL thought they had won the battle with the persistent intruder. But a few months later—long after their celebration—a letter arrived from a U.S. location requesting placement on the bogus offer's mailing list. The letter had obviously traveled from the intruder in Germany to a contact in the United States—and LBL knew it was now in the middle of a case of international *espionage*.

Most instructive (and scary) in the LBL investigation was watching the intruder manipulate the systems. He would use LBL as a host to connect to ARPANET/MILNET, and to other networks, including the Magnetic Fusion Energy network, the High Energy Physics network, and several LAN's at invaded sites.

From MILNET alone, the intruder attempted to invade 450 comput-ers—and, of those of major interest, he was successful almost 10 percent of the time by using even the most primitive of methods. Too, he often received system-manager status—or, once in the system, figured out how to give that to himself. Obviously convinced that he was uncatchable, he included among his many invasions files he had opened months earlier but hadn't touched since. Also among the government and government con-tractor files he accessed were a variety containing nuclear, biological, and chemical warfare information for central Europe.

But he *was* catchable: A few months later, United States and German agencies cooperated in arresting him (an East German agent) and his American contact, and charged them with espionage.

LBL is quick to note that this intruder was in no way a whiz—as some might imagine. They also note that such break-ins from abroad seem to be increasing, and that this individual's intrusions were different from many others only in that they were detected. *Many* intrusions have been detect-ed from European countries—as well as from Asia.

This case is complicated in that it is still unclear whether or not elec-tronic invasion is a crime. In most countries, including Great Britain and all of its dominion, it is little more than a misdemeanor, regardless of the sensitivity of the files accessed. Similarly, when a phone phreak of noto-riety is caught in the United States, he or she is often offered a high-pay-ing position with the victim company, to help test their systems. Even those who plant damaging viruses in the system networks have had little to fear from any legal repercussions. This may all change, however, now that terrorism is becoming a more visible, and thus much more viable, issue.

It is an undeniable fact that the same simple methods utilized by phone phreaks are now tools of terrorists—and so any company or government that allows itself to be victimized may well be accused of negligence in the future. In the past, electronic intrusion has been viewed as a *possible* theft of data, but it is now apparent that loss of control of entire systems, or even the alteration of data within systems, can ultimately result in thou-sands upon thousands of deaths. Such negligence may in the future carry a very high price for humanity.

Even now, this danger applies to almost everyone who has a computer linked via electronic transmissions of any kind. Just as police keep using advanced radar detectors, and in reply drivers find advanced fuzz-busters, the computer terrorists have all the technological tools available to outwit any protection devices the security forces come up with.

Intrusions have been made in every computer network, including the European Nuclear Research Center, the French Atomic Energy Commission, the French Space Studies Institute, and the NASA SPAN network (which includes facilities worldwide, such as the U.S. atomic research lab at Los Alamos, the European Space Agency, and the European Laboratory for Molecular Biology, in West Germany).

But if the telephone companies themselves are the greatest victims of phone phreaks, is there an effective defense for intelligent sabotage, short of shutting the systems down? Toll fraud—the theft or misuse of communications services—costs American business and government billions of dollars annually, according to a warning publication distributed by U.S. West to telephone company business users: "Virtually every communications system, be it Private Branch Exchange (PBX), voice mail, cellular or central office based, is vulnerable to toll abusers."

Crooks who penetrate communications systems steal authorization numbers, crack access codes with computer software programs, employ illegally altered cellular telephones, and take control of voice-mail boxes. One firm discovered—too late—that thieves had accessed its PBX system to place more than 30,000 international calls with a total value of $430,000.

In another case, a group of toll abusers whose efforts had been detected and who were shut down sought a unique form of revenge. They pried their way back into the user's system, and—for 45 minutes—dialed 911 to report numerous fake accidents and disasters. The local police, highway patrol, and medical emergency units were in chaos, endangering the safety of citizens who were trying to make legitimate calls.

In another stunning display of bravado, computer crooks targeted an office of the U.S. Drug Enforcement Administration, making $2 million worth of domestic and international calls over an eighteen-month period.

One of the reasons why toll fraud continues is this: Legal precedent has established that it is the victims, not the telephone service providers, who are responsible for the costs. There is thus little incentive for the telephone companies to take the elaborate and expensive steps required to thwart unauthorized access. Another important aspect is that it is questionable whether *any* action by the telephone companies would be very successful in stopping the unauthorized access.

The unauthorized users are hackers, crackers, and phreakers who range from the professional thief, the drug dealer, the corporate snoop, and the disgruntled employee to the recreational hacker who just wants to see what he or she can get away with. It is interesting to note that the U.S.

West warning publication does not bother to mention terrorists, who could raise the stakes astronomically.

The same systems that allow these crooks to rack up billions of dollars in costs to others each year will also allow terrorists and saboteurs the ability to take over or disrupt entire systems. The professional thieves use toll circuits, cellular phones, and voice-mail systems for profit. They steal both calling-card and credit-card numbers, and either steal or (using automatic "war dialer" software programs) crack access codes. Either the access can then be used by the initial intruder, or they can sell the access to others. In some cases, these thieves maintain complete phone rooms equipped with cubicles, and phone sets that operate with all the efficiency of a telephone company's, but at substantially discounted prices. Thousands of calls are billed to the victims' numbers.

Drug dealers steal authorization codes to voice-mail systems, which are then used to leave coded messages—sometimes to a worldwide distribution network. The calls are impossible to trace because they can be tracked only as far as the PBX or voice-mail system that authorized them and routed them over the public switched network.

Voice-mail systems are also the favorite tool for industrial espionage. An electronic intruder or unscrupulous employee can access the entire system for proprietary information, erase or alter important messages, or spread disinformation via bogus messages. Any idea of privacy over voice-mail systems is thus compromised.

A complete recreational hacker network with thousands of phone phreak members exists, with newsletters, electronic bulletin boards, underground software, and an in-place distribution network for sharing stolen access codes. Even these heretofore "innocent" hackers are now subject to infiltration by terrorists, who will use their codes as a resource for future infiltration or destruction of a business or government data base.

The toll fraud problem provides a good example of why terrorists are able to roam the electronic infrastructure of the country at will. Small businesses are not sophisticated enough to discover an intrusion. Large businesses and government agencies are too complex to notice increased charges and are manned by personnel who have no direct responsibility for the company's profitability. They don't notice even those massive fluctuations in bills which add up to millions of dollars over a short period.

Telephone companies are helpless to react without cutting the kinds of services subscribers want to have. They might be successful in helping to capture a fraudulent phone scam, but their lengthy efforts would pose little threat to a terrorist organization.

While one step toward a solution to computer terrorism is a decentralization policy, the main movement is in the other direction. Both industry and government are responding to economic and administrative problems by means of a tendency to consolidate operations into huge, centralized processing facilities.

In December 1991, Congress passed legislation which approved a $2.9 billion budget to upgrade the nation's computer infrastructure by 1996. The upgrades involve high-performing computing hardware and software, and networking capabilities, as well as education and training. By 1996 the Defense and Energy departments, the Space Agency, and other federal agencies are to be capable of transmitting at least a billion bits of data per second to millions of computer links with researchers, educators, and universities. For terrorists, this new system will offer, overnight, countless new weak spots which may allow them to enter not only the system, but that of each subscriber to the system.

The legislation included an attempt to thwart computer hackers by excluding classified documents from the system. This was spurred on by an electronic intrusion during the Gulf War, when Dutch teenagers managed to access the Department of Defense computer system. They were able to track military shipments of supplies and equipment.

But even unclassified material can be dangerous. Terrorists have at their disposal computer software that can compile the billions of bits of information—reports which in themselves are not classified—and combine them to develop a composite, the end result of which may be an otherwise classified conclusion.

One Department of Defense official has told the author that various government and military departments also do not agree with what should be classified:

"For example, our architectural and structural designs are not classified," the DOD official said, "But these designs might include instructions to contractors on how to make a building terrorist-proof. We have sophisticated computer equipment where we assimilate explosions at various structural points to determine impact, and based on these readings we adjust our designs accordingly. It's foolish to think terrorists have less sophisticated equipment, or that they do not have the ability to read our designs backwards."

Any building can be brought down if you have the computer plans or blueprints. If the terrorists who exploded the bomb in the World Trade Center had utilized such prior analysis, the results might have been immensely worse.

The DOD official explained that "They placed the bomb at the worst possible location, from their point of view. Had they parked directly beneath one of the towers, instead of the hotel, the explosion probably still would not have brought the tower down, but there is a good chance we would have to completely dismantle one of the tallest buildings in the world. The expense would have been astronomical."

Tied to this problem of clarification of information are two earlier governmental developments. The first development was as follows:

In 1988, the U.S. Department of Defense took steps to fully automate production of technical documents and manuals, accepting bids from dozens of computer firms. At stake is a $2 billion budget—large enough to actually shift the market share of the major companies.

The effort is a move to use electronic publishing to cut costs and streamline the publishing process—a process which previously required 270 days, on the average, to make a simple revision in a manual. There is good reason for the concern, of course. Documentation accounts for an estimated 10 percent of a weapon's total price, David Goodstein, president of Interconsult, told *PC Week* (March 15, 1988). "So if you have a $300 million nuclear submarine, $30 million is for its documents."

But those manual revisions could have a reverse message. Goodstein said that 5 to 8 percent of military accidents resulting in death can be traced back to errors in publications. If electronic publishing and on-line communications give terrorists access to the documents themselves, minor alterations which go unnoticed could have dramatic effects, indeed. (Even presumably unintentional alterations by staff members can do that. For example, a Soviet-manned space flight suddenly went out of control and began a direct approach toward the Sun. Disaster was narrowly averted when scientists finally discovered the cause: A keyboard operator had made a single-digit error.)

Small, intentional errors in nuclear plants, nuclear submarines, weapons, and oil or gas control centers can be the difference between efficiency and economic or environmental destruction. This problem is exacerbated by the parallel development of logical computers—those that build information within themselves. If the data are distorted or altered in any way, there is no human opportunity to catch the problem.

Major contracts with Boeing and NASA for space stations are already being developed via electronic technical documentation, and it does not seem that these systems are adequately protected from either external *or* internal sabotage.

A second development of the government's move to harden computer security through centralization—contradictory though it is—is the Air Force Logistics Command proposal to build a 105,000-square-foot computer center at Wright-Patterson Air Force Base in Ohio. It is designed to house over $40 million of equipment in a 67,000-square-foot section of the building. While the new building is meant to improve such things as energy efficiency, threat from damage by flooding, and basement sprinkler systems, it is also being justified by its consolidating of other sensitive military command centers, which were previously separate from one other.

The new building will also house both the Air Force's logistics system and its telecommunications hardware, along with the equipment it uses as part of the Worldwide Military Command and Control System, designed to allow officials from the separate programs more opportunity to interact. Making matters worse, the same building will house not only a 20,000-square-foot administrative office area, but also the center's 18,000-square-foot central power plant, "including a solid-state, uninterruptible power supply."

As Winn Schwartau points out in his book, *Terminal Compromise*, guns able to magnetically disable computer systems can be bought over-the-counter for about $2,000—guns which would have the capability of paralyzing a military, airport, telephone, or financial-institution computer center. One hopes that this would be more difficult to do at an elaborate center such as that described in Ohio, but it would be as easy as a drive-by shooting outside most banks, telephone control rooms, and airports. "On the one hand," Schwartau told Congress in November 1991 and reported in *Edge Publishing* magazine the same month, "there is the threat to the privacy of 250 million Americans. On the other, the threat to national security. These systems are virtually unprotected."

Unauthorized access remains the greatest threat. Douglas E. Campbell, a program manager for PSI International, wrote in an article titled "The Intelligent Threat" published as a March 1989 special section of the *Security Management* magazine: "In September 1984, a hacker with an interest in politics rummaged through the TRW credit report of incumbent congressional candidate Tom Lantos in California and turned up a prior small-claims court dispute over a price tag switched on a suitcase. Lantos had lost the case and refused to pay, putting the record of the court's collection efforts into his file. Lantos' opponent wasted no time in making sure certain local reporters were aware of the impropriety. What if this had occurred on the presidential campaign level?"

Social Security records, medical records, income-tax files, psychological reports, information about families (husbands, wives, and children)—all appear in huge data bases which are not protected from serious attempts to access them.

Private industry has turned information data bases into big business—one of the fastest-growing marketing tools of the decade. Each company compiles information, including buying patterns, and swaps it with others, in order to update all their records more fully. The Internal Revenue Service has been known to purchase these private files in order to improve its own.

Marketing analysis has moved, over just the past twenty years, from crude geographic analysis to more-advanced demographic analysis, which includes such data as average income, home ownership, marital status, and other information readily available from driver's license data and telephone books.

A relatively new practice is that of analyzing credit-card purchases at grocery stores and other retail outlets. This both assigns information to a specific individual or family, and identifies specific products bought by the purchaser—according to brand name.

It's all stored in a computer data base where the information compiler assists businesses in targeting more finite profiles of prospective buyers.

Most of the builders of these data bases hold to high moral standards with regard to the use of information. For example, they make certain that only the composite, calculated information can be used for research purposes—but not in such a way that clients can identify specific names or addresses of individuals. Rather, categories are profiled—and then the profiles are used to find customers of similar buying habits or other descriptions. However, regardless of the good intentions of these compilers of information, the credit-reporting files or the purchasing files (or whatever) all are on data bases in danger of being usurped.

This concern that *any* computer can be violated raises cries from all directions of Big Brother enemies—from the NRA's objections to the registration of handguns, to certain factions' complaints about centralized national health care. Unauthorized use by terrorists would move these files to the forefront of right-to-privacy issues, overriding the importance of gun control and access to health care.

Until the fall of the Berlin Wall, a convenient cause in support of the information privacy issue has been the threat of Soviet invasion of data files: Why give the enemy a convenient computer file showing the name, address, income, gun ownership (and on and on) of every American household? There has also been a resurgence of the Jeffersonian view that civilians should always be prepared to take their country back from a corrupt government. (Supporters of this view will be happy to know they can presently wipe out the government computer files at any time they choose.)

Although neither the threat of a foreign superpower nor that of a corrupt U.S. government is a realistic fear today, every computer scientist and security expert in the nation agrees that the threat of computer terrorism is real.

In July 1985, a group of New Jersey teenagers calling numbers at random discovered a phone line through which communications satellites were monitored and controlled. Their intrusion into the system was discovered when they began changing satellite orbits. Imagine one orbit irreconcilably changed so that the satellite entered the earth's atmosphere and crashed into a populated city.

Or, imagine a group of terrorists who, having completed their destruction of earth-based communications systems, now want to obstruct satellite communications as well.

The financial industry in general is perhaps the most vulnerable target of computer fraud and computer terrorism. For example:

People have been caught trading calling credit cards and cash credit cards over computer bulletin boards, using them to purchase thousands of dollars of merchandise on each card. But most credit card thieves are not caught.

Stanley Rifkin, who posed as a consultant in 1978 in order to collect computer passwords from a Los Angeles bank, and proceeded to transfer $10.2 million to a Swiss account, is unique only in that he got caught.

A recent report by the financial industry revealed even more incentive for computer theft: The average take from a traditional bank holdup for 1992 was $10,000; the average take from a computer holdup was $500,000.

It is not impossible for a clever terrorist group to attack the financial stability of the United States by accessing massive numbers of accounts and electronically transferring billions of dollars overseas—particularly if they have had the cooperation of a bank like BCCI.

Part III

RESPONSE

CHAPTER 15

Immigration—A Catalyst to Chaos

If a major terrorist goal is to create civil disruption within a target country, then stirring up a grassroots revival of racism will most certainly be a catalyst to chaos. But *only* a catalyst.

Whether the direct actions are those of neo-Nazis, white or black separatists, or Mideast terrorists, deep within the underlying themes of hate and prejudice lies a very real fear, held by the inheritors of the prosperity of the Industrial Revolution, of losing everything ever held to be important. Americans are not unique in this situation: Germany, France, Great Britain—indeed, all the industrialized countries—have a sense that their power and security are slipping away.

This fear is strengthened when we see dreams and values becoming ever more obscure, even without any outside help; when we are haunted by an undefined, nagging feeling that the society we knew and have grown to expect will go on forever is instead following some natural course of collapse. Economic hardship heightens these fears and prejudices, and a knee-jerk response is to find something—or some*one*—tangible to blame.

Hardened racists are not the real problem, but only a symptom of it. When unemployment reaches 20–30 percent, people who might not consider themselves racist or otherwise prejudiced often have a leaning toward stricter immigration laws, the elimination of benefits for immigrants, or a redefinition of basic democratic freedoms as they apply to immigrants. And they may well not consider themselves racists in these considerations, but rather economic survivalists.

The old patterns of the world certainly are changing, but there is a silver lining to all of this—which is that what we are experiencing is a temporary adjustment to a changing world, and not some doomsday gloom that has befallen us, never to be lifted. We can still look forward to a world filled with new, exciting, and rewarding challenges and opportunities. But terrorism most assuredly will capitalize on the immediate future, trying to bring to a head the racist attitudes simmering just below the surface of many societies.

Past experience predicates both a rise in antiblack activities and black riots in the streets. A wave of racist attacks on Islamic homes and businesses, in reaction to further Mideast-spawned terrorist attacks, is predictable—if not on the physical level then in the arenas of political policy and business activity. And an increased level of anti-Semitism and antigovernment alike will accompany any gross decline in the economy, as it always has.

The arrests of foreign-born terrorists involved in the World Trade Center bombing and the plot to attack other New York City targets happened to coincide with the accidental grounding of the *Golden Venture*, a smuggler's ship carrying almost three hundred bilked Chinese immigrants. Sitting in their comfortable homes while watching those sad souls being pulled out of the ocean, apparently penniless and helpless, might well have nevertheless set many viewers to remembering such other shocking events as bombing by Arab terrorists, or the firing of yet another multiple-thousands batch of employees (due perhaps to their company's move to a cheaper labor market)—and knowing that if those three hundred had *accidentally* been caught on the shores, who knows how many thousands more have come in undetected—it might be difficult to take pity on *all* those people. It is particularly difficult to relate to the misery the Chinese are fleeing when economists and political futurists predict that the country they escaped from has a good chance of eventually economically eclipsing the dominance of both Japan *and* the United States.

The question becomes: Should we harden both our immigration policy and our border security? And if we do, does something as vague as a hardened policy or attitude have the same dangers of becoming brittle—and breaking—as does a piece of steel or a complex web of computer networks? A climate of economic recession and slow recovery, of unimaginable national indebtedness combined with escalating immigration numbers and a rising awareness of terrorism, soon becomes a climate in which conservative voices are listened to that call for even furthering any existing hardening policy. In such a climate of insecurity, the liberal view comes across as totally irresponsible.

One of the most obvious reasons to reduce immigration is one of simple economics: If we stopped immigration altogether for a few years, perhaps we could wipe out the national debt without raising taxes or cutting back on benefits.

A new study by Donald L. Huddle, professor emeritus of economics at Rice University in Houston, indicates that more than $45 billion a year is spent by U.S. taxpayers on immigrants living in the United States. By the year 2000, the immigration cost to taxpayers will accumulate to over $450 billion—almost equal to the deficit-reduction goal of the 1992 presidential election campaign.

And Huddle's figures are conservative, based as they are on an annual influx of only 810,000 legal and 300,000 illegal immigrants. He doesn't count the suspected 4 million illegal crossings from Mexico alone each year, for example.

He did count the 18.1 million immigrants who resided in the United States in 1992, both legal and illegal—but it can be assumed that this figure was also conservative, by as much as 30 percent.

Some immigrants pay taxes, of course, but Huddle's $45 billion-a-year figures took that into account. His projections are *net, out-of-pocket* costs to *taxpayers*.

Education for immigrants devoured the lion's share of the costs: $12.8 billion for primary and secondary education in 1992; $2.4 billion for public higher education; $2.8 billion for second-language and bilingual education. Almost 40 percent of the annual immigration bill was for education. Part of the reason for this was that increasing numbers of immigrants have been bearing children on U.S. soil, then qualifying for the various government assistance programs designed to help the poor. Combined with low birth rates among whites, this makes for some interesting inequities.

Immigrant newborns automatically become U.S. citizens—even those born to illegals—and qualify for food-stamp and other assistance programs (which make payments to their parents or guardians).

The newborn-child rule comes into the spotlight in regard to the United States' immigration policy toward China, as well. The Bush administration left a gigantic loophole in the immigration laws dealing with Chinese in particular. While political asylum is an option for any foreigner to claim because of political persecution, the definition of persecution was expanded to include opposition to China's one-child rule. The expansion sent a message abroad that any Chinese who made it to United States shores were welcome to stay.

This also tied to special consideration for Chinese students. In the backlash of the military putdown of the student rebellion in Tiananmen Square, the U.S. government passed the Chinese Student Protection Act of 1992. Under this act, Chinese nationals (most of whom were students) and their dependents can become naturalized citizens. It allows students to obtain lawful permanent residence without applying for an immigrant visa abroad, provided they can prove they have resided continuously in the United States since 1990. The students are then placed on a "to be issued" list—but even those whose temporary visas expire will not be forced to return to China. In fact, after five years they may apply for permanent United States citizenship.

In Los Angeles County, an area which many demographers say represents a mirror for America's future, 62 percent of all births in 1992 (Chinese included) were to undocumented aliens—costing the county a net of $30 million.

Huddle's figures also argue against those who say that immigrants provide a positive contribution to the country, do not displace skilled workers, and provide a service by taking jobs that most Americans are unwilling to accept.

His report indicated that the 18 million immigrants in the country today have indeed displaced over 2 million American workers—and that this displacement eventually costs the U.S. taxpayer over $15 billion annually to cover unemployment, Medicaid, food stamps, and general assistance. It did not include any "private costs," such as wages and fringe benefits—just government (taxpayer) costs.

In July 1993, shortly after the arrests of the Arab terrorists, the foundering of the illegal Chinese aliens offshore, another six hundred illegal Chinese stopped in international waters and pushed south to Mexico, and thousands of Haitians with AIDS petitioning to be allowed into the country, USA Today coordinated with a Gallup poll to get a feel for how the American mood toward immigration is changing. Regarding methods to reduce illegal immigration, 90 percent favored stricter border controls. Fifty-seven percent would approve a national ID card. Forty percent would bar illegal immigrants from schools and hospitals. And 27 percent would even erect a wall along the Mexican border!

The survey also indicated that Anglo-Saxon America still holds to its heritage. When asked whether different nationalities cause more problems than they provide benefits to the country, 59 percent or more said that

Mexicans, Haitians, Iranians, and Cubans create problems. Forty-six percent said Vietnamese cause problems. By comparison Irish, Poles, Chinese, and Koreans had negative polls of only 11, 15, 31, and 33 percent, respectively.

The American attitude toward Asians, on the whole, was positive as compared to the attitude toward Latin Americans. Asians—especially the Chinese and Koreans—were viewed as hard workers who do very well in school, have strong family values, and do not end up on welfare. On the other hand, Latin Americans were viewed as poor students who significantly increase both crime and the taxpayer cost of welfare roles.

Again reflecting the attitude toward immigration as it is affected by economic conditions, Americans polled said that economic hardship was *not* a valid reason to admit aliens. On the other hand, if immigrants had job skills, and/or faced valid political or religious persecution, Americans were more responsive to providing a safe haven. Having American relatives or money to invest were far less important than having skills.

The poll, which was taken when economic woe, foreign terrorists, and immigration dominated the news, indicated that the American view toward immigration as a healthy process still exists, provided immigration is allowed on a *selective* basis.

The opinion polls indicate that most Americans do recognize the positive qualities of these particular nationalities, but they still fear that immigrants who refuse to assimilate into the culture will eventually make America un-American.

In response to the negative polls, some historical facts downplay the seriousness of any current anti-immigration moods by reminding us that a fear of new waves of immigration is nothing new in the U.S.

Woodrow Wilson said that Poles and Italians lacked intelligence. Benjamin Franklin claimed that Germans who refused to speak English threatened to turn Pennsylvania into a colony of aliens. Theodore Roosevelt wanted to require all immigrants to learn English, and return those who did not.

For America, the world's most renowned nation of immigrants who basically believe in the words written at the base of the Statue of Liberty, the problem of immigration has always been steeped in emotion.

Now, as in the past, the immigration issue is confused with the various waves of nationalism. James Madison, in the 1790s, argued that aliens who wanted citizenship must renounce allegiance to former nations. When the Irish arrived in great numbers in the United States in the mid-

1800s, a new wave of "Popism" soon followed: How could a citizen remain loyal to democracy and support the Pope at the same time?

Southern European and Eastern European immigrants followed in the late 1800s to find that old feelings of superiority still existed in their Northern European predecessors. In 1924, a strict quota system against Chinese immigration all but brought migration from China to a halt, not to begin opening up again until 1965.

The fear is that the new immigrants of any nationality not already predominant in the country will refuse to assimilate, and the United States will become not a nation of immigrants who appreciate their new freedoms and opportunities, but a nation of third world communities who have no loyalty or appreciation for their new place of residence.

This same fear is predominant throughout the industrialized world. While small countries throughout the third world fight for regional dominance and are experiencing a resurgence of long-suppressed nationalism, countries of the industrialized world are being influenced by such things as a global economy driven by global corporations and global government organizations. These social issues are also caught in a backlash of conservatism.

In fact, the American drift toward socialist policies has diluted the attitude toward immigrants in general. We remember now with romantic pride the millions of Jews and Irish and Italians and Europeans who came to this country poor and broke. They huddled into segregated slums and worked their way into the society. They were subjected to every kind of misery, from antisocial laws to subservient work duties, but with each generation looking upon their quest as an investment for the next generation.

Immigration advocates claim that a more open immigration policy will continue the positive aspects of bringing this vitality to a renewed America and could very well be the key to keeping America on the cutting edge of the future world economy. Other than the age-old argument that immigrants were either stealing jobs of Americans or driving down the wage levels, European immigrants prior to World War II were not a costly burden.

Today we tend to view the majority of third world immigrants as poor and needy who cannot resist the endless handouts our government is willing to give them. We blame the government for its ridiculous programs, too: How is it that only 18 million immigrants can cost $45 billion a year? If Huddle's figures are correct, we would save billions of dollars if we disbanded all of the programs and simply handed every legal and illegal immigrant in the country a million dollars. At least we could collect taxes on the interest earned over the next few years.

The irony is that immigrants are arriving to find that the land of milk and honey is not what they thought it would be. The Chinese illegals are duped by gangsters in their own country who work with organized Chinese gangsters in the United States. The price per head ranges anywhere from $25,000 to $35,000 to reach U.S. shores, through either sea or air routes, or the overland routes through Canada and Mexico. A 10 percent deposit can get them here, where they discover that they are now indentured servants until the balance is paid off. And the balance might *never* be paid off. Their position forces them to accept a job in—for example—a restaurant or garment factory which hardly pays enough to buy food, let alone find a place to live, or make payments on the loan—which of course keeps rising, due to interest.

Many of the women turn to prostitution. Local Chinese gangs resort to extortion and torture to force payments from the victims, or from their families back home.

Immigrants to America are also suddenly faced with their own challenge to decide what to hold on to from their past, and how to balance their religious views with American laws. In many Mideast countries, the painful female circumcision is customary—and a number of cases requesting asylum to avoid female circumcision have not yet been decided. Opponents fear that a favorable ruling will unleash a new wave of unwanted immigrants. But it remains a question, as the family becomes Westernized, will the women in the family pay homage to the age-old custom, and will the husband who works in a successful business and plays golf at the country club reject this custom, which he knows his peers would find abhorrent?

Will fundamentalist Islamic families forbid intermarriage—and break American law by killing their children for refusing to conform to the old customs?

At the same time, most of the immigrants who came from countries where they were persecuted echo the traditional advantages of coming to America. They are free to practice their religion, and free to get ahead if they can. Their children are not destined to poverty because of some ancient caste system.

Terrorism in the U.S. will challenge Americans' views toward immigration, both directly and indirectly. It is the terrorists' goal that sporadic terror acts, like the World Trade Center bombing, will cause revulsion against those from whatever country or religion the terrorists claim to represent.

Already there are bills in Congress dealing with different ways to manage "the immigration problem." And President Clinton has promised tougher enforcement of *existing* immigration laws. Similarly, Attorney General Janet Reno has promised to strengthen the Immigration and Naturalization Service (INS), in order to deal more efficiently with the immigration crisis—an office which admits to overseeing the facilities to hold only five thousand applicants at any one time but that has been dealing with a backlog of over two hundred thousand.

To the outrage of immigration advocates, most Haitians trying to enter the U.S. in recent times were returned to Haiti, where they were likely to face penalties. Three shiploads of Chinese were also stopped in international waters and redirected toward Mexico, from which they were immediately returned to China.

The economic consequences of terrorism will have a great backlash against immigrants—a pervasive and long-lasting setback—in that specific nationalities could end up being blamed for specific economic hardships. If the Islamic terrorists had killed four hundred thousand residents of New York with a biological weapon, or if they had crippled the U.S. monetary system through economic destruction, the outbreak of violence against that group's countrymen in the U.S., even for a short time, would have added to the chaos of their well-planned attack and would have been totally in keeping with terrorist goals.

CHAPTER 16

Counterterrorism

Having read the previous chapters, one could conclude that no amount of official counterterrorism activities will completely protect citizens from the whims of determined terrorists. This conclusion is valid. The population of the United States lies totally exposed to terrorist acts, protected by a security system that is designed only to respond to such a crisis, not to prevent it.

An important contradiction is that while government agencies have carefully defined terrorism, antiterrorist experts repeatedly claim that labeling criminal acts as terrorism somehow legitimizes the acts themselves—recognizes their political purpose—and, as a result, allows these cowardly lawbreakers to not be treated with the same disgust as are any other indiscriminate killers. But this attitude again flies in the face of the current rash of proposed laws that would label terrorism itself as an illegal act with punishment treated more along the lines of espionage.

The current attitude of government agencies and most antiterrorist experts indicates their general refusal to recognize the potential sophistication and commitment of future terrorists. This refusal to view terrorists as anything other than common thugs leaves our global network of intelligence agencies chasing the grunts of terrorist organizations, allowing the leaders to operate unhampered. This is also the reason why terrorist leaders are more apt to die of old age in freedom than they are to die of bullets, or in prison.

The need to awaken official agencies to a new level of threat is not a new problem. In a June 1985 report, *Terrorism: The Worldwide Threat and Protective Measures for the U.S. Military*, the United States Intelligence and Threat Analysis Center concluded that the primary reason the rash of terrorist attacks against U.S. foreign military facilities throughout the 1970s was so successful was that U.S. troops had not been properly trained to respect their enemy.

Now much the same situation exists on the domestic level. After the World Trade Center explosion the news media quoted various antiterrorist experts on such things as the "lack of a population base to support terrorists," and with "no sea for the fish to swim in." These statements encouraged a lackadaisical attitude toward taking steps to prepare for future terrorist actions.

A New York City detective interviewed in the World Trade Center bombing said that the best way to defend against terrorism is the same as for any other criminal activity—just good old gumshoe detective work. While persistent detective techniques are the basis for any investigation, they run into some interesting barriers when the case involves terrorism on domestic soil. One of these is the Constitution itself. In the land of free speech, it is difficult to find that fine line where the talk of disgruntled civilians leaves the rhetorical and enters the realm of actually plotting illegal action.

Sometimes the investigators who have infiltrated a particular group grow impatient for the arrests, and make the mistake of spurring on the suspects. In both the 1993 plot to blow up targets in New York, and the 1993 white supremacist plot to attack black targets in Los Angeles and elsewhere, information released after the arrests indicated that it was an undercover agent who urged the conspirators to put their theories into action. The defense lawyers in each case could be expected to scream entrapment, and the terrorist plotters to more than likely go free.

Surveillance became yet another touchy investigative issue after government abuses against U.S. citizens were revealed in the 1960s and early 1970s. Targets of the Watergate era, Vietnam protesters, and civil-rights groups all were bugged by the executive branch in the name of national security. The matter was brought to new heights by a paranoid President Richard Nixon and a frustrated administration overwhelmed by the civilian dissidence they saw in the streets. Suddenly, much of America was looked upon as a potential enemy—not an enemy of the people, but an enemy of the administration. In the insular world of Nixon's White House, this was a far greater crime.

The Foreign Intelligence Surveillance Court

In an effort to protect constitutional rights, Congress passed the Foreign Intelligence Surveillance Act in 1978, which stripped the executive branch of the authority to give final approval or disapproval for national-security surveillance. This law allows eavesdropping against foreign governments and their agents within the United States, but specifies that when it is likely that an American citizen will be overheard in the process, any government agency involved must first get approval from the Foreign Intelligence Surveillance Court—a supersecret court which convenes in a bugproof "vault" on the sixth floor of the U.S. Justice Department in Washington, D.C. The walls of the chamber, although insulated, are regularly searched for snooping devices.

The members of the court are seven federal judges selected from around the country by the Chief Justice of the Supreme Court. They serve seven-year staggered terms on the court. On an alternating schedule, one of the court's judges uses the secure vault, called a Special Compartmented Information Facility (SCIF), semimonthly for two days at a time to consider surveillance applications. The attorney general must also approve the applications which must be renewed every ninety days.

Mary C. Lawton, the Justice Department's counsel for intelligence policy, has said that the end of the cold war was expected to produce a drop in the amount of electronic snooping by federal agents within the United States, "but Desert Storm got a lot of people nervous on the terrorism front." Critics of the court have said that the rights of citizens may be violated during government wiretapping in national-security cases, but Lawton counters that the applications are well "scrubbed" to make sure they are done properly. There are reasons to doubt this cleansing process, however. Since the inception of the court, almost seven thousand applications have been submitted for surveillance by the FBI, the National Security Agency, and even the armed forces. *All* applications have been approved, according to a 1993 *St. Louis Post-Dispatch* article.

How is it that if all these applications have been so well scrubbed, nary a one submitted since 1978 has been turned down? The fact that they are apparently *not* being all that well scrubbed no doubt makes them suspect—and, in some future trial, a good defense lawyer could find leeway thereby to have vital evidence declared invalid.

The court came to the forefront in the trial involving the 1989 stabbing death of Tina Isa in St. Louis (see Chapter 3). The FBI had wiretapped the Isas' apartment with a remote, unmanned recorder, and happened to pick up the murder itself on the tape. Since the recorder was automated, the FBI did not realize they had taped the murder until after they read about it in the newspaper. They retrieved the tape and had it translated from

Arabic to English. During the trial, the jury sat mesmerized as they listened to the murder taking place.

This was the first time a tape approved for national-security purposes was allowed as evidence in a state court. When the defense lawyer argued that the tape was illegal, the court ruled that since the wiretap had been approved by the Surveillance Court, it was admissible. Since part of the justification for approval was the idea that the wiretap requests are carefully scrubbed, this may not hold up in the future if it becomes commonly known that all wiretap requests of the Surveillance Court are approved.

A key factor in many cases is that foreign terrorists have become naturalized United States citizens. That is one reason why intelligence agents stress the importance of keeping their information-gathering network in place in foreign countries—in an effort to locate developing trouble before it reaches home.

In many ways, it is no less difficult to deal with terrorists on our own soil than it is to deal with them elsewhere. The first intelligence operation designed to bring a terrorist from a foreign country to stand trial under the laws of the United States was a good example of both extraordinary intelligence work and extraordinary obstacles. It follows.

Operation Goldenrod

In 1986, President Reagan ordered the U.S. raid on Colonel Muammar Qadhafi. And, breaking an age-old code of conduct, one of the primary targets of this raid was the Libyan leader's personal home. The raid was in retaliation for an attack by Libyan agents on a discotheque in Germany. Shortly after the attack on the discotheque, President Reagan had sent a warning to terrorists everywhere: "You can run, but you can't hide."

That fall, the members of the administration's Operation Sub-Group (on terrorism) convened in the White House Situation Room and plotted how to make good on the warning. Of all the suspected terrorists they had under surveillance, twenty-nine-year-old Fawaz Younis was the best target for what would be an historic change in the U.S. counterterrorism policy: Though not a leader of any terrorist group, Younis would be the first foreign terrorist to be captured on foreign soil and returned to the United States for legal process. They named it Operation Goldenrod.

Younis had been part of a small team of terrorists who had stormed a Jordanian airliner. Although they released all of the passengers before blowing up the airliner, they had terrorized the passengers, including three

Americans, and had brutalized the armed guards. It was holding the Americans hostage that would be Younis's big mistake.

American security forces wanted the Younis arrest to demonstrate that American agents could mount an effective attack on terrorists abroad, particularly following the Iran-Contra debacle; and they also wanted to demonstrate to other countries that the United States was capable of doing the job with or without their assistance.

Cooperation from other countries had been a problem. It was the U.S. Navy that intercepted the hijackers of the cruise ship *Achille Lauro*, and it was U.S. intelligence that informed West Germany that the attackers of the discotheque had been Libyan. But in both cases the final outcome was unsatisfactory. The West Germans never charged *anyone* with the discotheque bombing. And, after Egypt allowed the hijackers to attempt to return to Tunis, U.S. jets were sent to force their plane to land at a NATO base in Italy. The Italians then let the notorious leader, Mohammed Abbas, go free! And Abbas has gone on to commit some of the more vicious terror acts of the PLO.

Two important official actions then took place: President Reagan authorized what is known as a "finding," allowing the CIA to identify terrorists who had committed crimes against Americans abroad, and to assist with bringing them to the United States; and, at the same time, Congress passed legislation authorizing the FBI to investigate *all* terrorist acts against Americans, and to go after the perpetrators. The FBI was thus no longer officially restricted to U.S. soil.

Because Operation Goldenrod was the first of its kind, it was "one of the most important counterterrorism operations ever staged by the U.S. government," Noel Koch, who was in charge of the Pentagon's elite counterterrorist units until 1986, told the *U.S. News & World Report* (September 12, 1988). If agents could capture Younis in his own backyard, that would send a message that the President's warning was more than just words.

Pulling it off was a nightmare, however. Over the next three months, the CIA and DEA gathered information about Younis's friends and his daily movements. Almost a year later, however, they still had uncovered no plan of attack. Crucial to their own plan was getting Younis on a boat or a plane that could carry him back to the United States without entering the territory of any other country. Their experience with other countries had already shown that local authorities could very well intervene, and even release the prisoner.

By coincidence, a DEA agent had "signed on" a Lebanese named Jamal Hamdan as an informant. Hamdan had lived in Beirut, from which (after serving a short jail sentence) he had moved to Cyprus. The DEA agent put him on retainer in order to acquire information about the seamy underworld of crooks and conspirators who operate out of Cyprus. But, most importantly now, Hamdan was an old friend of Younis—having served as a driver for him in Beirut, and eventually even shared an apartment with him for six months. In 1985, while Hamdan was in Poland, Younis had come to visit him.

In Hamdan, the U.S. finally had the bait with which to attract Younis. In March 1987, the CIA directed Hamdan to renew his friendship with Younis, and shortly the first of nearly sixty telephone calls took place. The two men talked over old times, the war in Beirut, and Younis's obsession with money. Every conversation came back to money—of which Hamdan had plenty, thanks to the DEA—and now too the CIA payroll.

Hard evidence was still missing, however, because Younis had not revealed much over the telephone. But then Hamdan persuaded Younis to visit his apartment in Larnaca, and U.S. technicians wired the place with listening devices. When Younis started talking, the agents knew they had the evidence they needed to get a conviction—and, as a bonus, Younis told of the leaders who had sent him on the Jordanian airliner mission, as well as of the TWA Flight 847 affair.

After the first visit, Hamdan invited Younis to return to Larnaca twice more, each time throwing around a lot of money in five-day jaunts through nightclubs, restaurants, and bars. And when Younis complained about having no money, Hamdan tossed him four thousand dollars and told him to keep it.

Now it was time to reel in Younis. The investigators instructed Hamdan to tell Younis that he had arranged for him to meet "Joseph," a fictitious drug dealer who could make Younis rich. Younis, who had two young sons—one aged ten months and the other four years—was anxious to start on his new financial prospects.

Then the agents had to face squarely what had been their overriding problem from the start: how to get Younis to the United States without entering the legal territory of any other country. It was a four-thousand-mile trip from the Mediterranean, and there was no way the agents could risk letting another Egypt or Italy free their prisoner on some technicality.

When Younis arrived for his last visit with Hamdan, he was not surprised that he was to meet Joseph on a luxury yacht. On September 12, Hamdan and Younis stayed overnight at the Sheraton hotel in Limassol, then took a speedboat from the hotel marina the next morning. Although it was a ninety-minute ride in the boat, well into international waters, Younis did not become suspicious.

When they pulled up beside an eighty-one-foot yacht, Younis was greeted by Joseph—and was frisked immediately, as Hamdan had warned he would be, by two of Joseph's bodyguards. They then proceeded to the stern, to "talk." No sooner had they reached there than the bodyguards signaled each other and knocked Younis's feet out from under him. He landed on his stomach, breaking both wrists in the fall. He was re-dressed in a green jumpsuit, handcuffed, and bound in leg irons. Within an hour the yacht rendezvoused with the U.S.S. *Butte*, a 564-foot Navy ammunition ship, and four days later the *Butte* met up with the U.S.S. *Saratoga*.

During the cruise to join the *Saratoga*, the agents interviewed Younis—who had given up his right to an attorney—and he signed a confession. (This would later cause a problem when they reached domestic soil.) In the meantime, Philip Voss, commander of the *Saratoga*'s S-3 flight squadron, had been waiting to carry out a top-secret mission. He knew only that he was to fly some sort of "cargo" nonstop from somewhere in the Mediterranean to somewhere in the United States, and could use no assistance in planning the logistics of the trip. In order to make the thirteen-hour flight, he would have to refuel twice in the air.

A CH-46 helicopter ferried Younis from the *Butte* to the *Saratoga*, where Voss was already waiting in the pilot's seat. Minutes later, the S-3 took off with Younis, the agents, and a Navy physician.

The second refueling midway across the Atlantic went off without a hitch, but now Voss faced yet another hurdle. Because of the secrecy of the mission, he was left to find out only while en route that the agencies had not informed the FAA either of their plans or of Voss's arrival. He would have to *sneak* his fighter jet into the United States!

The FAA knew that the second refueling plane, a KC-10 tanker, would be returning to Andrews Air Force Base in Maryland, but they didn't know about the secret flight of the S-3 fighter plane that had been refueled. To avoid radar, the inventive Voss positioned his jet just ten feet below the belly of the tanker—which was fifteen times larger than the jet. (Voss said it was "like flying formation on the Empire State Building.")

It didn't work: The FAA challenged him. But then the federal agents, who had been monitoring the transmissions, broke in and ordered the FAA not to "bug" them, but rather to "Just let them come in." Voss landed in a driving thunderstorm at Andrews a few minutes later—and the plane was immediately surrounded by fifteen FBI sedans. Younis was at last on United States soil.

Within days of Younis's reaching the United States, however, his lawyer challenged the validity of the confession. The judge agreed, and lambasted the FBI for their methods. He ruled that because Younis had been suffering two untreated broken wrists, and was dehydrated, seasick, and confined for four days in a small room (where he was continuously questioned in eighty-five-degree heat), the agents had procured Younis's statement, and the waiver of his rights, against Younis's will. Now the agents would have to go into court against Younis with only the information they had from the tape recordings of his conversations with Hamdan, and a video they had of Younis making a statement shortly before he blew up the Jordanian airliner.

Regardless of its problems, U.S. agents still consider Operation Goldenrod a success, in that it sent a message to terrorists that the United States is willing to go after them wherever they are. And, even though there may have been legal difficulties in the courts for the government agents, one reason for the success inherent in bringing Younis to the States was the agencies' ability to keep the operation *secret*.

Time after time over the years, this secrecy issue has been a major problem in counterterrorism. Internally, both the CIA and FBI have had troubles keeping classified information to themselves—to the point where Count de Marenches of the French secret service says he refused to share details of *any* important plots with the CIA during his tenure as head of the French Intelligence. He knew that anything he shared might very well appear (at the very least) in the newspapers the next day.

An even greater problem for those involved in governmental secrecy has been the American press in general. There is a constant battle between sides taken on the issues of national security and the public's right to know—as well as an ongoing debate aimed at defining the differences between reporting a newsworthy event and sensationalizing the story for the sole purpose of (for example) selling newspapers and magazines.

The News Media

In 1986, when Operation Goldenrod began, William Casey, director of the Central Intelligence Agency, published an editorial in *USA Today*. It was titled "Conquering the Cancer of Terrorism." The article detailed how terrorism in general was spreading, particularly in South America, along with the rise of state-sponsored terrorism. Libya was giving upwards of

$100 million a year to the Sandinista government in Nicaragua, where Marines in a sidewalk cafe had recently been killed.

Casey went on to report how the raid against Libya had awakened many of the European nations to the United States' commitment against terrorism. For example, within a few months of the attack, suspected terrorists had been expelled from France, and a total of nearly fifty Libyan diplomats had been tossed out of Spain, Italy, France, and West Germany. Casey estimated that these joint efforts had helped to avoid as many as one hundred planned attacks against U.S. targets by Libya.

But the main point to Casey's article was not to talk about terrorists, their weapons access, or their state-sponsorships. Casey wanted rather to address what he called "the greatest single impediment to protecting our interests and our citizens from the scourge of international terrorism"— the news media. And he did so as follows:

"Congress, shortly after it established the National Security Agency to gather 'signals intelligence' [through electronic surveillance], enacted a law which prohibits the publication of information about communications intelligence. Nevertheless, there has been widespread violation of that law and much damage has been done. Kay Graham, the publisher of the *Washington Post*, in a very thoughtful and constructive speech, cited the kind of damage which we have sustained. She told how a television network and a columnist had obtained information that we were reading the messages of people arranging the bombing of the U.S. Embassy in Beirut. Shortly after this public disclosure, that traffic stopped. This undermined our efforts to capture the terrorist leaders and eliminated a source of information about future attacks."

The problem with journalists either exposing confidential information or exploiting situations, and thereby playing right into terrorists' hands, has in fact been a continual governmental (and military) complaint. And one well taken—witness the following startling breach of secrecy.

Everyone remembers watching the amphibious landing of U.S. troops in Somalia in the spring of 1993. The soldiers came from ships stationed offshore and landed expertly on the beaches, weapons ready and faces blackened for night work. But as they reached the shore and crawled on their bellies to the nearest cover, hundreds of lights suddenly came on— with television and flash cameras capturing every anxious moment. A crowd of reporters had spent the night in the dark waiting for them to arrive!

A viewer could not help but wonder how easily every one of those reporters might have been wiped out by gunfire from even one frightened or overeager soldier. And, had the situation been only slightly different, how easily all the soldiers could have been killed if the enemy had been at hand.

But the millions of dollars' worth of free publicity given the World Trade Center bombers and the plotters of the other (would-be) New York targets are the most recent cases in point.

Intelligence officers do not argue the public's right to know, but somewhere along the line the press crosses the point where they are no longer reporting events but are sensationalizing them instead. These relatively minor players, and perhaps the stupidest terrorists ever, have now become living martyrs to the Islamic fundamentalist terrorist world.

Michael Yarley, who developed the concept of MACE, the Multinational Alliance for Criminal Emergencies, said in the November 1, 1986, *International Defense Review*:

"Terrorism and terrorists have been given special attention and space by the drama-hungry and frequently irresponsible news media. Governments and their people have become victims because they have allowed this situation to develop, and also because there has been no concerted psychological warfare campaign against these politically motivated criminals. The initiative needs to be regained."

As William Casey pointed out, the release of information (even the release of *faulty* information) can not only hamper investigators' efforts—it can cost lives. He has recalled a 1985 incident in which the following occurred:

"A well-known reporter called the information officer at the Central Intelligence Agency and told him he had a story that we had helped the security service of a friendly nation stage a car bombing of the headquarters of a terrorist organization which had resulted in death or injury to a large number of residents and passersby in the neighborhood. Our officer told the reporter that his information was incorrect and that the CIA had no knowledge of [it] and no involvement, direct or indirect. He was also told that, if he charged U.S. involvement, he might wind up with blood on his hands. The story was run in his newspaper. It got around the world and created a false impression of U.S. involvement in the bombing.

"The House Select Committee on Intelligence investigated the matter and concluded that 'no complicity of direct or indirect involvement can be established with respect to the March 8, 1986 bombing in Beirut.'

"However, this came too late. A month . . . after the misleading story was published, terrorists hijacked a TWA plane and its 153 passengers and took them to Beirut. When the hijackers shot and killed an American sailor, they claimed it to be in retaliation for the bombing in Beirut. . . ."

Casey went on to suggest some solutions.

"The trick is to recognize the potential for damage and to consult on how it might be minimized. We are always ready and available on short notice to help on that.

"I hasten to add, however, that the first line of defense and the most effective way of preventing these types of leaks is to increase discipline within the government. The inability to control sensitive information is destructive of the morale of people who do keep secrets, as well as damaging to our security. . . . We have increased and must intensify our efforts to uncover those who violate this trust. We are studying procedures and possible new laws needed to deal with federal employees who decide on their own to disclose classified information. . . . I would like to emphasize that all of us have a very serious challenge in coping with a rapidly growing terrorist threat."

Casey also wrote about the consideration of new laws to handle the press as well as government employees. With regard to the press at least, a new system of self-imposed limitations may supersede the need for restrictive laws or censorship, either of which could also lead to a loss of constitutional rights. The resolution of all this will be difficult, what with today's media, wherein news programs are among the leading profit centers for television networks, and news personalities (instead of reporters and investigative journalists) are getting the big bucks. The result of this misdirected trend is "event journalism"—a kinder, gentler name than the "yellow journalism" of the early part of this century, when publishing empires were being built—which concentrates on headlines without delving deeper into a story, or following up on one if it is no longer *au courant*.

In the emerging age of guerrilla warfare, or low-intensity warfare, which will be more reliant on secrecy than firepower, along with increased reliance on electronic surveillance, cooperation between the press and the intelligence agencies will become vital. And now the emergence of privately owned satellites and inconclusive arguments over privacy and security issues regarding surveillance of other countries moves the argument to outer space.

Spy Satellites

Many people remember marveling at the pictures taken of Cuba from a U-2 spy plane miles above the earth in October of 1962. As the photographs were shown to various heads of state worldwide in order to elicit a united protest, the leaders were more shocked by the pictures themselves than they were to learn that Russia had managed to place missile installations on the island. From many miles up, here were photos that clearly showed ground images incredibly highly magnified.

When Nikita Khrushchev backed off, the Cuban missile crisis became the political victory needed to solidify John F. Kennedy's administration—even wiping out the terrible 1961 Bay of Pigs fiasco for which Kennedy had rightly taken full responsibility.

Today those photographs would seem quaint. A satellite in orbit can now take pictures of Earth with such a fine resolution that the writing on the sides of missiles can be read.

When the realization of the power of spy satellites first became obvious, some nations considered them an inadmissible means of spying, a subtle violation of airspace—but then gradually came to accept them as a legitimate means of remote sensing for intelligence-gathering purposes—especially when they got their own. That was back in the days when the business of spacecraft was in the hands of the only two superpowers, however. Now, in a popular move to privatize the space industry amid both the economic woes of nations and the realization of multiple economic benefits for private industries having their own satellites in space, the question of intelligence-gathering from outer space suddenly takes on new meaning.

For the first thirty years of the space race, the United States and the USSR enjoyed mutual exclusivity in the satellite business, although sometimes sharing selected information with allies. But often this piecemeal approach resulted in misinformation, and it is no wonder these nations now have a desire to get their hands on the raw data before it has been filtered by another nation's intelligence agency.

The superpower monopoly began to disintegrate in 1986, with the launching of the French–Belgian–Swedish SPOT satellite. Now, high-resolution images and pictures are available commercially—and (at least in theory) virtually anyone who can afford to is able to have a close look at any part of Earth's surface.

The SPOT satellite's successful private launching coincided with the unfortunate space shuttle *Challenger* accident in 1986, which temporarily limited the United States' launching capability and delayed further expansion of its spy satellite program. Concerns for national security took on an interesting contradiction with government contracting private satellite spy services while it concurrently lobbied to pass restrictions against the private owners.

To fill the intelligence gap, the United States contracted to receive satellite pictures from SPOT, which had poorer resolution than those of the intelligence satellites. It was the SPOT satellite that first gave the Western countries a look at the Chernobyl nuclear accident later that same year, showing that SPOT *could* be useful in rather immediate circumstances.

But by then the stage was set for a legal shootout setting the limits of access to high-resolution images of Earth. In July 1987, the U.S. Commerce Department issued a final regulation that gave the Foreign Affairs Department and the Pentagon the right to veto license applications for private ownership of satellites offering sharp images of Earth. This rule allowed the government to invoke a national-security ban in order to block such projects as Mediasat, a concept for a remote-sensing satellite solely owned by the electronic and print news media.

Media critics now argue that the government is restricting the free flow of information, and point out that the rules apply only to U.S. spacecraft, leaving the foreign competition (including state-sponsored terrorists) a wide-open field for space-based news gathering.

This is a fast-growing problem as developments in sensor technology advance. The SPOT satellite, for example, has three spectral bands (measures images based on wavelengths and produces pictures in color or black and white). The symmetric mapper of the Landsat satellite has seven bands, and in the future there will be satellites with perhaps hundreds of bands, opening up remarkable new possibilities for image analysis.

Infrared sensors are of growing importance in the new low-intensity warfare arena, because they show objects which would otherwise remain hidden—underground facilities and other objects identifiable by their heat transmission even through cloud cover.

With these facts in mind, it is easy to understand the devastating loss the CIA felt on August 2, 1993, when a seventeen-story-tall Air Force Titan IV rocket exploded over the Pacific Ocean shortly after liftoff. The missile carried the CIA's next generation of satellites—three secret ocean-surveillance units (each about the size of a medium-length automobile) designed to monitor surface fleets and nuclear submarines. With losses in excess of $1 billion, it was the most expensive economic catastrophe in United States space history. As one senator lamented, the explosion completely wiped out all CIA budget cuts. Understandably, launches of such satellites were once again put on hold until the Air Force could determine what went wrong.

Scheduled launches of military payloads also were delayed—for perhaps a year or more. One was to deliver the first in a series of Milstar communications satellites designed to allow military communications even in the aftermath of a nuclear war. A second one was to carry classified materiel—some experts say the powerful SIGNET satellite designed to intercept radio and telephone signals.

News stories covering the billion-dollar bang provided a good example of the media problem discussed earlier. The August 5, 1993, issue of the *Los Angeles Times* reported: "Government officials still almost never discuss U.S. surveillance satellites openly. So civilian analysts must piece together their picture of the secret military space effort through clues gleaned from budget documents, closed-door congressional testimony, leaks, gossip and technical data. The identity of an individual spacecraft also can be determined through orbital tracking and deep-space photography conducted by a network of foreign observatories and from technical details of the launch itself." (In other words, the press can rely on foreign or private services to determine information the U.S. military holds secret.)

We still have a long way to go to address the objections put forth by Casey back in 1986.

Given the idea that any foreign country with a satellite can sell images and other advanced phenomenon to any other country of their choosing, and keeping in mind that these same countries have demonstrated no restraint in selling weapons and nuclear bomb components to terrorist-sponsoring countries, the growing problem of how to regulate space-based sensing devices moves close to the forefront of negotiations—right up there with nuclear proliferation.

How to Find a Nuclear Needle in a Haystack

Nuclear extortion has been meat for the media but poison for security officials. Movies depict an efficient team of SWAT-type government experts moving swiftly in on their subject and saving the day. But in 1974, when the government received its first major nuclear extortion threat, the response was more typical of that of the clumsy World Trade Center bombers. The mayor of Boston received a note demanding two hundred thousand dollars, lest Boston be blown to smithereens, Fenway Park included. (As this book was being written, a movie with a similar theme was being shot in Boston.) A federal squad was thrown together to find and deactivate the explosive weaponry. The idea was that even small nuclear arms emit a spectrum of recognizable radiation, and so the right sensitive gear can use that as a beacon.

The team flew in by commercial airliner. They were delayed at the airport because their luggage was lost. Then they rented a fleet of vans, but couldn't find any electric drills to help install their radiation detectors. Luckily, the threat was a false alarm—but the result was the realization of the need to form a NEST—a National Emergency Search Team.

New York Times reporter William J. Broad sought out present and former members of NEST to learn how they were affected by both the World Trade Center bombing and the rise in the threat of terrorism on United States soil. As Broad reported, the search team comprises volunteers from nuclear labs and contractors, "and is always ready to zoom off day or night in its own special fleet of vans and aircraft." Chris West, a spokesman for the team, told Broad they have all kinds of detection gear—most of it very unobtrusive, about the size of a small briefcase or large purse. "The people are supposed to blend in," West said. The team also has a warehouse of disguises which allow them to literally keep an eye on things almost anywhere, more or less unnoticed.

Since 1974, the team has had experience with eighty false bomb threats. In the meantime, they have taken radiation readings in many large cities, including New York, Washington, Boston, Los Angeles, San Francisco, Spokane, Reno, and Wilmington. In theory, at least, they will be able to fly over these cities and record marked fluctuations from previous readings—potential indications of nuclear devices.

Mahlon E. Gates, a retired Army general who led the federal bomb-hunting team from 1975 to 1982, published a book titled *Preventing Nuclear Terrorism*, which explained the team's limitations in terms such as these: "If an improvised nuclear device were hidden in a large metropolitan city such as New York or Chicago, with no further information on its location, it would be next to impossible for NEST to find it within a limited period of time."

If, however, an extortionist had indicated that the bomb was located near Times Square, for example, then NEST might have a chance of detecting the emitted waves of energy. Even then, the terrorists would have had to leave the nuclear device uncovered—because neutrons, according to the report, can be stopped by thick concrete, gamma rays by lead, beta particles by aluminum, and alpha particles by skin—and nearly everything else.

This of course means that the NEST team is still searching for ways to improve their capabilities.

Carl N. Henry, the program manager for the team at Los Alamos, told Broad, "There are improvements we can make, and should make, since the emerging era appears to be more dangerous than the recent past for nuclear terrorism."

The best solution to stopping the proliferation of nuclear weaponry is to cut off the supply of plutonium—but that would be next to impossible. Plutonium (like other materials needed for a nuclear device) is identical to materials needed for nonmilitary use. Paul Leventhal, president of the Nuclear Control Institute, told Broad that it is difficult to regulate industrial items that have both civil and military uses, "as the Iraqi nuclear buying binge made clear." The best choke point, Leventhal said, is to stop the making of bomb-grade materials. "They are too hard to control once you bring them into existence."

After looking at all of the advanced tools at the disposal of federal and local agencies, it is difficult not to concur with the gumshoe's comment regarding the World Trade Center investigation: The best weapon is just good old detective work.

Fighting Terrorism on the Streets

The FBI and their Joint Task Force groups cooperating with police throughout the country can make many boasts. They have stopped hundreds of would-be terrorist attacks, and have captured almost one hundred terrorists in the United States since the beginning of the 1980s, when the FBI counted more than 170 terrorist attacks over the previous five-year period, with seventeen people left dead and sixty-three wounded. That was small change compared to European numbers, which were averaging almost five hundred terrorist attacks annually—but it was enough to cause concern that the numbers would become ever larger.

When the FBI's person in charge of antiterrorism was interviewed in 1986, shortly after the arrest of Mutulu Shakur on a West Los Angeles street corner, he was quick to provide a dose of reality: "It only takes one person to plant a bomb," he said. "No democracy can carry out police actions at a level that could totally deny terrorists an opportunity."

Shakur was said to be the ringleader of a terrorist group that robbed a Brink's armored car in Rockland County, New York. They killed two policemen and one guard, and made off with over $1.6 million. The arrest of Shakur five years later was the culmination of unprecedented cooperation among the FBI, the New York City police department, and local authorities in California.

In investigating the Brink's robbery, the task force uncovered an extensive network of underground political extremists who had carried out a series of robberies and jailbreaks over a five-year period in order to finance their operations in five states. The network was an accumulation of at least four radical groups—the Black Liberation Army, the Black

Panthers, the Weather Underground, and the May 19 Communist Committee.

The frightening part of the discovery, the FBI official said, was to realize that this terrorist cooperative was operating actively, "without law enforcement agencies even being aware of it." Up until the Brink's investigation, law enforcement was aware only of the Puerto Rican independence groups, the Jewish self-defense groups, and the neo-Nazi white supremacist groups.

In March 1986 the FBI had managed to cripple the United Freedom Front, a left-wing group that had set off at least eleven bombs at military, business, and diplomatic targets in the New York City area. The group opposed U.S. policy in both Central America and South Africa. One reason why the black militant groups had managed to operate in relative obscurity may be tied to the FBI's own problem with internal racism: An antiblack attitude inherited from the FBI's founder, J. Edgar Hoover, has persisted within the organization. Thus, without black agents in the right strategic or tactical positions, a natural gap was created in the FBI's connections to workings of the criminal world in black communities. But steps are being taken to balance the playing field.

On July 29, 1993, FBI director Louis U. Freeh, then a nominee to become the next director, told a Senate Judiciary Committee that one of his top priorities would be to recruit more men and women of diverse ethnic backgrounds to become bureau agents: "We need diversity because without it the FBI cannot function to its maximum potential. We need diversity because it is simply the right and fair thing to do."

Freeh's predecessor, William S. Sessions, had antagonized the agency's power structure by being sympathetic to black agents. It is thought that Judge Freeh, previously a respected FBI agent himself, will have an easier time transforming the agency because his actions will be seen as practical revisions designed to update the effectiveness of the agency, rather than as acquiescent political gestures.

Intelligence-gathering, both at home and abroad, remains the most important job of the FBI and CIA in fighting terrorism. If a more diverse agent force gives these agencies more diverse channels of information, then the move can be harmful only to the illegal elements of minority dissidents.

From the lessons learned in the 1970s and 1980s, security forces on the federal, state, and local levels recognized the threat of transnational terrorism. This, combined with a general increase in ruthless crime, encouraged the creation of special units trained to handle situations requiring more expertise and firepower than ordinary security forces are prepared to provide. These forces usually were referred to by the name we've cited before, SWAT (Special Weapons and Tactics) teams—but they also took such other monikers as Emergency Response Teams, Tactical Response Teams, and Crisis Intervention Units—designations indicating their special training in tactics and the proper use of sophisticated hardware and weaponry. In many cases, the growing reputation alone of these SWAT teams, spurred on by both actual field battle and romanticized television and movie accounts, is quite enough to defuse dangerous situations.

One of the biggest differences between the training of SWAT teams and that of regular military units, including the Marines, is that the SWAT teams assume they will be fighting an enemy holed up in an area surrounded by innocent American civilians. This is a marked difference from the battle settings that regular Marine, Army, Navy, and Air Force personnel are traditionally trained to anticipate.

A terrorism-related problem recognized by the government late in the 1980s was that the typical field-readied Marine (for example) was prepared, at least in a typical combat situation, to engage an enemy and destroy him without worrying about the surrounding civilian population. If a group of terrorists were there, holed up in a building, destroying the building would therefore be a viable Marine option. But this option would not hold if terrorists were hiding in—for instance—a high-rise in Manhattan.

Starting in 1987, the Marines increased their training for urban-warfare techniques and, importantly, turned to civilian law-enforcement agencies for advice. In addition to utilizing FBI and SWAT input, they used big-city police departments to help make their Corps more streetwise, so as to survive more easily in complex urban environments to which they might be called.

As delved further in Chapter 18, the differences in the ways we train and order our soldiers to fight battles at home and to participate in low-intensity warfare on foreign soil appear to be formulating yet another problem for our country's military: For one reason or another, we are helping to *create* terrorists—or at least unfriendly civilians—when United States (or United Nations, or NATO) forces are seen to be occupying troops instead of the friendly saviors they were intended to be.

CHAPTER 17

A National Energy Security Policy to Combat Terrorism, Save Money, and Reduce Dependence on Foreign Countries

If a terrorist wants to get the most bang for the buck, then the nation's energy system is the obvious target. As we have already seen to some extent, our gas, oil, nuclear, and electrical delivery systems are so complex and so interdependent on each other that even a slight vulnerability could give a single terrorist the opportunity and power to crash the entire national system.

The possible cost in lives is astounding. And the possible cost in dollars is beyond imagining. But the realization of this vulnerability in our national security is nothing new to government officials. Only now is the knowledge that terrorism is becoming an increasingly sophisticated weapon being added to the risk equation.

Our energy systems are not designed to be protected against the improbable. Until recently, the threat of a serious sabotage attempt was considered improbable. And the improbable also includes natural disasters or technical failures, either of which could occur at levels of severity that exceed what experts have concluded are likely.

The nation's energy system was designed with a Utopian attitude that everything will always work the way it is supposed to according to blueprint, including acts of Mother Nature as programmed by a benevolent Creator. In truth, Murphy's First Law ("If anything can go wrong, it will") has never been more evident than in our complicated gas, oil, nuclear, and electrical distribution systems.

We do not find this "Law" surprising—after all, most of our personal and business experiences, to one or another degree, are built on trial and error. But never before have we been subjected to a system wherein even a slight error could prove so devastating. And the results of not expecting the unexpected are made evident in our own lives almost daily when the unexpected not only occurs but also turns out to have been more or less predictable.

In 1993, rainfall in the midlands of America broke century-old records, and hundreds of millions of dollars that taxpayers had paid over the years to build dams, dikes, and channels went down the sink. Earthen dikes designed to withstand high water levels for only a few days became saturated and turned to liquid mud flows. All along the Mississippi and Missouri rivers, dams and dikes built high enough to withstand normal floodwater levels proved useless when the flooding exceeded "normal." The few dikes built high enough simply managed to send the damage elsewhere, backing floodwaters up smaller rivers and tributaries and destroying towns and farms which would not have been damaged at all if dikes downstream hadn't been built. Even entire cities were inundated—and some, weeks later, still had sewers backed up in basements, and residents without water suitable for drinking, bathing, cooking, or laundry.

The 1993 summer floods have been recorded as the most economically costly natural disaster in United States' history, their primary cause our failure to foresee that the rivers might well behave exactly as they have in the past, and to prepare accordingly for battling the elements. From a sociopolitical point of view, another battle began even before the floodwaters subsided: Lobbyist groups argued that anyone foolish enough to build a home, a business, or an entire city on a floodplain did not deserve government aid, and any farmer whose livelihood depends on the weather should have been forward-thinking enough to anticipate a year of total loss. In a climate where government spending cuts were the major focus, these arguments did not go unheard.

Not mentioned in most of these arguments were the number of nuclear plants, built next to the rivers on the floodplains, which came dangerously close to being affected by the flood-stage waters. Even now our experts—civil engineers and civic planners—are assuming that next year's flooding will probably be "normal."

As most people watched the massive flooding on television, it must have seemed ridiculous to them that anyone could ever have thought that a body of water so potentially destructive as the Mississippi would forever, even at floodtide levels, be kept from swamping everything in sight (and well beyond) by shallow, rigid channels designed only for her worst *past* experiences with overampleness. After all, it was the river that determined the floodplain a millennia ago—and all of those little dikes and bridges and buildings fell like Tinker Toys in that great old river's natural flow to its natural boundaries.

The problem with the waterway security system was that it *was* rigid. In other words, if the river ever exceeded the limits that had been (as it were) *designed* for it, all was lost. There was *no* system designed to let the river stretch without destroying billions of dollars of property and disrupting hundreds of thousands of lives!

The same rigidity is true of our energy system—and this rigidity represents the single greatest threat to our national defense, the single greatest target for smart terrorists. Perhaps even for dumb ones.

Particularly with our complex energy system, and its interconnected reliability on our equally complex communications and computer systems, it is simply beyond human capability to anticipate all of the possible consequences of a mistake, a failed piece of equipment, an operator error, or an act of sabotage. When expert engineers design a complex energy plant or nuclear facility, they anticipate many events—but a standard designed to prepare for normal, probable dangers forces them to ignore as insignificant the many thousands of weak spots that might cause problems therein if a danger exceeds the probable level. However, because one fault in a system sets off a cascading effect on every other potentially faulty part of the entire system or facility, these small, insignificant vulnerabilities can collectively add up to calamity.

For this same reason, most problems or failures in the space program or in nuclear facilities typically begin with a relatively simple problem—a brittle or frozen "O" ring, for example—which kicks off a course of destruction causing death and the loss of billions of dollars. In *any* mechanical system a physical weakness will reveal itself sooner or later. There is no question about that. The real question is: Once a weakness reveals itself, how much damage is the system designed to allow it to do?

Today, our energy system is designed very much like the dikes along the Mississippi River—either to work as planned or to collapse, with no middle ground or flexibility. This is what makes our energy system such a juicy target for terrorists. On the other hand, if we design a system that reduces the risk of massive failure caused by a single incident or series of incidents, then we reduce the seduction to terrorists, because now the target gives them less bang for their buck.

Decentralization of the Energy System

Computer experts now agree that a system made up of smaller parts, interrelated but able to operate separately, is a much better and safer system than that of the central mainframes that dominated the growth periods of the 1960s, 1970s, and early 1980s. The reason is simple: A problem with one component does not crash the entire system. Recognizing that failure is more severe in huge, centralized systems, we now continue to build an *energy* system that is more and more centralized.

If you compare the evolution of the animal kingdom and that of engineering, you find that the two are often at odds. In biology, the species that still evolve—change as they react to a changing world—are alive because of their flexibility, while those that were inflexible—hardened to maintain their original design—disappeared. Unfortunately, our technological process has followed the line of hardening, and that has put our system in danger of collapse.

This all leads to a few simple principles:

•Failures are less severe in small systems than they are in large systems.
•The more centralized the system, the more vulnerable it is to sabotage at more points.
•Alternative sources provide diversity, and diversity protects the entire system from collapsing.
•Complex systems reduce reliability with each higher level of complexity.

With regard to our energy system, all of these principles can be applied in the negative because our reliance on oil, gas, and nuclear energy puts us immediately into a reliance on massive, centralized systems—which are in turn dependent on nonrenewable sources that create harmful and dangerous waste.

And other negative factors can be applied to centralized systems: They are beyond the control of the individual user, they are beyond the understanding of the user, and the user is totally dependent on them.

Of particular interest to the terrorist is the fact that the centralized systems have little storage or buffer capability in the event of sabotage, and also require lengthy distribution routes for the delivery of gas or oil, thus offering any number of thousands of points at which to be sabotaged. In other words, our present energy system is a perfect recipe for disaster.

The key ingredient for changing this recipe is the increased use of dispersed, diverse, local, and redundant sources. An increase in the use of solar, small hydro, and wind energy, for example, would almost immediately wipe out all of the negatives of our energy system and—ironically—save the country trillions of the dollars now being spent in the wrong areas.

This does not mean we should reexamine the government tests which were conducted in building gigantic solar and wind generators. Those massive projects were ill-conceived, a byproduct of an attitude that even wind and solar projects *had to* fit the mold of massive centralization. Rather, the key to success, in addition to efficiency, is the rapid and ongoing placement of tens of thousands of small wind and solar energy units across the country.

Some politicians argue that a decentralized energy system would lead to a decentralized society—an immediate threat to the centralized government in Washington, D.C. This does not at all have to be the case, but it is important to note that many sociologists believe that a decentralized government *is* in fact the key to progress in the twenty-first century—that the diverse masses of people who now make up our country can no longer be treated as one mass, all of whom need the same thing at the same time.

Smaller technologies conserve energy even while giving the consumer a range of choice. They can reverse the long-standing trend of depending on centralized plants which can use more energy than the consumers they serve. *Big* should not necessarily have to be equated with *power* in the future. If we concentrate on the goal of delivering energy, and not just on having a gigantic capacity to do so, then diversified energy sources are the obvious answer.

Today's energy systems—whether oil, gas, or nuclear—consume in excess of 80 percent of the energy of their nonrenewable resources in order to deliver the remaining 20 percent (or less). Small, simple, easily accessible technologies can contribute much more to the energy system in a shorter time than can any of the conventional, large-scale systems. Ironically, not only could the use of wind, solar, ethanol, and small hydroelectric generators provide the nation with unlimited energy, but also they could do so less expensively, using renewable energies, without creating waste or pollution.

Furthermore, alternative technologies would all but eliminate the energy system as a terrorist target, and guarantee that the country would never again be held hostage by an oil embargo, or be forced to go to war over the threat of a hostile country taking over large oil reserves. In this scenario, energy conservation would not mean going without, but rather getting more—less expensively.

A diversified system would limit the immediate effects of sabotage, in that the failure of a part of the system would both be isolated and occur more slowly. Rather than one act shutting a system down, it would merely shave peak-load delivery. Designing a system around our own inexhaustible energy resources would indeed eliminate the fear that our lifestyle could be changed suddenly by a foreign country or terrorists.

A Huge Step Backward for the Nuclear Industry

One of the biggest roadblocks to stopping both the proliferation of nuclear war materials and the further development of nuclear technology is that ordinarily there is a fine line between the materials needed for peaceful use and those needed for weapons. But sometimes the line isn't there at all, because the materials are identical.

The International Atomic Energy Association is both the police force for over nine hundred nuclear facilities around the world, and the biggest promoter of nuclear usage. Its only problem is that it is a better promoter than it is a policeman, helping countries "go nuclear" while watching Iraq and North Korea build nuclear weaponry capabilities.

If the third world countries realized that nuclear is not the answer to their energy needs, just as it is not the answer to the United States' energy needs, the incidents of proliferation would be reduced considerably. The need for the spread of nuclear expertise would be reduced, and the difference between nuclear energy needs and nuclear weapon needs would be more discernable.

But proliferation of nuclear technology and materials is just one of the problems that would be solved by a new, forward-looking energy plan. Another is the proliferation of nuclear waste, and what to do with it. Waste sites present dangers in themselves, and are terrorist targets as well.

On August 14, 1993, the Hanford Nuclear Reservation outside Richland, Washington, closed down after a worker became contaminated when he lowered a rock on a rope into one of the nuclear waste storage tanks. Hanford is the nation's largest nuclear waste site, with 177 underground tanks containing 61 million gallons of radioactive waste from 40 years of plutonium production for nuclear weapons. Many of the tanks have leaked, and others, according to a *Wall Street Journal* report, are in danger of explosion.

Just one week later the nuclear industry, with 110 plants producing electricity across the country (and many of these running out of storage space while still others are already preparing to shut down due to age), announced that it is looking for a central (albeit temporary) place to store radioactive wastes. Some utilities are faced with a cost in excess of $21 million a year *per plant* to maintain storage pools for waste at the reactors! (An interesting side note here is that Native American tribes are discussing the idea of leasing an area of just a few acres to the industry, at a cost of $50 million a year, for at least 20 years.)

Actually, a whopping $3.8 billion is being held in reserve for both the building of a permanent storage facility, and a temporary one in the meantime. Until they find a place to store the materials, even plants that have closed must be staffed and operated to control the waste—sometimes (again) at a cost of over $20 million a year.

Keeping in mind that all of these utilities which are dumping money into these plants are making a lot of money, it gives one an idea of just how cheap one's utility bill might otherwise be, if the savings were passed back to consumers.

All of this points to the ridiculous ideas that nuclear energy can ever be cost-effective, and that it can survive even a year without government subsidies of billions of dollars. Too, efforts to transport nuclear energy technology to third world countries is patently close to immoral—even without nuclear weapons consideration.

Revising our national energy system would lead us into the twenty-first century without a nineteenth-century attitude, and it would begin to eliminate our most vulnerable and devastating terrorist targets.

CHAPTER 18

Foreign Policy: Should the United States and the West Fight Terrorism With Terrorism?

In August of 1993 I was at a marina in New Hampshire, about three miles upriver from the historic seaport of Portsmouth. Along with spending a day with good friends on their boat, I wanted to see firsthand the accessibility of terrorists to the nearby nuclear-submarine pens. We would pass the subs on our way both to and from the ocean. There were two of them in the shipyard, moored just off the river a few feet and looking very much like a couple of humpback whales trying to crawl onto a beach. The only visible security was a sign warning us that we were near a restricted area: KEEP OUT.

When we returned to the marina, a neighbor in the next slip was struggling to inflate a rubber dinghy and to install the awkward, collapsible wood floor panel. I offered my assistance, which he didn't need, and we struck up a conversation.

He was an ex-CIA agent who had retired during the Carter administration "when Carter decided he had to clean up the CIA."

"We were trained to hate our enemy," he recalled, "and now Carter wanted us to love our enemy. I got out, along with a lot of other guys. Luckily they offered early retirement to anyone who didn't feel he could go along with the transformation, and it was that same ruling which allowed us to tell people what we used to do for a living."

He discussed briefly how the new attitude promoted by Carter had shackled agents by restricting their mobility, tactics, and options during clandestine missions in the field. He was glad he was not involved with the new directives, which he felt instructed agents not to employ the same low tactics used by the enemy.

According to the Count de Marenches, who dealt with terrorists during his tenure as chief of the French secret service, a major change required in order to fight terrorism is a revised foreign policy which encourages the use of unauthorized actions, as well as revision of congressional restrictions. Marenches suggests that both the President and the heads of the CIA and FBI be allowed more freedom to move in secret. He also suggests that the definition of proper covert conduct be revised— to exclude such restrictions as assassination of foreign leaders. This broadening of the powers of the executive branch of the government would fly in the face of laws passed by Congress throughout the 1970s and the 1980s.

The recommendations of Marenches would give the green light to such unconstitutional actions as Iran-Contra and would mark a return to a foreign policy that has not worked for at least fifteen years. Marenches's suggestion not only promotes a return to a cold war mentality, but a resurgence of the worst aspects of that cold war thinking—the kind of thinking that encourages the proliferation of still more terrorist cells.

But What Is Terrorism?

Throughout the summer of 1993, United Nations troops and American special forces sought to arrest the Somalia warlord Mohammed Farah Addid. It is against Western rules of fair play to hire someone to assassinate a warlord, so the alternative was to send troops after him in the 1990s' version of low-intensity warfare. United Nations peacekeeping troops searched cities for arms and weapons storage centers located in the middle of business and residential districts, and U.S. troops searched for the leader's secret headquarters in the same areas. In order to avoid military losses they destroyed buildings, using bombs or rockets, knowing there would be civilian casualties.

Would it not have been more humane, more moral, simply to target the individual rather than the neighborhoods?

Earlier (December 1989–January 1990) we faced a somewhat similar dilemma when it suddenly became imperative to arrest or eliminate Manuel Noriega in Panama. Using a loophole in the War Powers Resolution, President Bush ordered twelve thousand troops sent in to get Noriega. If they were in and out in less than sixty days, the action was legal. They were out before the end of January. Human-rights group estimates of civilian casualties in the Panama action vary from hundreds injured or killed, to thousands. Official U.S. figures never reached such numbers, and came in even lower than originally estimated.

Would it not have been better to assassinate Noriega in order to avoid the civilian losses as well as the millions of dollars spent finally to capture him? If an individual has been targeted for military action, with no declaration of war, does not calling this a police action rather than terrorism simply present a blatant form of hypocrisy?

This question was even more obvious when President Reagan ordered an attack on Libya in retaliation for a terrorist bombing of a German discotheque frequented by American soldiers. From a third world point of view, was not this action in Libya merely an act of terrorism? Does not the use of advanced Western weaponry somehow escalate terrorism to an acceptable form of military action? If the definition of terrorism is the deliberate killing of civilians for political purposes, our missiles and troops directed into civilian population centers may well be definable as terroristic.

Compare a similar situation if it occurred on the home front: If a mafia leader was known to be holed up in an office building in New York, the local police and FBI probably would not bomb the area or expend warehousefuls of ammunition in an attempt to get him out of it.

When the action is taking place in what we consider a hostile country, however, our attitudes and methods change. Human lives are suddenly part of a military equation whereby the end justifies the means, just as Company Commander Myron Harrington reported in Vietnam: "In order to save the village, we had to destroy it." This mentality still operates in our present definition of low-intensity warfare on foreign soil. Without arguing the pros and cons of specific military actions, the greater question concerns the ability of the Western world to recognize the difference between military actions and political actions.

The tendency to use our technical superiority to warn or punish an enemy suffers from a number of fallacies, as is demonstrated by two fairly recent events. In Somalia, within two weeks of troops landing to feed the starving and restore order, United Nations teams were no longer viewed as peacekeepers—they had become yet another of the many warring tribes in the country. Our presence actually strengthened local support of the local warlords. As for the U.S. attack on Libya, investigators of the crash are now satisfied that PanAm Flight 103 was exploded over Lockerbie in retaliation for the attack on Qadhafi's home.

When Egos Fly

Thanks to President Clinton and (at least) his two immediate predecessors, we have seen costly actions that did little more than salve individual egos or prop up personal political stature. A recent case was Clinton's order to attack Baghdad in retaliation for the assassination attempt on ex–President Bush.

Having won the Gulf War but losing his reelection campaign, George Bush had traveled to Kuwait to accept an award from the newly established dictator, knowing full well that this trip to the heart of the Mideast was insensitive to the leaders of every Arab country, and a foolhardy exposure to any assassination attempt. Weeks after the would-be assassins were captured, President Clinton ordered a missile attack on the intelligence headquarters in Baghdad. The missiles did little military damage, but managed to kill a number of civilians.

Sometime in the future another PanAm 103 or similar catastrophe may occur, being Iraq's retaliation for the missiles into Baghdad. At the very least, that attack managed to transfer the Bush-Hussein personal animosities over to Clinton, along with the personal animosities of future terrorists whose loved ones may have died in the attack. It is here where terrorism again brings these worldly actions to a personal level, creating new generations of potential enemies.

Many of the politico-military actions around the world today—on all sides of all issues—are remnants of the cold war mentality, and it will be difficult to expel that attitude until all of the politicians and government leaders who grew up during the cold war have gone into retirement. It is this same mentality which drives our definitions of terrorism and power alike.

Weak Foreign-Policy Laws

The War Powers Resolution of 1973 was passed, despite President Nixon's veto. It was designed to prevent a President from getting the country into another "undeclared war" like the one in Vietnam. This effort was reinforced in 1976 with the amendment of the Arms Export Control Act, designed to limit the President's ability to approve arms shipments to friendly countries. In 1980, limitations were also placed on the President's theretofore unlimited freedom to use the intelligence agencies abroad, which until then were able to operate in total secrecy.

As more and more information is revealed about the secret operations of our government over the years, Americans have learned that our foreign policy has often done a poor job of representing the image we would like to project to the rest of the world. These revelations add to our national distrust of government, and as we become even more distrustful of politicians, the idea of strict limitations of power becomes more and more desirable.

The cold war mentality of the late 1940s and 1950s resulted in such initiatives as the National Security Act in 1947, which allowed the creation of the CIA and the National Security Council—both initially designed to allow the executive branch unlimited power to fight a cold war by any means necessary, short of a declaration of war itself.

This virtual carte blanche is now recognized as outmoded, but the fear of terrorism could allow a similar era of secret government to sweep in, as Marenches is actually recommending. Even with our suspicions that presidents will abuse their powers, however, Congress has been lax in enforcing its powers, allowing substantial abuses to go unpunished.

The divisiveness of Congress does not allow it to readily or convincingly enforce its own guidelines or make decisions. In case after case, congressional gridlock has forced presidents to take action on their own. Presidents Reagan, Bush, and Clinton all have bypassed Congress in order to proceed with limited warfare tactics—Reagan in Libya, Bush in Panama, and Clinton in Iraq. In the Reagan-Bush administration, secrecy was the code of the day when bypassing Congress and the opinions of the American people. In all three cases, the presidents believed that if they handed the Americans a quick success, public opinion would force Congress to accept the victory. And for the most part they were right.

Reagan and Bush funneled millions of dollars to Saddam Hussein in order to support Iraq's war with Iran, sidestepping all legislation by using members of the security staff, who then subcontracted the tasks out to shady arms dealers and money-launderers. Many of the deals were disguised as legitimate transactions made through the Department of Agriculture. Concurrently, Reagan and Bush took similar actions to support the Iran-Contra debacle.

One of the biggest legal loopholes is the one that allows presidents to send troops to war abroad for fewer than sixty days—a loophole which resulted in Grenada, Panama, and the increasing involvement of the Navy in Kuwait. In all cases, there is a possibility that a gridlocked Congress all but invites the executive branch to ignore some of the more sacred parts of the Constitution. If it is perceived that decisions are not being made by consensus, U.S. foreign policy can then be perceived as essentially without law, resulting in both its unreliability and a distrust of American promises.

Such distrust leads to any legitimate uneasiness that non-Western countries have of an American superpower stumbling around their territory. It leads to countries concluding that they must defend themselves by any means necessary. The authority of a foreign superpower loses credibility if it is perceived as being manipulated by the whims of personalities.

This leaves only confusion. And confusion is not a good weapon against terrorism or all the foreign and domestic issues which result in terrorism or civil dissidence.

Americans have become accustomed to the idea that government is not a source from which to expect either honesty or justice, and Oliver North's announcement in 1993 as a senatorial candidate may be the final, ironic act of hypocrisy in the Iran-Contra scandal, which could be accented only by his victory in the campaign.

War Is the Result of Failed Diplomacy

Politicians are elected to serve as diplomats. Military leaders are paid to defend and prepare for action. When the diplomats fail, we send in the military. So why do the politicians and diplomats wind up taking the bows for a military victory? Perhaps in the new century we will finally realize that it is not contradictory to cheer our military to victory, and then fire the diplomats and politicians who have allowed an undeclared war to happen.

Whether there is a Democrat or a Republican sitting in the White House, the presidential powers invite deceit and corruption. While it may be true that the President needs the ability to take quick action when necessary, the method of giving this ability should not allow the breakdown of the basic principles of a democracy and a consensus of the people, as occurred with Iran-Contra.

In basic, rudimentary, and painful experience, acts of terrorism bring Americans the experience with which other countries are all too familiar. Terrorist acts are far different than the penalties of trade sanctions, embargoes, or economic bailouts, which are all watered down or obscured by the national debt or the ebb and flow of the economy. There is nothing that insulates the explosion of a bomb, nothing that asks a victim more clearly: How do you like our foreign policy now?

The problem with Marenches's idea of fighting terrorism with terrorism is that governments would have to imply that they have somehow divined right from wrong, friend from foe. But we have learned that these distinctions, too, change rapidly as the course of the world changes.

Had Yasser Arafat been assassinated a couple of years ago, the Israeli-PLO peace accord might never have taken place. It remains to be seen what comes of it. Some things are certain: more terrorism in the near future, friction between Arab nations, attempts to pull the United States into the middle of the fray, either a pulling together or a slow disintegration of Islamic fundamentalist extremists.

The same holds true of Nelson Mandela. He was branded a terrorist and held in prison for years, but now he is one of the hopes for a unified South Africa with black majority rule. This too is a matter of destiny yet to be played out, but both sides of the issue agree that if Mandela had been killed or executed a few years ago, the violence which erupts sporadically in South Africa today might be continuous instead.

It is one thing to change the course of history, but it is another to attempt to do so in secret. One can only wonder what would have happened if the CIA's plot to assassinate Fidel Castro had succeeded, or if numerous secret attempts to topple governments had succeeded or failed—but one does not have to wonder whether these history-changing moments have a right to be carried out in criminal secrecy. That is the primary fallacy of the suggestion that our government needs to give our FBI and CIA greater freedom to carry out actions in secret and to fight terrorism with terrorism.

CHAPTER 19

When Cultures Clash

S ince we have not spent a great deal of time publicly examining what would happen after the end of the cold war, many people feel that the world is falling into chaos—as evidenced by terrorist acts, declining economic systems, a surge of Islamic fundamentalism, a resurgence of mass-genocide policies, and a rise in racism and anti-Semitism. The list goes on and on. This sense of disorder runs deep in national and individual psyches, leaving many people with a strong feeling of being left in a state of limbo in an undefined post–cold war climate.

At the same time, without much direction or definition from our politicians, our academics, or our media, we have a positive sense that all of the eruptions happening around the world in a seemingly helter-skelter manner contain a clue to what our world will be like over the next hundred years. How we deal with current situations may very well determine whether or not the new world will be a peaceful or warlike community. It is a natural process to seek order—any kind of order; a defining moment which outlines the problems we must deal with or absorb.

Although many terrorist acts have happened in the United States with far greater consequences to human life than the World Trade Center bombing, because *that* bomb was planted by Islamic fundamentalists it is *the* one that has captured our attention. The World Trade Center bomb was more than our wake-up call to the foreign terrorist threat. It was our wake-up call to a changing world bringing a new clash of civilizations.

Samuel P. Huntington, Eaton professor of the Science of Government and director of the John M. Olin Institute for Strategic Studies at Harvard University, has predicted the next pattern of conflict in a 1993 report, *The Changing Security Environment and American National Interests.*

211

According to Huntington until the Iron Curtain was rent, for all political purposes the world was divided between two Western superpowers with the rest of the countries governed by the needs and demands of these powers—which carried with them the ancillary threat of nuclear annihilation. It was the superpowers, and they alone, that determined the world's battle lines.

Now the old battle lines have been obliterated in the disintegration of the Soviet Union—and the new ones are being redrawn as much more meaningful borderlines. These new parameters are not defined by capitalism versus communism, but instead by the much deeper motivations of religion and culture.

In theory, this should be good news, because every true religion of the world is rooted in the teachings of peace and fellowship. This was the message at the Parliament of the World's Religions, which met in Chicago for nine days in August 1993. (It was the first time the Parliament had convened since its inaugural meeting in 1893 at the Chicago World's Fair!) Most "formal" religions were represented—even those professing no belief in any kind of god.

Disruptions during the meeting revealed that, even among this nonsecular group of representatives, the mix of religion and politics was a volatile combination. And even though each religion was rooted in peace, the varying degrees of fundamentalist and extremist interpretations could be applied in very brittle patterns. Evangelical and Christian fundamentalist groups did not show up at all, though liberal Protestant groups did, but only quietly observed the proceedings. Eastern Orthodox Christians walked out midway through the conference in protest of the presence of neopagans and goddess worshipers, as did four Jewish groups when Louis H. Farrakhan of the Nation of Islam took the speaker's platform.

The goal of the gathering had been to create a Declaration of Global Ethics—but the "short" five-thousand-word document they crafted was indicative of the problems the world faces when religion and politics mix. To placate the diverse assembly, the word "God" (even in its uncapitalized form) was omitted; and, rather than address specific issues, it promoted general goals of nonviolence; environmental responsibility; economic justice; honesty in politics, culture, and the media; and the end of sexual discrimination.

A keynote speaker on the final day, the Dalai Lama, summed up the meeting in the same way he would sum up the world situation: "We will see."

But what we are already seeing is not as obscure as it might seem at first glance. As we read world headlines, we are witnessing the globe being divided into eight major civilizations, according to Huntington: Western,

Confucian, Japanese, Islamic, Hindu, Slavic-Orthodox, Latin American, and African.

The differences among these civilizations are very real and very basic. They have to do with history, language, culture, tradition, and religion. They are the product of centuries of development, and are not soon to disappear.

These differences pose a far greater need for understanding than do the conflicts that existed between the two superpowers. We have long felt that we had a basic understanding of the Soviet Union (which, however, most Americans have considered to be *only* Russian) because tens of thousands of its people had already immigrated to the United States prior to the cold war. Too, we felt that the people they left behind were also essentially like us, only stuck in a system that did not reward individual achievement.

Most Americans cannot make these same claims of the Islamic, Confucian, Hindu, or other groups. Here many of us cross more than ideologies—we cross civilizations.

This difference in perceptions based on cultural background was made profoundly clear during World War II. Although we were convinced that the German and Italian soldiers were our hated enemies and their unwitting dupes, respectively, we were largely able to separate all that from their fellow citizens. The civilians were people who shared our ancestry and were not (especially in the case of the Italians) to any great extent accountable for the actions of their dictatorial governments.

When it came to Japan, however, we went to war against a foreign culture epitomized by such alien things as samurai warlords and kamikaze suicide missions. It would have been unthinkable to drop the atom bomb on Germany or Italy—but when it came to Japan, it was not only thinkable, but was deemed the practical thing to do because of the millions of U.S. lives it saved due to our demand for unconditional surrender.

Throughout history it has been the *cultural differences*—not the conflicts between economic ideologies—that have caused the most violent and most prolonged conflicts. And, with the widespread current trend whereby these differences are being promoted even as interaction among civilizations is increasing in this shrinking world, the differences are becoming grossly intensified and magnified.

With the confusion of governments and the struggle of economic policies in almost every country, many traditional governments have lost their power to hold their nations together. This includes dictatorial, socialist, and democratic governments alike. Religion has attempted to move in to provide the unifying force in many countries.

In Iran, the goal is to rule the nation through Islamic fundamentalist beliefs, and with a demonstrated anti-Western doctrine. The West views this movement as fanatical and alarming. But it is meaningful that the leaders of this movement are not the poor masses rallying behind a radical rabble-rouser—the leaders are the young, educated, middle-class professionals and businessmen.

This rise of religious fundamentalism to overshadow and direct political authority not only transforms the workings of a nation, it transcends national boundaries and unites the worldwide diaspora of their respective believers, particularly the extremist element. Signs of this are evident throughout the more moderate Arab lands, where "unenlightened" intellectuals, politicians, writers, and media personalities have been brutally assassinated. Anyone who believes in secularism or simply accommodates secularism is targeted as a nonbeliever, an enemy of the greater cause, who must be killed.

If future threats from Islamic fundamentalists caused the Christian West to respond with a conservative or even a Christian fundamentalist protection, it is frightening to ponder the results of a confrontation. If *cultural* religious morality is the bottom line, what solution remains other than the annihilation of the enemy? And yet it is not impossible to imagine this.

In President George Bush's reelection campaign, the Republican Party suspected that it was being taken over (or at least manipulated) by a strong coalition of Christian conservatives, with evangelical preachers lining up behind Jerry Falwell to put a Christian conservative policy in the White House. But Americans have long believed in the separation of church and state; we feel it is one of the basic constitutional principles meant to assure freedom of democracy. And the religious aspects of George Bush's campaign, mixed with the issues of abortion and family values, may well have contributed to his downfall, in addition to his lethargic participation.

Americans who believe in strong family values also believe that the subject of family values should not become another government program. But *any* government drifting toward becoming a social-welfare state tends to intrude on what was once considered personal or religious territory. It becomes involved in such issues as abortion and euthanasia—and, as proponents of both sides of the issues run to government to legislate a solution, both sides give over to government the power to make such life-and-death decisions.

This initiates a dangerous progression, to the point where it is not impossible to imagine the predictions of science-fiction writers coming true, whereby government institutes such things as mandatory death at age sixty-five in order to settle economic or population problems. An extreme example, to be sure, but not as extreme today as it was only a few years ago.

Currently the problem for the West is that it is stuck in a quandary: to police the world while at the peak of its own power while non-Western nations are undergoing a "return to the roots" movement which rejects much of what the West stands for.

When talking about the future of terrorist-sponsoring countries, William Colby, the ex-CIA director, had a message of hope that he tied to economic progress in an interview for this book. He pointed out that if you look at the countries that have isolated themselves from the West—Cuba, North Korea, Libya, and others—you'll see that they are now paying the price of having been left behind while the rest of the world prospered.

This makes sense, from a *Western* point of view: It assumes that the West will continue to dominate both the politics and the economics of the world. It also assumes that the West will continue to be liberal. Since we in the West have not completed our own "return to the roots" movement, we don't really *believe* that Muslims want to annihilate us—rather, we assume they would prefer to live beside us in peace and prosperity. But as each nation succeeds in its resurgence of its own definition of culturalization—the "Keep Japan Asian" movement, the forces of Hinduism in India, the growing Islamic fundamentalism throughout the Middle East, and the split between East and West in the former Soviet states—the cultural differences become more defined and more difficult to compromise.

All this may be hard for most Americans to understand. We live in a nation of immigrants, which now includes sizable numbers from every nation of the world. We eat together in restaurants. We work together. Interracial relationships have become common. And because of our mix of races, we are (for the most part) taught that racism is ignoble and abhorrent. This contrasts greatly with what is going on in many other countries, where racism is a common teaching in most culturalization programs.

Even in the United States, where it is still common for people whose families have lived here for three hundred years or more to identify themselves as one-tenth German, one-fifth Italian, three-tenths Irish, and so forth, religious fundamentalists insist that it is not possible to say you are part Christian and part Muslim.

The lines of the eight civilizations are self-defining, and such interruptions as the domination of the Soviet Union or of the United States are only that. They do not break the cultural ties that bind peoples (rather than nations) together. But, as we are seeing in Bosnia, Croatia, and Serbia, the fractures along these cultural dividing lines can be opened like unhealed wounds.

Perhaps even more meaningful is the trend to divide the world into economic regions. These also must occur along cultural dividing lines—because if they don't, they won't work.

The European Economic Community is a coalition of Western European states made up of people with common religious and cultural backgrounds. Former East-bloc countries that do not fit the predominant Christian description are not allowed into the EEC. Even poor Turkey, which tried to "go West" by cooperating during the Persian Gulf War, and thereby excluded itself from the East, has been rejected by the EEC—and now finds itself alone, with only a distant hope of recreating the Turkish Empire up to the borders of Iran.

China, Hong Kong, Taiwan, Singapore, and the Chinese overseas diaspora will be an economic unit.

Iran, Pakistan, perhaps a placated Turkey, Azerbaijan, Kazakhstan, Kyrgyzstan, Turkmenistan, Tudjikistan, Uzbekistan, and Afghanistan will be an economic unit. The reformed Soviet Empire of Yeltsin's dreams will likely not happen because his plan calls for a joining of cultural civilizations—and this contradicts the people's natural, deeper tendencies.

Latin America and Central America will each be economic units, as will Canada, the United States, and Mexico.

The bottom line is, according to Huntington, that people of common cultures will band together, and peaceful interaction across cultural lines will occur, *only* if these moves are in the best interests of *both* parties. This is a unique concept for the West, which has had the luxury of laying down most of the world's rules for the past three hundred years or more.

It is difficult for the West to suddenly acknowledge the emerging civilizations. We have seen it as our moral duty to promote the properties of democracy and liberal ideologies. We see these as universal values, and anyone who does not agree is perceived as backward, unenlightened, ignorant—even barbaric. These beliefs, rooted in evangelism, were the mainstay behind both the preservation of our military dominance and our justification for promoting our brand of economic interests throughout the world. But we have never quite understood that the hymn "Onward Christian Soldiers" does not play well in Islam. All of our most basic beliefs and universal justifications receive a direct counterresponse from the non-West, which perceives us to be imperialistic.

When the Soviet economy collapsed along with all of the communist states of the East bloc, that was hailed as proof of the superiority of democracy and capitalism, and the inferiority of totalitarianism and communism. But the arguments along these lines of inquiry continue, particularly now that most of the Western nations are *also* struggling to restructure their economies in order to meet a changed world.

Students of Marxism argue that the communist dictators bastardized the original theory—that Marx predicted socialism would be the natural progression of an open, democratic society—and they point to the United States as an example, not the Soviet Union.

Even more perplexing to Western analysts is the fantastic economic growth occurring inside China under what the West perceives as an oppressive regime. In just the past fifteen years, the level of poverty in China has fallen from 30 percent to 10 percent—and health-care quality is among the highest of all nations, with the chances of a newborn baby surviving in China better than those of a baby born in New York City.

For most Chinese—regardless of China's record on human rights and regardless of our opinion of their standard of living—there has never been a better time to live there than right now. Most people in most other nations cannot make that same claim, including Americans (who certainly are better off than the Chinese, but can easily remember better times).

An important element the West will have to remember is that its half of the world, which lives in relative tranquility, represents just 15 percent of the world's population. The remaining 85 percent lives in relative turmoil. They have different priorities. Most would rather eat than vote.

The Shifting of Cultural Plates

Huntington looks at today's rising turmoil and compares the fracturing among the eight civilizations to a series of deep faults causing violent earthquakes along the cultural battle lines. But aren't these cultural movements rather more comparable to those related to continental drift—the shifting of the loosish upper layers of earth (plates) that has been going on for eons? Let us see.

In many ways a political map of the world today is eerily similar to one from 1900. Eerily, because we remember that the old maps had to be redrawn because of World War I and (more to the point) World War II, the latter of which kicked off the cold war, the Korean War, Vietnam, the isolation of Cuba and North Korea and China, the creation of Israel, and the Mideast conflicts. Eerily, because we have long been told that history repeats itself—and we've found that, in a way, the only difference between then and now, militarily speaking, at least, is in the massive

destructive capabilities of our weapons. Eerily, because it seems that—
after all of this turmoil—we have simply come full circle *again*.

In the final analysis, it is the deep faults that better represent the cause
of the fracturing that goes on among the eight civilizations—a war between
Iran and Iraq, for example, or an economic battle between Sweden and
Finland, or Italy and France. These "earthquakes" are short and violent,
and do not have the lasting impact of the kind of cataclysm we have represented as continental drift. When continental plates shift and collide, they
create mountain ranges and cause climatic changes, form deserts and rain
forests, and otherwise change the face of the globe forever.

Something like that is true of the shifting *cultural* "plates," the major
difference being that we do have the option of controlling them—or at
least of insulating their impact points. And we have good incentive to
respond to these options, because the next World War will undoubtedly be
a clash between civilizations—a clash of biblical proportions wherein
everything that defines cultural and religious beliefs is on the line and per-
taining to which there is no compromise or withdrawal.

A Redefinition of Power

Most Arab countries are either openly or privately proud of the actions
of Saddam Hussein in the Persian Gulf War. He stood up to the massive
strength of the combined West, and he is still in power.

The Persian Gulf War was the culmination of a conflict that had been
building for sixty years. It began when the West found oil in the Middle
East, and then was accentuated when World War II ended Western colo-
nialism and coincided with the beginning of the growth of Mideastern
nationalism and Islamic fundamentalism. This conflict between Islam and
the West is likely to keep on growing, particularly if the West continues to
rely on oil as its energy mainstay.

Each time the West uses its massive military power or advanced technical weapons, it reminds the non-West countries that they can be humil-
iated by that power and that they are not yet in control of their own des-
tinies. Even the Arab countries that have moved toward a more
democratic reform have ironically found themselves leading a populace
with a growing anti-West attitude. Any nation in which people are moving toward new degrees of self-empowerment can expect those same people to reject symbols of authority and superiority—and once again societal divisions move beyond the borders of nations, to the more meaningful
divisions of peoples.

The West's knee-jerk reactions to immigration problems only strengthen these divisions. As European borders close to burgeoning populations of the East, the barriers highlight division and exclusion. And there is always a counterresponse. The counterreaction becomes a form of racism, which is reinforced by religious and cultural movements that encourage ethnic separation. And, as we have seen, when the battle is between people of different cultures, ethnic cleansing and persecution are not only severe but (in the fevered minds of fundamentalist) wholly justified.

A Redefinition of Responsibility

If we want to avoid conflict between East and West, we will have to redefine our priorities, understanding that a redefinition is not a show of weakness, but rather of strength.

The non-West civilizations face a near future filled with turmoil, not only along their cultural borders but within them. The West will have to decide whether it should involve itself with these inner struggles, realizing that with each meddling it increases the danger of escalating a local or regional problem into a cultural war with global consequences.

For years, the United States attempted to balance the powers of Iraq and Iran, to play one against the other, to preserve Mideast stability, and to offset Soviet influence in the area. Iran and Iraq squared off against each other in brutal combat which killed tens of thousands of their soldiers and civilians. They used chemical and biological weapons against each other, and wreaked havoc upon their respective economies as they locked in mortal conflict. Today, Iran and Iraq still harbor resentment against each other—but they both agree on one thing: a hatred of the United States for messing around in their territories.

In theory, if the West weren't interfering in these internal conflicts, it would have the option of sitting back and watching the other civilizations handle their own battles, without becoming the scapegoat for both sides. And it keeps holding up that if both sides of the conflict are of the same culture, then only the foreign interloper will be blamed in the end.

Is it the responsibility of the West to interfere, or is it more responsible to stay out? The answer to this becomes confused when it includes such issues as human rights, arms proliferation, nuclear and biological weapons proliferation, and the economic needs of the "free world."

The West views as one of its duties the responsibility to impose Western concepts on the rest of the world. But everything the West stands for with regard to individualism, equality, liberty, judicial freedom, democracy, and freedom of religion holds little value in many other cultures. Only the West has had the idea of a universal democracy, or a New World Order. On a global scale, 85 percent of the population has other priorities, and they view this Western doctrine of a kinder, gentler democratic world as just another form of imperialism. If a non-West country does not want to succumb to Western preaching, then it has two options: It can either isolate itself, or it can begin its own version of a cold war and build to balance itself against the West—as China is doing.

Throughout the non-West, the trend is to institute forms of modernization without succumbing to the doctrines of westernization. The trend is to use their (for example) oil-rich resources to get their own weapons— their own stockpile of nuclear, chemical, and biological weapons. They are actually more interested in obtaining these items to strengthen their positions in their own regions than they are to reach global dominance, but the West does not trust the trends to stop at regional borders.

If the West does not want internal clashes to lead to cultural battles, then it will have to recognize that the non-West is no longer willing to sit on the sidelines. The non-West will help shape the future of the world's physical, spiritual, and economic characteristics *with* or *without* permission.

To accommodate a peaceful future, the West will have to get over its cold war attitude before it creates another cold war on a variety of fronts. Rather than playing civilizations and countries against each other, as we did in our ploys to counteract Soviet ploys, we should realize that promoting cooperation between countries is in our own best interests.

We should recognize that almost every institution operating today is viewed by the non-West countries as a pawn of the West, and of the United States in particular. This includes the United Nations, NATO, the International Monetary Fund—all representatives of Western interests regardless of how they feel justified "for the common good."

Since neither the globe nor human leanings toward war will change overnight, it is important for the West to *maintain* military and economic power—but also to recognize that power *includes* the ability to allow other countries their differences and self-empowerment.

CHAPTER 20

Democracy Versus Terrorism

This final chapter is written with the urge to pull together all of the loose ends of previous pages, solve all the problems, and anticipate what lies around the next bend. These are difficult assignments because there is no conclusion to a story based on a living world. As I hope the previous chapters adequately demonstrated, the terrorist threat is as changeable as global events, with danger levels rising and falling as fast as the barometer of political turmoil depicted in the daily newspaper headlines.

While the threat of terrorism will grow, and will likely become an even more common war tactic, there is much a democratic society can do physically to protect itself from terrorists and politically to prevent the escalation of grievances from reaching catastrophic levels.

This book began with a look at events that took place within a sixty-day period of the World Trade Center bombing. While we watched authorities sift through the rubble and track the suspects, we also watched the drama of the fifty-one-day siege of the Davidian cult group in Waco and, at the same time, we waited to see if another race riot would explode in Los Angeles as the jury brought in the verdicts against the police officers who had been accused of beating Rodney King. As those events were only starting to become clear, we discovered that another group of Islamic extremists had been stopped short of setting off more bombs at the United Nations and other New York City targets, and we also learned that a group of Skinheads had been stopped short of a misguided attempt to start a race war by bombing a black church in Los Angeles. Almost as a backdrop to all of these happenings, heated political debates raged regarding inner-city economic problems and what to do with the flood of legal and illegal immigrants.

Looking back on those events a year later, the view was both encouraging and frustrating. Encouraging, because in each of those potentially explosive situations the system of democratic due process prevailed.

The Waco Siege Verdicts

On February 26, 1994, eleven Branch Davidians were acquitted of all murder and conspiracy charges. Their primary defense was that they had acted in fear and self-defense when their group killed 4 of the 76 federal agents who had raided their Waco compound almost a year earlier. Officials saw the verdicts as a loss, but later admitted the case had caused the Federal Bureau of Alcohol, Tobacco and Firearms (ATF) to do a great deal of soul searching that would change the nature of the agency. Jurors later said they hoped their verdict sent the dual message that both sides were wrong. They also indicated that they had earlier been impressed when the top three ATF officials who had planned the raid had consequently been forced out.

Seven of the defendants were convicted of manslaughter or possession of illegal weapons while the other four were acquitted of all charges. The judge later reversed a ruling that had freed seven defendants of a weapons charge, which kicked off a series of legal appeals and an examination of constitutional protection against double jeopardy and federal sentencing guidelines. The experience should help change the siege mentality of law enforcement agencies as they deal with individuals or groups who in the future choose to hide behind barricades but do not pose an immediate danger to others.

Another aspect of the Waco siege had to do with the press. News media involvement was intense before, during, and after the raid on the compound, resulting in both praise and criticism. The Waco *Tribune Herald* began an investigative series on the Davidians the day before the raid. A Dallas radio station, KRLD, allowed David Koresh to air a Scripture passage every two hours in return for his releasing children from the compound. All in all, a thousand journalists showed up to surround the federal and state agents who were surrounding the compound. At times the reporters became so bored during the 51-day siege that they began writing about each other. A Society of Professional Journalists task force found no evidence to blame news organizations for the disastrous raid, but a Treasury Department review said that a lost cameraman inadvertently disclosed the ATF plans when he asked a passing mailman for direction to the raid. The mailman was a Davidian sect member who raced back to the compound to warn the others.

With the verdict, it was generally concluded that murder charge acquittals could not be seen as a victory for David Koresh since none of those on trial had been part of his inner circle. Had Koresh or one of the other leaders been on trial, the verdicts for them might have been different. More important, it was pretty much agreed that the jury had done its job.

The World Trade Center Verdicts

Six days later, on March 4, 1994, a Federal jury convicted all four of the World Trade Center bombing defendants. They were pronounced guilty on each of the 38 counts against them. Immediately afterward, one of the defendants shouted in Arabic, "Victory to Islam." Two others cried out, "Allah is great!" And the other shouted insults at the jury.

Although the prosecution in the World Trade Center case faced formidable challenges, and periodic lapses in ideal testimony (including one witness who identified a juror as representative of what a suspect looked like, rather than pointing directly to one of the defendants; and a bomb expert who admitted that it was nearly impossible to positively identify all components of the bomb), the prosecution presented a blizzard of evidence that allowed the jury to bring the verdicts without doubt.

It remained to be seen what effect the verdicts would have on the trial of the defendants who were arrested in the plot to attack other New York City targets. That trial was scheduled for September 1994. But authorities were comfortable that the verdicts had sent a message to other would-be terrorists that the American justice system is ready to deal with them.

A comparison of how the Waco siege and the World Trade Center cases developed, as well as their respective verdicts, provides a reminder that there is a difference between terrorism and dissidence—regardless of the added complexities when the cases involve religion and nationalities.

The picture of the national scene a year later was also frustrating, however, because it seemed that some lessons that should have been learned had not taken.

As reporter Matthew Wald wrote in the *New York Times*, March 6, 1994, after guilty verdicts were brought against the suspects in the World Trade Center bombing, "larger issues—like how a society can protect itself from terrorists—remain unresolved." When he posed this as a question to Nestor Michnyak, a spokesman for the FBI, Michnyak responded, "Do we have any different, modified response? No, is the bottom line." He said, "We respond—that's the problem. We can offer advice on what we are finding, based on experience and what history is showing, but everybody is responsible for themselves."

Michnyak was referring to targets similar to the World Trade Center (businesses, government buildings, office towers, monuments, and landmarks), but when I met with William Colby in 1993, the former CIA director applied the same reality to society in general—that we each have a responsibility to ourselves and to our communities, and a personal vigilance against unusual happenings in our neighborhoods is the best deterrent to terrorism.

This idea of law enforcement being reactive and citizens acting responsibly goes to the very roots of our democratic ideas. A crime is not a crime until it has been committed. A journalist is not censored prior to publication, and so forth. These principles are challenged when ruthless acts are carried out in total disregard for society, whether it is gang violence or terrorism.

But how does one awaken a society to accept its responsibilities so it neither lays itself open to terror nor invites stricter government control?

The Oxford Companion to Politics of the World, edited by Joel Krieger, provides one of my favorite examples of democracy in action. It refers back two decades when the governments of the United States and Canada jointly announced that on a specific date both countries would switch to the more practical metric system of weights and measures. The Canadians readily complied, but over two hundred million Americans simply ignored the new policy and the government was forced to abandon the change. Krieger used the quiet defeat of the "go metric" movement to exemplify America's proud disdain for authority and our refusal to conform to rules laid down by the state.

It is this silent strength, a consensus of democratic free will, which is needed to combat the perpetrators of terrorism. Our local, state, and federal law enforcement agencies need to be supported by the vigilance and alertness of our 240 million citizens.

Privacy Versus Intelligence Gathering

That uniquely American disdain for authority, however, has also created a distrust for a government "Big Brother" image in the modern, computerized world. In 1991, the *Readers' Digest* magazine conducted a reader survey to determine what subscribers felt about a proposed electronic health-care claims processing service. Although the responders agreed that such a service would relieve them of what had become a nightmare in paper shuffling and confusion, the overwhelming majority referred to "enough of this Big Brother" mentality in the comments section of the survey form. The idea that their names and addresses, along with their detailed medical history, would be in yet another computer data file was perceived as further encroachment upon their privacy. This attitude, which is particularly strong among older age groups, has not been given a great deal of consideration in the various political debates over national health-care proposals, but it is a powerful force that may very well have an impact similar to the metric conversion if the concepts are ever put up for a vote or if participation is voluntary.

In regard to terrorism, however, the conflict between personal freedom and Big Brother's invasion of privacy is coming to the forefront as federal agencies try to find ways to become proactive and to keep up with the technology now available to criminals and terrorists. The urgency felt by these agencies to respond grows greater as the possibilities of war with North Korea (or with any of a number of countries developing nuclear weapons capabilities) move from a war-room game toward reality.

One of the keys to moving our national defense into a proactive status will rely heavily on proper and creative intelligence gathering, which may require a revamping of our FBI and CIA intelligence-gathering capabilities and methods. In March 1994, CIA agent Aldrich H. Ames and his wife, Rosario, were arrested on espionage charges for selling information to Russia—collecting as much as $2.7 million since 1986, and resulting in the deaths or disappearances of a dozen or more CIA agents and counter-agents over the eight-year period. Because of Ames's enormous access to information, the Ames case may be the most damaging spy mission to the U.S. since the beginning of the cold war, and the Ames case also revealed a number of lax policies within the CIA itself.

From a political standpoint, the arrest of Ames and his wife could not have come at a worse time for the CIA. Just a few weeks earlier it had been revealed that North Korea had developed nuclear weapons capabilities—apparently without the CIA having a clue. By the time of the arrests, North Korea was already posturing as if for war, and U.S. military sources were admitting that if North Korea responded to a loss of a conventional war with a nuclear weapon, U.S. losses would be catastrophic. All of this was on the tail end of any number of complaints about the CIA's past performance, ranging from misinformation regarding the U.S.S.R. throughout the cold war, to failure to foresee the collapse of the Berlin Wall, to misinformation during the Persian Gulf War.

In reaction to the Ameses' arrest, CIA director R. James Woolsey promised on March 10, 1994, to appoint an outside panel of experts to study weaknesses in the agency's counterintelligence and internal security departments. However, Senator Dennis DeConcini, who heads the Senate Select Committee on Intelligence, angrily asserted that such a panel would not change the "culture and mentality" within the departments responsible. Nebraska Senator Robert Kerrey, who had earlier stated that he wanted to be named chairman of the Committee after his reelection, said he intended to be one of the chief architects in reorganizing the CIA. Perhaps a major part of this reorganization should be a decentralization of the Central Intelligence Agency.

With more than a little irony, on the same day the Ameses were arrested, the Clinton administration announced that it would allow private U.S. companies to market sophisticated spy satellite technology to commercial customers around the world. The CIA was in a weak position to argue that such a move would put the technology in North Korea's hands, and the counterargument was that the technology was becoming available from foreign sources anyway, so American companies might as well profit from the sales.

On either side of these controversies, two additional proposals were being presented to combat terrorism and criminal activities. On February 4, 1994, the Clinton administration adopted the "Clipper Chip," an encoding device that would allow law enforcement agencies to intercept coded telephone and computer communications. Designed in cooperation with the National Security Agency, the Clipper Chip creates a portal through which agencies can intercept and unscramble the billions of bits of digital information that flow through information networks. Computer companies and telephone companies have argued against the device, along with civil-rights groups concerned about privacy, but the administration's original idea was to make installation of the chip a voluntary decision while it uses the government's huge purchasing power within these industries to force their participation.

By March 1994, however, the plan to introduce the Clipper Chip was a part of legislation. On March 19, 1994, FBI Director Louis Freeh said, "Unless Congress creates a new law, law enforcement's ability to protect the public against crime will be gravely eroded and the national security will be placed at risk." Freeh recognized the serious privacy arguments. "The costs are high," he said, "but you have to do a cost-benefit analysis." He said the intent was to fight terrorists and criminals, not play Big Brother to the citizenry. Freeh stated that an FBI wiretap had recently prevented a terrorist plot to shoot down an airline passenger plane in Chicago with a Stinger missile, but had the terrorists not used conventional telephones—had they used cellular phones or computer messages—the FBI's conventional wiretap would not have intercepted the phone calls which had revealed the plan.

The question of greater authority at some expense to individual privacy is a difficult one, but in many ways the new law would simply give authorities the same capabilities the terrorists and crooks already have. This was demonstrated by an official warning sent by the Computer Emergency Response Team to users of the international Internet computer communication network on February 4, 1994. The warning reported that Internet had been "flooded" with computer break-ins during the previous week and that all of the fifteen million computers linked directly to Internet or indirectly to another, interlinked network, were in danger of being invaded by unauthorized users, if indeed they had not already been compromised. The tremendous rash of break-ins reminded authorities that there are plenty of hitchhikers and unlicensed drivers all along the information superhighway.

The problem with the ease and convenience offered to terrorists by electronic transmission networks was exemplified in a different way in a February 22, 1994, article in the New York *Daily News*. The article reported that a confidential Secret Service memorandum alerted credit card companies that a Mideast religious group had smuggled thousands of counterfeit credit cards into the United States as a way of financing terrorism. According to the memo, the cards were manufactured in Beirut and were being shipped via Iranian and Armenian couriers to Nigerian and Asian accomplices in the U.S., Canada, Europe, and Latin America.

The credit card scam is an example of how the information superhighway can connect the financial institutions of the world, and how more sophisticated terrorists are learning to attack the financial stability of countries. A 1993 government report had shown earlier that Iran had obtained printing equipment to reproduce U.S. currency so perfectly that the bogus bills were undetectable to even a trained inspector. The Iranian plan was to flood Europe and Asia with as much as $200 billion in fake U.S. currency—a potentially serious threat to the U.S. economy. Credit card access, the BCCI-type of money transfers, and the possibility of computer break-ins, which can drain entire bank accounts for transfer overseas, all demonstrate that the superhighway allows quite a number of ways to attack the financial industry to benefit terrorist goals.

The Clipper Chip would allow authorities to intercept such illegal trans-actions. While the cost to taxpayers would be in excess of $500 million to develop the software and hardware required to implement the Clinton administration's proposed legislation, called the Digital Telephone and Communications Privacy Improvement Act of 1994, Freeh said the ter-rorist threat to the country through communications manipulation is con-servatively estimated in the neighborhood of $5 billion. This makes the investment a good one, according to Freeh, and he said he would be will-ing to work with the privacy groups to set a higher limit of standards required by law enforcement agencies to gain access.

Nuclear Proliferation and "Soft Targets"

The March 1994 North Korean threat to invade South Korea brought both nuclear proliferation and nuclear terrorism to the forefront as the Pentagon responded to the growing crisis. Pentagon officials admitted in a March 22, 1994, *Newhouse News Service* release that the nuclear proliferation issue had been "relegated to dusty academic study." Suddenly North Korea was going ahead with nuclear development in complete disregard of international treaties, inspection teams, or trade sanctions. A North Korean official warned that any attempt to counter their actions would assure that South Korea would become "a river of fire." This was not taken lightly by the Pentagon. A recent war game which pitted U.S. troops and technology against an irrational, third world dictator had turned out disastrous in terms of loss of U.S. life and capabilities.

Although Congress and the Pentagon and the past five administrations had been warned that what was now happening was inevitable, not much had been done to prepare for a fight with a small country holding nuclear weapons. We learned in the Persian Gulf War that our weaponry did little either to destroy or to neutralize Iraq's vast underground storage of nuclear and biological weapons—weapons our foreign intelligence resources had limited knowledge of at the time.

Suddenly the Pentagon was aware not only that North Korea had the ability to build as many as forty nuclear bombs a year, but that the same problem would start popping up all around the world in any country that chooses to follow North Korea's lead. Iran, Libya, Israel, India, and Pakistan all have nuclear weapons or the ability to assemble them quick-ly, and the list of nuclear states is expected to expand quickly.

"Somewhere, some time in this decade, someone is going to set off a nuclear weapon in deadly earnest," the director of naval intelligence, Rear Admiral Edward Schaefer Jr. told *Newhouse News Service* in 1993.

With the wake-up call provided by the World Trade Center, Pentagon officials were also mindful of the fact that any battle against the U.S., regardless of where the center of conflict is located, would probably be augmented by terrorist attacks at home. "Soft targets," including nuclear reactors that have little or no real protection from attack, would be the primary targets of any such attempt.

A Global Intelligence Network

We need to respond to the rising dangers of nuclear proliferation and terrorism with an effective global network of intelligence resources working closely together. This shared network must operate in regard to all terrorist activity, never withholding information from friendly countries, even when doing so might be politically beneficial.

Rational countries must ban together in efforts to identify, track, arrest, and punish terrorist criminals. In order to accomplish this effectively, these countries must rise above the current arguments over the distinctions between terrorists and freedom fighters. Those who use terrorist methods, regardless of their cause, must appear on the network's list.

There is a similar problem of selective sharing of information within the internal workings of our own FBI and CIA. Law enforcement and intelligence gathering often conflict, as they did in the case of the World Trade Center bombing. Intelligence gatherers often don't want their sources to be arrested, so information that might have allowed another agency to arrest the perpetrators of a crime is often not passed on. A simple change in procedures to create an effective synergy between various agencies would deal a serious blow to terrorism as well as to many elements of organized crime.

Trade Sanctions

As a means of avoiding physical confrontations, the U.S. and other Western countries have relied heavily on economic sanctions against countries that spurn the global community. But these sanctions are seldom fully effective. Loose laws and lax enforcement can still allow American corporations to conduct business with the countries in question. Most

important among the offending companies are the all-powerful grain cartels (Cargill, Continental, Bunge, Louis Dreyfus, and André). Their business is so close-vested and complicated due to multibillion dollar telephone deals without paper trails, wrote Dan Morgan, author of the book
Merchants of Grain, that a majority of the world's grain trade is, for all
practical purposes, virtually under the control of just seven individuals. If
one of these cartels decides to profit from a trade sanction by skirting it
via a foreign subsidiary, the sanction fails. The December 27, 1993, *Wall
Street Journal* detailed how Cargill, along with nongrain companies,
including the Brown & Root, Inc. engineering firm in Houston and The
Price Brothers Company, a consulting and machinery company headquartered in Dayton, Ohio, used loopholes in the law to supply grain to Libya
and Cuba. This list of American and foreign companies that ignore the
trade sanctions is long, and as we saw with closer inspection after the
Persian Gulf War, the list includes many companies that supply weapons
or the materials to make weapons.

The defense offered by these multinational companies, the grain cartels
in particular, is that the secret of their value to the global community is
their "nonpolitical" stature. But if the global community has decided that
trade sanctions are a viable alternative to war or terrorism, is not a decision to ignore them a political decision? Responsible countries must not
only vote to support sanctions, but act to enforce them. These countries
must let multinational companies and subsidiaries located within their
borders know that if they are not going to be part of the solution, then they
will be treated as part of the problem.

A Global Grievance Organization

To be sure, there are leaders of groups and countries whose irrational
goals are the annihilation of other cultures. But it is also clear that a great
deal of terrorism is born of despair and frustration. As recently as 1992 did
the CIA remove both Nelson Mandela and Yasser Arafat from its official
terrorist listing. In 1994, the Mideast peace negotiations between Isreal
and the Palestinians moved along in fits and starts, as did the efforts to
move toward a black majority government in South Africa. Both of these
processes continued against tremendous obstacles not only from the
opposing sides, but from factions within each group that wanted to disrupt
the proceedings.

The fact that both of these conflicts were being played out in full view
on the world stage led the players from senseless acts of violence to the

negotiation tables. The conflicts themselves, along with the differing opinions and perspectives, became part of the world dialogue and subjected all sides to international scrutiny. Such exposure can be a terrific force of reason to any political group whose goal is being accepted by other nations. Some kind of a global grievance organization may accomplish a similar purpose, bringing even obscure groups a degree of democratic strength and, along with it, a measure of democratic responsibility.

The U.S. legal system may be the best model for such an organization. Because U.S. citizens have a right to address their grievances through a variety of legal avenues, their ability to receive a judicial judgment eliminates the impulse to report to violent demonstration in the vast majority of cases. Conversely, if an individual or group rejects the legal system and resorts to violence, it is easier to classify their actions as wantonly violent transgressions against the government and society.

If a global grievance committee offered a legal system, it could possibly reduce the risk of local and regional conflicts escalating to national and international terrorism. This organization should not be another NATO or United Nations. It should not be perceived as a tool for either Western or non-Western countries. It would receive a rebel with the same consideration as it would an official ambassador. The committee would be comprised not of nations but of individuals from diverse nations representing all cultures and religions. Each grievance would be heard, with committee conclusions published and delivered for world inspection, providing a kind of instant global opinion poll for both sides of the grievance to take into account.

This may be an overly simplified blueprint for the creation of such an organization, but even a minor success could save untold thousands of lives at relatively no cost as compared to the destruction of even one nuclear weapon or a prolonged ethnic war.

The Difference Between Dissent and Terrorism

Not since the 1960s—the turbulence of black revolt against discrimination and the student antiwar demonstration—has the justice system been so challenged to reexamine where the constitutional protection of civil disobedience ends and where outright crimes against society begin. Supreme Court Justice Oliver Wendell Holmes said that the rights to dissent and free speech carry with them some social responsibilities—they do not include the right to spread panic and endanger others by shouting "fire" in a crowded theater. Abe Fortas, Associate Justice of the Supreme Court, expanded upon this definition in his 1968 book, *Concerning Dissent and Civil Disobedience*. He emphasized that while members of a democratic society not only have the right to disobey, they sometimes have the duty to disobey against injustice, and the Constitution has the duty to protect their right to do so, thereby providing an alternative to violence.

Because of the existence of terrorists and terrorist supporters in our country, we must question this constitutional protection, particularly when projected on a worldwide scale. We are inadvertently left in a position of harboring terrorist organizations which are outlawed in other countries. Israel's March 1994 decision to outlaw the Kach and Kahane Chai Jewish extremists as terrorist groups once again brings our policy into question. Both of these groups are active and growing in the U.S., sending both money and hate propaganda domestically and abroad. Likewise, for the past forty years the German government has attempted to convince the U.S. to crack down on the neo-Nazi groups located within our borders that have been fomenting hate and personal, racist attacks against Jews and foreigners. In both Israel and Germany membership alone in these outlawed groups is illegal, as is the spreading of their propaganda and symbols.

The U.S. must determine a way to protect the rights of disobedience without protecting killers of innocent people. It is one thing to protect an individual's right to talk of the overthrow of a government, but is not a pamphlet calling for violence against individuals akin to shouting "fire" in a crowded theater? As Abe Fortas said in the conclusion of his book, "it is part of the dynamics of democracy which depends for its vitality upon the vigorous confrontation of opposing forces. But we cannot and should not endure physical assault upon person or property." He also said that in our nation the deliberate violation of law is never justified unless it is the law itself that is the target of protest.

Our ability to find an acceptable way to avoid providing safe harbor to terrorists will become more important if terrorist actions rise to their predicted levels and governments attempt to respond. We currently have what may be a brief period of quiet in which to calmly and rationally debate this issue. The debate must take into account not only our responsibility to our citizens, but also our responsibilities to the citizens of other nations.

A Struggle for World Peace

The struggle for world peace was never confined to the conflict between two superpowers, although so much emphasis was placed on the cold war that it sometimes seemed that way. With nuclear proliferation and terrorism leading the way in the post–cold war world, it is clearer now that world peace cannot be achieved by governments alone.

If nuclear proliferation and terrorism are likely to continue to grow, we must prepare for these eventualities even as we search for solutions. But world peace requires a consensus of the world's people. If various governments or religions do not want to lead the search for peace, then perhaps we, the people, can force them to follow along.

Bibliography

Books

Adam, James Ring, and Douglas Frantz. *A Full Service Bank. How BCCI Stole Billions Around the World.* New York: Simon & Schuster, 1992.

Al-Khalil, Samir. *Republic of Fear: The Inside Story of Saddam's Iraq.* New York: Pantheon Books, 1989.

Barnet, R. *Real Security: Restoring American Power in a Dangerous Decade.* New York: Simon & Schuster, 1981.

Clark, W., and J. Page. J. *Energy, Vulnerability, and War: Alternatives for America.* New York: W.W. Norton, 1981.

Fallows, J. *National Defense.* New York: Random House, 1981.

Fortas, Abe. *Concerning Dissent and Civil Disobedience.* New York: Signet Books, 1968.

Gearty, Conor. *Terror.* London: Faber and Faber, 1991.

Kah, Gary H. *En Route to Global Occupation.* Lafayette: Huntington House Publishers, 1992.

Kotkin, Joel. *Tribes: How Race, Religion and Identity Determine Success in the New Global Economy.* New York: Random House, 1992.

Krieger, Joel. *The Oxford Companion to Politics of the World.* New York/Oxford: The Oxford University Press, 1993.

Kupperman, R., and D. Trent. *Terrorism: Threat, Reality, Response.* Stanford: Hoover Institution Press, 1980.

Lovins, Amory B., and L. Hunter Lovins. *Brittle Power: Energy Strategy for National Security.* Andover: Brick House Publishing Company, 1982.

———— and Seth Zuckerman. *Energy Unbound: A Fable for America's Future.* San Francisco: Sierra Club Books, 1986.

Marenches, Count De, with David A. Andelman. *The Fourth World War: Diplomacy and Espionage in the Age of Terrorism.* New York: William Morrow and Company, 1992.

Prange, Gordon W. *At Dawn We Slept: the Untold Story of Pearl Harbor.* New York: McGraw-Hill Book Company, 1981.

Truell, Peter, and Larry Gurwin. *False Profits: The Inside Story of BCCI, the World's Most Corrupt Financial Empire.* New York: Houghton Mifflin Company, 1992.

235

Yergin, Daniel. *The Prize: The Epic Quest For Oil, Money & Power.* New York: Simon & Schuster, 1992.

Government Documents

Congress of the United States Office of Technology Assessment. *Physical Vulnerability of Electric Systems to Natural Disasters and Sabotage.* June 1990.

Department of State Bulletin. *Countering Terrorism in the 1980s and 1990s.* February 1989

Emergency Management Institute, National Emergency Training Center. *State and Local Continuity of Government.* SM250.1, 1990.

Federal Emergency Management Agency, Emergency Management Institute. *The Emergency Program Manager.* HS-1, 1989.

Federal Emergency Management Agency. *Civil Defense Systems, Programs and Policies.* SM 66.1, 1989.

—*Disaster Mitigation Guide for Business and Industry.* FEMA, 1990.

—*Guide for the Development of State and Local Emergency Operations Plans.* CPG 1-8, 1990.

—*Guide for Increasing Local Government Civil Defense Readiness During Periods of International Crisis.* SLG 100, 1990.

United States Department of State. *Terrorist Group Profiles.* U.S. Government Printing Office, 1988.

—*Patterns of Global Terrorism: 1992.* U.S. Government Printing Office, 1993.

U.S. Army Foreign Science and Technology Center. *Protection from Terrorist Devices.* Special report by Ronald E. Fischer. Declassified, 1985.

U.S. Army Intelligence Agency, U.S. Intelligence and Threat Analysis Center. *Terrorism: the Worldwide Threat and Protective Measures for the US Military.* A special briefing, 1985.

Vice President's Task Force. *Public Report of the Vice President's Task Force on Combatting Terrorism.* February 1986.

Magazines

Business Week
    4-19-93   "Robber Bank."
International Defense Review
    6-1-86   "Chemical Deterrence—Will It Work?"
    11-1-86   "Mace: A Multi-national Approach to Countering Terrorism."
    9-1-88   "An End to Chemical Weapons: What are the Chances?"
    8-1-90   "Biological Weapons; How Big a Threat?"
Jane's Defense Weekly, International Edition
    1-6-90   "NATO: Facing Up to the New Europe."
    2-10-90   "Thorn in the Side of Middle Eastern Peace."
Jane's Intelligence Review
    11-1-91   "Biological Warfare Developments."
National Review
    6-17-87   "The Making of a Terrorist."
Newsweek
    7-5-93   "The New Terrorism."

New York Times Magazine
    8-23-92   "The Party Crasher."
    3-7-93   "How the Foreign Policy Machine Broke Down."
    2-27-94   "Don't Send in the Marines."
    3-6-94   "Out of Sight, Out of Our Minds."
Parade
    2-27-94   "None of This Had to Happen."
Scholastic Update
    5-16-86   "FBI Efforts to Make the U.S. a 'Hard Target.'"
    5-16-86   "The U.S. Stand Against International Terrorism."
    5-16-86   "Terror Groups Around the World."
    5-16-86   "Five Who Support Terrorism and Five Who Fight It."
    5-16-86   "Faces of Terrorism."
    5-16-86   "What 19th-Century Terror Tells Us About Today's."
Security Management
    1-89   "The Case for Continuity."
    5-89   "Terrorism in Your Own Backyard."
    6-90   "A Time to Redefine Policy?"
    1-91   "Terror Marches On."
    3-91   "The Democratic Dilemma."
    4-91   "Is America Next?"
    1-92   "Terrorism in the United States: 1990."
    5-92   "Profiling for Terrorists."
    6-92   "Trends for Terrorism in the Nineties."
Time
    1-14-91   "The Life and Crimes of a Middle East Terrorist."
    5-31-93   "Diplomacy of Terror."
    7-5-93   "The Terror Within."
    7-5-93   "We Distorted Our Own Minds."
    7-5-93   "A New World for Spies."
    7-5-93   "Striking Back."
    7-12-93   "Laying Hands on an Unwanted Guest."
    7-26-93   "Today Los Angeles, Tomorrow . . ."
    8-9-93   "Where Have All the Nazis Gone?"
    8-9-93   "When White Makes Right."
    10-4-93   "The Secret Life of Mahmud the Red."
    1-3-94   "Men of the Year Peacemakers."

Newspapers

New York Times
    6-6-93   "Signs of Blast at Trade Center Fade, But for Many, its Tremors Remain."
    7-18-93   "Ideas & Trends; a Split in Thinking Among Keepers of Artificial
               Intelligence."
    7-29-93   "Ethnic Recruiting a Priority."
    7-29-93   "Florio Signs Law to Impose Death for Terrorist Murders."
    7-29-93   "Manhattan Hit by Bacteria in Water, Puzzling Experts."
    8-1-93   "Preparing to Meet Terrorists Bearing Plutonium."
    8-18-93   "Egypt Fights Militant Islam With More of the Same."
    8-18-93   "Germany's Anti-Terror Unit Buffs its Image."

8-19-93   "U.S. Says Sudan Helped With Logistics of Terror."
8-19-93   "Qaddafi Says He Won't Surrender Bomb Suspects."
8-26-93   "U.S. Indicts Egyptian Cleric as Head of Group Plotting 'War of Urban
           Terrorism.'"
8-28-93   "Conspiracy Case Against Sheik Involves Risky Strategy, Legal Experts
           Say."
10-1-93   "U.S. Border Crackdown Enrages Mexican Town."
10-22-93   "Germans Sense New Strength in Nazi Movement."
10-29-93   "A Day in Belfast: Fear and Funerals."
10-31-93   "Bomb Informer's Secret Tapes Offer a Rare Glimpse Into Dealings With
           the F.B.I."
11-18-93   "150 Windmills to Test Elusive Power Source."
11-25-93   "F.B.I. Shaken by Inquiry Into Idaho Siege."
11-28-93   "Book on Nazi Murder Industry Stirs French Storm."
12-1-93   "GAO Says Accidents Slowing Disarmament."
12-8-93   "Cold War Secret Revealed: 204 Nuclear Blasts by U.S."
12-9-93   "U.S. Destroys Missile Silo; 499 Still to Go."
12-9-93   "U.S. Rebukes Manager of Nuclear Site."
12-10-93   "Airport Security Found Lacking in U.S. Inquiry."
12-15-93   "Germans Ask if a Film Hurts or Helps Neo-Nazis."
12-16-93   "Map of All Chromosomes to Guide Genetic Hunters."
12-25-93   "Policy Questions Leave C.I.A. Chief Out in the Cold."
12-31-93   "Victims of Bias Try to Guide Skinheads Off Road of Hate."
1-6-94   "Neighbors of Bomb-Test Site: Unlucky and Now Embittered."
1-8-94   "Shamir Remarks on New York Bomb Attack Draw Criticism."
1-11-94   "3 Skinheads Cut a Swastika on a Disabled German Girl."
1-25-94   "Harassment of Jews Rose in '93, Anti-Defamation League Reports."
1-28-94   "Wiretap Technology Plan Pushed by F.B.I. Director."
2-1-94   "The I.R.A.'s Advocate."
2-3-94   "Klan Chapter in Texas Seeks to Collect Trash Near Blacks."
2-5-94   "A Rise in Internet Break-Ins Sets Off a Security Alarm."
2-5-94   "Death and Domesticity Mix at Trial of 11 Cult Members."
2-5-94   "U.S. Plans to Push Computer Coding Police Can Read."
2-6-94   "Los Angeles Debates Quake Aid for Illegal Aliens."
2-13-94   "Ideas & Trends; Cyberspace Under Lock and Key."
2-16-94   "U.S. to Charge Immigrants a Fee When They Seek Political Asylum."
2-16-94   "Some Israelis Fret as Congo Hires Their Young Ex-Soldiers as Army
           Trainers."
2-19-94   "Montana City Reacts Early to Subdue Racist Organizations."
2-20-94   "Legacy of Tower Explosion: Security Improved, and Lost."
2-22-94   "U.S. Links Terrorists, Credit Fraud."
2-25-94   "CIA's Lie Detector Must Have Lied."
2-28-94   "Oliver North Finds Himself a Candidate Under Siege."
2-28-94   "Questions Linger After 11 Cultists' Trial."
2-28-94   "Sect Trial Jurors Sought to Send a Message: 'Both Sides Did Wrong.'"
3-1-94   "Suspicions on Spy Suspect Were Long Out of Focus."
3-4-94   "An Ancient Ritual and a Mother's Asylum Plea."
3-4-94   "Terror Made Easy."
3-5-94   "Bomb Verdict Could Cast Shadow on Second Case."
3-10-94   "4 Are Convicted in Bombing at the World Trade Center That Killed 6,
           Stunned U.S."
3-6-94   "How Does the World Look Through the Eyes of Aspiring Terrorists?"

3-9-94   "Pentagon Suggests a New Plan for Verifying Nuclear Disarmament."
3-11-94   "C.I.A. Director Plans to Review Spying Policies."
3-16-94   "Russia Paralyzed in Effort to Dispose of Vast Chemical Arsenal."
3-16-94   "North Korea Said to Block Taking of Radioactive Samples from Site."
3-16-94   "A Flogging Sentence Brings a Cry of Pain in U.S."
3-17-94   "Court Favors German Who Denies Holocaust."
3-19-94   "Senators Want Atomic Plants Protected Against Car Bombs."
3-20-94   "Italy's Ex-Communists Now Have a Shot at Power."
3-20-94   "North Korea, on Long Leash, Runs Circles Around Its Foes."
3-20-94   "War to Keep Apartheid Spawned Terror Network."

The Omaha World Herald
4-2-93   "Alleged Terrorist Cell Indicted."
5-20-93   "Paper Reports Trade Center Bomb Cost $3,200."
7-3-93   "Islamic Zealotry Again in Spotlight."
7-13-93   "Huge Cold War Security System Becomes Expensive Dinosaur."
9-20-93   "Poles Give Old Leaders New Chance."
9-26-93   "U.S. Likely Underestimated Soviet N-Supply."
9-26-93   "German Unification Remains a Struggle."
11-1-93   "Hackers Bedevil Superhighway of Information."
11-17-93   "U.S. Urged to Buy Plutonium to Ease Threat."
11-29-93   "Probe Looks Deeply into How FBI Handled Siege in Idaho."
12-8-93   "Pentagon to Focus on Mass Threats."
12-15-93   "German, U.S. Hate Groups Probed for Possible Ties."
12-17-93   "Superconductive Material Found."
12-27-93   "North's Foes Aim to Derail Senate Run."
1-19-94   "Doctors Link War Ailments and Viruses."
1-19-94   "New Solar Panels Cut Costs in Half."
1-25-94   "League Says Anti-Semitic Acts Increased."
2-7-94   "Subs Run Undercover Missions."
2-14-94   "Rushdie's Death Sentence Is 5 Years Old."
2-23-94   "Agent Had 'Enormous Access.'"
3-6-94   "Kerrey Has His Eye on Intelligence Work."
3-6-94   "Waco: Were News Observers Too Involved?"
3-7-94   "East German Files Credited for Helping Find Alleged CIA Mole."
3-7-94   "Plan to Abduct Kissinger Tied to U.N. Bombing Plot."
3-19-94   "Freeh Says Bill Needed for Wiretaps."
3-19-94   "Report: S. African Police Helped Black Terrorists."

Rocky Mountain News
10-10-92   "State Raiders Seize Guns at Group's Remote Camp."
10-11-92   "Women, Kids Took Raid in Stride."
10-17-92   "Hare Krishas Fear Targeting."
10-17-92   "Islamic Sect Suspected in Krishna Temple—Fuqra Members Eyed in
            Denver, Philadelphia Firebombings."
10-18-92   "Not Linked to Raided Group, Say Black and Orthodox Muslims—
            Colorado Leaders Deny Knowledge of Fuqra."
10-18-92   "Sect Suspected in Crimes Across U.S.—Toronto Also is Among Cities
            Where Cops Say Fuqra Has Been Tied to Terrorist Violence."

St. Louis Post-Dispatch
1-17-90   "Murder Suspects Bugged—Secret U.S. Inquiry Netted Chilling Tape of
            Killing."
11-18-91   "Secret Court Ok'd Bugs."

USA Today
   11-86   "Conquering the Cancer of Terrorism."
   3-2-93   "From N.Y. to Calif., security concerns vary."
   3-18-93   "New breed of terrorists."
   7-6-93   "Terrorism talk swirls around 'Muslim pope.'"
   7-28-93   "Vets feel painful vindication."
   8-3-93   "2 plead innocent in Los Angeles race war case."
   8-18-93   "Terrorism woven through three continents."
   8-20-93   "Islamic militants vow further violence in Egypt."
   8-26-93   "New acts of terror feared."
   2-17-94   "Lawyer: Iraqi duped trade center suspect."
U.S. News & World Report
   9-12-88   "Taking on Terrorists."
   2-18-91   "Holes in the security web."
The Wall Street Journal
   6-16-93   "A Trail of Terror."
   3-20-94   "A Satellite System Is Planned to Link Most of the Globe."

Index